THE MONETARY
APPROACH TO
INTERNATIONAL
ADJUSTMENT

THE MONETARY APPROACH TO INTERNATIONAL ADJUSTMENT

Edited by
Bluford H. Putnam and
D. Sykes Wilford

Foreword by
J. Richard Zecher

PRAEGER PUBLISHERS
Praeger Special Studies

New York • London • Sydney • Toronto

Library of Congress Cataloging in Publication Data

Main entry under title:

The Monetary approach to international adjustment.

    Bibliography: p.
    Includes index.
    1. Foreign exchange--Addresses, essays, lectures.
2. Balance of payments--Addresses, essays, lectures.
I. Putnam, Bluford H. II. Wilford, D. Sykes.
HG3821.M66   332.4'5   78-19753
ISBN 0-03-046711-X

The views expressed in this collection of essays are solely those of the respective authors and do not necessarily represent the views of the authors' supporting institutions.

PRAEGER PUBLISHERS
PRAEGER SPECIAL STUDIES
383 Madison Avenue, New York, N.Y. 10017, U.S.A.

Published in the United States of America in 1978
by Praeger Publishers,
A Division of Holt, Rinehart and Winston, CBS, Inc.

89   038   987654321

Printed in the United States of America

To Mary Etta
and Jane

FOREWORD
J. Richard Zecher

THE MONETARY APPROACH
TO INTERNATIONAL ADJUSTMENT

Much of the recent work in international economics, including the studies in this volume, reflects an evolving theoretical and empirical framework that has several prominent characteristics. First, there is an emphasis on market efficiency and rational expectations in both domestic and international markets, in the sense that price or interest rate differences are quickly eliminated or totally avoided to the extent they can be anticipated, through the rational behavior of market participants. Second, there is an emphasis on general equilibrium in the stock markets (bonds and money) and in the flow markets (commodities and labor). And, of course, there is the prominent role assigned to the supply and demand for money. This emphasis follows naturally from interest in issues relating to the balance of payments, which is the international flow of money, and the exchange rate, which is the price of one type of money in terms of another.

My reading of the recent and not so recent literature suggests that most, if not all, of the propositions known as the "monetary approach" have been around in some form for a long time. Yet it is useful to identify three modern general equilibrium theorists—Lloyd Metzler, Robert A. Mundell, and Harry G. Johnson—who brought these propositions together and developed the general equilibrium outlines of the monetary approach to international adjustment.

Many scholars have been attracted to work on the monetary approach by its richness of testable implications. This has led to what is, for the field of international economics, a large and rapidly growing body of empirical literature. These studies are too recent to have withstood successfully the test of time, but they do provide very substantial encouragement for further work on the monetary approach.

Others have been attracted to the monetary approach mainly because of its strong policy implications, particularly for those actions of the central bank and fiscal authorities that affect the domestic supply of money and, therefore, the balance of payments and the exchange rate. The monetary approach's general equilibrium nature allows, in a refined form, the policymaker to observe and be aware of the key variables determining international adjustment. Implications of the monetary approach are applicable equally to the reserve currency-creating country, the United States, and to the small, open economy. The approach, already being used to evaluate and promote economic performance in the developing (as well as the industrialized) world, is fast becoming an important tool for the practitioner of economic policy.

The coeditors of this volume have made a major contribution by successfully integrating a series of papers that deal with the broad historical development of the monetary approach, its theoretical and empirical application in a wide variety of circumstances, clarification of previously ambiguous parts of the theory, and refinements in variables in the model and in the statistical tools used to test the model's implications. The result is a self-contained volume that provides the reader with a clear picture of where the monetary approach came from, the current state of the art, and the most promising avenues for further research.

PREFACE

With the breakdown of the Bretton Woods international monetary system in the early 1970s and the emergence of a system of managed, floating exchange rates, a number of economic realities have clashed sharply with received economic doctrine. First, the balance of payments problems that undermined the fixed exchange rate system were not those of unsustainable current account or trade account deficits. Instead, the primary problem lay with the very large capital flows from the United States to the rest of the world, fueled by the relatively expansionary monetary policy in the United States. And second, floating exchange rates, managed or not, assure that the foreign exchange market clears, but do not equilibrate nations' current accounts and do not provide an insulated environment in which nations can conduct an independent monetary policy.

The monetary approach to international adjustment goes directly to the heart of these economic realities and has made some impressive strides in providing a consistent framework in which to analyze international adjustment problems under any exchange rate regime. This book is a collection of essays that present the basic theory, trace its historical origins, demonstrate its empirical relevance, and then, in limited ways, extend the basic theories into more sophisticated and complex forms directed toward the many unanswered questions that remain.

This collection is testimony to the complexities and directions of international monetary studies that have developed through the years. In the days of Adam Smith and David Hume, domestic policies geared to acquiring and hoarding monetary wealth—principally gold—were shown to be fallacious at best. Essentially, Hume told us that the price level, the income of a country, and the supply and demand for money were interrelated variables searching for some equilibrium. In his work, the balance of payments or change in holdings of international reserves were part of an automatically adjusting system, determined by market forces. Mercantilistic policies aimed at hoarding reserves were doomed to failure by these forces. The pursuit of mercantilistic policies by various governments would only undermine trade and create a less than optimal level of real trade among nations. Consistent with Hume's view of money and trade were the laissez-faire notions of Adam Smith. His appeal to the "invisible hand" is consistent with modern arguments for market-determined international transactions in goods, services, and assets. Mercantilistic value judgments that trade deficits were bad and surpluses good had no meaning to a man who realized a country's wealth was found in its actual output potential and not its stock of gold.

Such arguments as these are strongly embedded in the monetary approach to international adjustment. The emergence of the monetary approach in the late

1960s and 1970s marks a major swing in economic thought back to the concepts of Hume and Smith, and away from the balance of payments theories that emerged from the Keynesian revolution. In particular, economists schooled in the Keynesian tradition tended to focus on the balance of payments, and specifically the current account, as a policy variable. Depreciation policies could be used to make exports more competitive and thereby increase employment at home. Trade account imbalances were viewed as employment problems deserving of protectionist policies if the imbalances could not be corrected with exchange rate changes. In the economic models, capital flows were often ignored and changes in the exchange rate were assumed to cause equal changes in the terms of trade. Partial equilibrium frameworks became the standard for viewing trade imbalances.

The changing reality of the international monetary system, however, began to challenge these approaches. World markets were important for many goods and capital markets developed internationally at impressive rates. At the same time, domestic monetarism was a rising force, emphasizing the importance of money and the general equilibrium nature of domestic economies. Given that world goods and capital markets were becoming more and more integrated, international theorists were forced to rework their models; simultaneously, the importance of monetary demand and supply relationships on a world level was becoming integrated into this new general equilibrium approach to balance of payments questions. The resultant work by Robert Mundell, Harry Johnson, Arthur Laffer, Richard Zecher, and their students and colleagues at the University of Chicago and elsewhere is now known as the monetary approach to the balance of payments. In some sense, then, the monetary approach is not a restatement of Hume, but is more properly viewed as the refinements of international adjustment theories prevalent in the 1950s and 1960s, after these theories had been reworked with a view toward global markets in the context of a general equilibrium framework. The basic argument, under fixed exchange rates, became that excess supplies of and demand for money led to changes in international reserves. Trade was viewed as only one portion of the country's international account, as was the capital account. If one viewed trade as representing the goods market and the capital account as reflecting the bond market, the balance of these or the change in international reserves would reflect money market (using Walras' Law) equilibrium or disequilibrium. An excess supply of money implied an outflow of reserves as the country's domestic money stock adjusted to the demand for money within the country.

The development of this literature opened a new chapter in the development of international monetary theory. In the course of changing international monetary relations, and during the end of the Bretton-Woods exchange rate system, this basic theory is leading to new ways of analyzing and forecasting exchange rate movements.

This collection of essays, developed from this heritage, Hume to Mundell, challenges the old theories as well as the new and, it is hoped, contributes to the further understanding of how the international economic system functions.

ACKNOWLEDGMENTS

This volume has benefited in no small way from the services rendered by two professionals who also happen to be the editors' spouses. For this reason we wish to express more than the usual passing gratitude and compliments to our wives. Jane Micholet Wilford, currently a librarian at Columbia University, prepared the index and provided critical advice concerning the compilation of the bibliography. Jane's extensive library experience, and in particular her training in indexing, proved indispensable. Mary Etta Schneider Putnam, currently with Citibank, used her experience in international economics gained at Citibank and the Federal Reserve Bank of New York to provide valuable assistance and to aid with the final manuscript review.

CONTENTS

Chapter		Page

LIST OF TABLES

LIST OF FIGURES

FIXED EXCHANGE RATES

PART I

INTRODUCTION
Bluford H. Putnam
D. Sykes Wilford

The present theory of international adjustment addressed in this volume, the monetary approach to the balance of payments, is a product of the Bretton-Woods period, or as one might argue, is a product of the decay and demise of the Bretton-Woods period. In either case, the monetary approach's initial development focused upon balance of payments adjustment under fixed exchange rates. Of course, as we see in the second part of this volume, the literature has been speedily applied, with success, to the flexible case as well. But for the first set of papers let us return to the period of fixed exchange rates.

As many authors have noted, the monetary approach traces its roots back to David Hume's classic essay, "Of the Balance of Trade," in his *Essays, Moral, Political, and Literary*, published in 1752. The concepts that there is automatic adjustment of the balance of payments, that the existence of expected arbitrage possibilities would in itself lead to speculative arbitrage and then to purchasing power parity, and that a country's stock of money is determined by demand factors not under the control of the authorites—all these are fundamental implications of the monetary approach and are contained in Hume's essay. Indeed, Hume had much more to contribute to balance of payments theory than just the price-specie-flow mechanism so often recounted in economic texts. Thus, before moving on to the present-day extensions of Hume's work, a close look at exactly what Hume said will lead to a fuller appreciation of the monetary approach's debt to him.

After laying the foundation for his analysis of the balance of payments by providing pedagogical illustrations of the price-specie-flow mechanism, Hume takes a general equilibrium view of the world. He states,

> Now, it is evident, that the same causes, which would correct these exorbitant inequalities, were they to happen miraculously, must pre-

vent their happening in the common cause of nature, and must forever, in all neighboring nations, preserve money nearly proportionable to the art and industry of each nation.[1]

Hume is very definite here in his perception of a world in which monetary stocks are consistent with the real income of the nation. He is arguing that the forces that determine the money stock are so strong as to preclude any significant inequalities. To make certain his readers understand this point, Hume likens money to water:

> All water, wherever it communicates, remains always at a level. Ask naturalists the reason; they tell you, that were it to be raised in any one place, the superior gravity of that part not being balanced, must depress it, till it meet a counter-poise; and that the same cause, which redresses the inequality when it happens, must forever prevent it, without some violent external operation.[2]

Hume's statement suggests a perception of the world quite similar to the framework of the monetary approach to the balance of payments. Hume is arguing that the money stock is demand determined by the "art and industry" of the nation. Furthermore, he is suggesting that prices among countries are also linked. Hume's specific statement on prices is as follows:

> And any man who travels over Europe at this day, may see, by the prices of commodities, that money, in spite of the absurd jealousy of princes and states, has brought itself nearly to a level; and that the difference between one kingdom and another is not greater in this respect, than it is often between different provinces of the same kingdom.[3]

Here, Hume is making the case for the purchasing-power parity doctrine, and his arguments are similar in nature to the monetary approach assumptions of unified world markets.

Building on these basic points contained in Hume's writing, studies of the monetary approach to international adjustment have elaborated these propositions, expressed them in mathematical formulations, and applied modern statistical techniques to evaluate them. The collection of works in this volume is designed to give the reader a broad picture of such studies, from basic theory and historical origins to frontier extensions and new statistical tests.

The collection is opened by Michael Connolly's "The Monetary Approach to the Open Economy: The Fundamental Theory," an overview of the monetary approach in its basic form as well as a survey of new developments in theory and empirical work. Following this study is Robert Keleher's extensive investigation of the historical origins of monetary approach concepts studied titled "Of Money and Prices: Some Historical Perspectives." More than any other historical essay to date, this work documents the thoughts of early economists who grappled with the problems of international adjustments, as they related to the monetary approach, and refined and extended the theories associated with Hume and his contemporaries.

Initial studies of the monetary approach tended to focus on the small, open economy, but application of the approach to the United States is extremely important given the role of the dollar in international trade and finance. The next two studies, "A Monetary View of the Balance of Payments," by Donald S. Kemp, and "Money, Income, and Causality in the United States and the United Kingdom," by Bluford H. Putnam and D. Sykes Wilford, analyze the special case of the large country providing the international system with a reserve currency.

Empirical studies have provided an extensive body of evidence supporting the usefulness of the monetary approach, and two such investigations are included in this collection. The first, "International Reserve Flows: Seemingly Unrelated Regressions," by Bluford H. Putnam and D. Sykes Wilford, empirically evaluates the approach for eight European countries and provides evidence on the purchasing power and interest rate parity assumptions within a reduced-form specification. Michael Cox's study, "Some Empirical Evidence on an Incomplete Information Model of the Monetary Approach to the Balance of Payments," integrates expectations of monetary policy into the theory and estimates the resulting formulations, using Canada as its test case. This study is of particular interest since it explicitly recognizes the interdependence of the monetary policies of Canada and those of the United States.

Applications of the monetary approach to developing economies are becoming increasingly important, as the approach has much to say concerning the interdependence of these economies and the world financial structure. In "Some Observations on the Monetary Approach to Balance of Payments and the Third World," Walton T. Wilford addresses the issue of how a basic monetary approach model applies to developing economies, taking care to note the points that are unique to these countries and embody them in his analysis. His conclusions concerning the applicability of this approach to Third World nations deserve critical attention.

The final study in the fixed exchange rate section is by M. A. Akhtar. Here, in "Some Common Misconceptions about the Monetary Approach to International Adjustment," the analytical problems of the monetary approach as noted by its critics and opponents are given special attention. Since many authors of works on the monetary approach concentrate on extending the standard approach rather than on responding to questions and criticism, this study is a valuable contribution to the monetary approach literature.

NOTES

1. David Hume, "Of the Balance of Trade," *Essays, Moral, Political, and Literary* (1752), Essay V, Part II, reprinted in *International Trade Theory: Hume to Ohlin*, ed. William R. Allen (New York: Random House, 1965), p. 35.

2. Ibid.

3. Ibid., p. 36.

Michael Connolly

1

THE MONETARY APPROACH
TO AN OPEN ECONOMY:
THE FUNDAMENTAL THEORY

"Suppose four fifths of all the money in Great Britain to be annihilated in one night," David Hume speculated in 1752 ". . . must not the price of all labor and commodities sink in proportion," giving England a competitive advantage in trade which must quickly "bring back the money we had lost, and raise us to the level (of prices) of all the neighboring nations?"[1] This adjustment process was to be christened the Hume specie-flow mechanism, and is, in a fundamental sense, the earliest known statement of a monetary approach to the balance of payments. Hume's statement also raised specific issues such as the now controversial so-called law of one price. This law, apparently contradicted in particular for traded goods by Hume's theoretical adjustment process was, however, firmly held by him: "Any man who travels over Europe at this day, may see, by the prices of commodities, that money . . . has brought itself nearly to a level; and that the difference between one kingdom and another is not greater in this respect, than it is often between different provinces of the same kingdom."[2]

(This latter criterion has in fact provided the basis for one of the first modern empirical tests of the law of one price.[3] Hume further noted: "The only circumstance that can obstruct the exactness of these proportions is the expense of transporting the commodities from one place to another.")[4]

This is so because "the same causes, which would correct these exorbitant inequalities, were they to happen miraculously, must prevent their happening in the common course of nature."[5] Consequently, price differences would not be an observed part of the species flow adjustment process, and the apparent contradiction with the law-of-one-price is resolved.[6]

While the first statements of a monetary approach to the balance of payments stressed commodity trade more than adjustment in asset markets, they nevertheless laid out the fundamental principle of a demand for money that, if not satisfied, led to a surplus to provide the additional money desired or, if exceeded, led to a deficit, thereby depleting the excess balances. This is the basic modern monetary view. It consists of three elements: a theory of the demand for money, a money supply process, and balance of payments surpluses in instances of excess demand for money and deficits in cases of excess supply.

In the context of flexible exchange rates, an excess supply of money would induce an exchange depreciation rather than a loss in foreign reserves, and an excess demand results in an appreciation in lieu of a reserve accumulation. Finally, the monetary model has offered an explanation of both reserve and exchange rate changes in the context of a managed float.[7] Once again, the fortunes of a country's reserves and/or exchange rate depend upon the balance between the supply of and the demand for money.

In what follows, we try to develop somewhat more formally a minimum monetary model for the uninitiated. Modern monetary views are stated more completely elsewhere in a number of articles by Harry Johnson, Robert Mundell, and some of their former students, such as Rudiger Dornbusch and Jacob Frenkel.[8]

A MINIMUM MONETARY MODEL

The most succinct monetary model is that of the "small, open economy" facing given world prices and interest rates.* With interest rates unchanged or simply omitted from the demand for money, we can write a straightforward Cambridge demand for money equation:

$$L = kPY \qquad (1)$$

where P is domestic prices, and Y permanent income. A stable demand for money, no matter what the variant it assumes,† is the cornerstone of the monetary approach to an open economy. If one agrees that the demand for money is stable in the Friedman sense, the monetary approach to the balance of payments is the natural consequence.[9] Put more forcefully, the notion of a stable demand for money and the monetary approach to an open economy are one and the same thing. Harry Johnson put it this way in his nontechnical guide to the monetary approach to the balance of payments: "A proper test of the monetary approach must be essentially a test of the stability of the demand for money (in Friedman's terminology) "[10]

---

*Empirically, this model has been fruitfully applied to a number of seemingly large countries, so that it applies to most large ones, if not the United States.

†A slightly more complex one used in empirical studies is $L = kPY^{\epsilon}i^{-\eta}$, where ϵ and η are income and interest rate elasticities of the demand for money respectively.

The second essential ingredient of the minimum monetary model is a specification of the money supply process. The simplest one is that of Robert A. Mundell,[11] which consolidates private and central banks into a consolidated banking system whose monetary liabilities, the money stock, M, are matched by the sum of its foreign and domestic assets, denoted by R and D respectively, in the following identity:

$$M = R + D \tag{2}$$

This identity states that changes in the money stock are either from foreign or from domestic sources, for example, a change in foreign reserves via the balance of payments or a change in domestic credit extended by the consolidated banking system.*

The third relationship essential to the simple monetary model is the link between domestic and international prices via the exchange rate. It is assumed to hold partly because of arbitrage and partly because of the monetary adjustment process. The purchasing power parity relationship is shown by

$$P = EP^o \tag{3}$$

where P is domestic prices, P^o is foreign prices, and E is the exchange rate.

This relationship, while it need only hold in terms of changes (for example, $p = e + p^o$, where small letters denote percentage changes), is perhaps one of the more controversial ones in the monetary model. Further, it is an important one in that it is part of the transmission mechanism whereby exchange rate changes and world price movements disturb domestic prices and, consequently, the demand for money. In favor of the purchasing power parity relationship, one can invoke commodity arbitrage and/or the neutrality of money in an adjustment process. Against it, one can argue that it holds only for purely monetary disturbances. Empirically, the evidence on this law-of-one-price is mixed.† In some instances,

---

*The supply of money equation is closely related to the IMF definition: Foreign Assets + Domestic Credit = Money + Quasi-Money of the consolidated banking system. If M_2 is used, they are the same; if M_1 is used, Quasi-Money must be deducted from Domestic Credit as defined by the IMF, and the result defined as domestic credit. If we wish to separate central and private banking systems the money supply process becomes $M = m(R^o + D^o)$, where m is the money multiplier, R^o official reserves, and D^o net holdings of domestic assets by the central bank. Empirical studies have taken both forms with little difference resulting, in that typically most foreign reserves are held by the central bank and there is little change in money multipliers over relatively short periods.

† J. M. Keynes was the first to dub purchasing power parity the law of one price, in his comment on Gustav Cassel's 1916 paper: "The effect of Professor Cassel's interesting calculations . . . seems to me to be that even with the hindrances to free movements of goods which prevail in war time, *real* price levels in different countries tend to equality. That is to

the weakness of the evidence on the law of one price has diminished the predictive power of the monetary model.*

Finally, it simplifies matters greatly to assume that the money stock in existence adjusts rapidly to the quantity demanded, either by a deficit (running down the money stock) or by an exchange depreciation (increasing the demand) or by some combination of the two, so that monetary equilibrium holds:†

$$L = M \tag{4}$$

With fixed exchange rates, the nominal money supply adjusts to the demand via payments imbalances, while with flexible exchange rates the demand for money adjusts to the nominal supply via changes in the exchange rate. In a mixed system, both the demand and the supply of money adjust to achieve equilibrium.

Substituting equation (3) into (1), and equations (1) and (2) into (4), taking logarithms of both sides, differentiating with respect to time, we have, after manipulation: $r + e = -d + p^0 + y$ where r is the change in foreign reserves (the balance of payments) as a proportion of the money stock, e is the percentage appreciation (if positive) of the home currency, p^0 the world rate of inflation, and y the rate of growth of permanent income (assumed to be determined exogenously).‡

Two polar cases of the minimum monetary model can be distinguished. First, with fixed exchange rates $e = 0$, giving:

$$r = -d + p^0 + y \tag{5}$$

which states that an increase in the rate of growth of domestic credit will cause an equiproportionate loss in reserves for a given rate of world inflation and growth in

---

say, the index numbers of local prices corrected by the world-value of local money, as measured by the exchanges, tend to equality."[12] Keynes' later empirical studies in *Monetary Reform*, despite his theoretical reticence regarding real disturbances, such as in Germany, found that the "Purchasing Power Parity Theory, even in its crude form, has worked passably well"[13] for the United Kingdom, Italy, and France relative to the United States between August 1919 and June 1923.

*On the side of integrated markets and one-price are H. Genberg, P. Isard, D. McClosky, and R. Zecher, while against are R. M. Dunn, and Michael Bordo and E. Choudri. Richardson reports mixed results. M. Connolly and J. da Silveira find that purchasing power parity predicts well for postwar Brazil where disturbances were frequently monetary.[14]

†A more sophisticated model allows for less than immediate adjustment. Specifically, in R. Dornbusch's notation, $H = \pi(L - M)$, where H is hoarding, for example, the change in reserves, and π the speed of adjustment. Here we suppose $\pi = \infty$, which implies $L = M$. The Dornbusch model is of interest also because it provides a two-country monetary framework.

‡ Note that for notational simplicity both the change in reserves and the change in domestic credit are expressed as a proportion of the money stock, that is, $r = (dR/dt)/M$ and $D = (dD/dt)/M$, since $d \log (R + D)/dt = (dR/dt)/(R + D) + (dD/dt)/(R + D)$ and $R + D \equiv M$.

permanent income. (Parenthetically, the higher income growth is, the *more* favorable the balance of payments as a result of the increase in the demand for money, contrary to post-Keynesian import demand arguments.) This relationship (or variants of it) has been tested for a good number of countries under fixed exchange rates. The majority of the studies strongly support the negative relationship between domestic credit (for example, monetary policy) and the state of the balance of payments. Put briefly, monetary expansion is at the expense of foreign reserves.

A second polar case is that of fully flexible exchange rates, that is, $r = 0$ with no intervention on foreign exchange markets, giving:

$$e = -d + p^0 + y \tag{6}$$

With fully flexible rates any increase in the growth rate of domestic credit causing an excess supply of money results in an equiproportionate depreciation of the home currency. Consequently, the monetary approach provides a theory of exchange rate determination in the event of flexible rates.*

Finally, a mixed case in which exchange market pressure is absorbed partly by reserve losses and partly by exchange depreciation is given by

$$r + e = -d + p^0 + y \tag{7}$$

where, once again, r and d are changes in reserves and domestic credit as a proportion of the money stock, while the other variables are percentage changes.

This model was first proposed by L. Girton and D. Roper[15] for the Canadian-managed float from 1952 to 1962, and is an extremely useful way of viewing the current mixed exchange regime. Basically, the monetary authorities have, for a given rate of growth of domestic credit, world prices, and permanent income, a choice between reserve losses and exchange rate changes that will absorb a given level of pressure on the exchange market. Or it makes clear that an expansionary domestic credit policy will cause a loss in reserves, an exchange depreciation, or a combination of the two.†

For the purpose of an introductory essay, this is the current state of the art. The fundamental monetary model presented here captures, I believe, the essential elements of the monetary approach to an open economy. To sum up, its foundation is a stable demand for money in the Friedman sense coupled with a money

---

*This formula applies to freely floating rates, and not to the discrete, discontinuous devaluations of the adjustable peg system of the postwar period until the 1970s. Such once-and-for-all exchange rate adjustments are analyzed by M. Connolly and D. Taylor for 18 devaluations that took place in the 1960s.[16]

†Connolly and da Silveira have recently applied the exchange market pressure model to postwar Brazil.[17]

stock composed of an external component (foreign reserves) and an internal component (domestic credit). In cases of excess money supply over demand, exchange market pressure results in a loss of foreign reserves, thereby reducing the supply of money, and/or an exchange depreciation, which restores equilibrium by increasing the demand for money. In one sense, that is all one need know about the principal elements of the monetary approach. In another, it is an incomplete picture because the state of the art is rapidly changing. In the next section, some special issues and further extensions of the monetary model to an open economy will be touched upon.

FURTHER ISSUES AND EXTENSIONS

Expectations

Probably the most important issue regarding exchange rates in particular has to do with expectations. Some recent studies in this area are suggestive of the delicate problems involved. R. Barro, for instance, has devised a scheme of exchange rate dynamics that revolves around individuals and firms distinguishing between a permanent and a transitory component or any exogenous change in the rate of monetary expansion.[18] The greater the permanency perceived by the public of an increased monetary expansion rate, the more immediate and the greater the exchange depreciation. This raises the question of the formation of expectations, which has been explored in a number of interesting papers by John Bilson[19] in the context of rational expectations.

The basic principle is that the spot and forward rates fully incorporate all current information and expectations regarding the future. In this light, J. Frenkel has devised a clever shortcut for measuring expectations in the demand for money by using the forward exchange rate rather than, for example, adaptive expectations.[20] For the German hyperinflation, the forward rate for the mark performs well as an explanatory variable in the demand for money, and has the property of conforming to rational expectations theory, in that spot exchange rates are correlated with the last period's forward rates but not with previous ones. That is, the most recent forward rate incorporates all currently available market information.

A different approach in a monetary context is that of Rudiger Dornbusch.[21] The main interest of his approach is that it provides a "monetary shock" rationale for overshooting of exchange rates. Consider increasing the domestic monetary stock by means of open market purchases in a flexible exchange rate regime. This lowers domestic interest rates instantaneously through a liquidity effect, and immediately depreciates the exchange rate, but by *more* than its ultimate depreciation. That is, overshooting takes place. The reason for this is the Fisherian relationship:

$$i = i^0 + \rho \tag{8}$$

which states that domestic interest rates, i, must equal foreign ones, i^0, plus ρ, the expected rate of depreciation of the home currency. (Irving Fisher puts it succinctly: "... Two rates of interest in ... two diverging standards will, in a perfect adjustment, differ from each other by an amount equal to the rate of divergence between the two standards.")[22] Consequently, if monetary expansion depresses domestic interest rates through a liquidity effect, and foreign interest rates remain unchanged, the home currency must initially depreciate *more* than its eventual decline. Thus the expectation is that it will recover somewhat in value, but not return to its initial value. This satisfies the Fisher rule since it implies $\rho < 0$. Of course, not all reversible exchange rate swings are necessarily caused by monetary supply shocks; they can also arise from shifts in demands for national monies as assets. This latter view, while admittedly not entirely new, possibly sheds light upon current exchange rate swings. Further, it shifts the emphasis away from relative rates of inflation (or purchasing power parity) toward an asset or stock market determination of exchange rates. While purchasing power parity may in the long run (and occasionally in the short run) be a good predictor in instances of widely diverging monetary policies, it cannot account for dramatic, sometimes reversible swings in short periods of time.

Neutralization

In the framework of the monetary approach to the balance of payments under fixed exchange rates it has been suggested that the direction of causation may be from changes in reserves to changes in domestic credit rather than, as the monetarists would have it, the other way around.[23] This occurs with a policy of neutralizing the effects of payments surpluses or deficits upon the high-powered money base via an offsetting domestic credit policy. In the notation of the minimum monetary model:

$$d = a - \beta r \tag{9}$$

where β, the sterilization coefficient, ranges from zero (no offsetting) to unity (complete sterilization) and a is a constant.

This argument merits further attention. As Pentti Kouri and Michael Porter[24] note, neutralization would tend to bias empirical tests in favor of the domestic credit aspect of the monetary model. (Their study stresses capital outflows in response to monetary expansion. A framework for the analysis of this problem is found in Alexanda Swoboda.)[25] In separate tests by Hans Genberg for Sweden, Lance Girton and Don Roper for Canada, and Michael Connolly and Taylor for a cross section of 27 countries, the evidence suggests that some neutralization takes place, particularly in developed countries, but that even in its presence, the bias in favor of the monetary view is negligible. Further tests would, however, be in order.*

Currency Substitution and Competition Among National Monies

Recent theoretical developments have stressed the importance of currency substitution among asset holders. A number of papers provide a theory of multiple currencies that circulate within the same region (or rather are held by individuals within the same region) and are viewed as substitutes by holders of money. Russell Boyer's early "nickel and dime" paper neatly posed the problem, which, in the context of stability, involves Gresham's Law. Girton and Roper find that the greater the degree of substitution among national monies, the less stable the exchange rate. G. Calvo and E. Rodriguez add rational expectations to the picture, and find that exchange rate responses to monetary shocks exceed price responses but that with perfect foresight paths, instability does not result. David King, Bluford Putnam, and D. Sykes Wilford examine exchange rate stability and the independence of monetary policy with currency substitution.[26]

A natural companion to currency substitution is the implied existence of competition among issuers of national monies. (On this, see Benjamin Klein and Gorden Tullock for opposing views.)[27] The situation is analogous to the era of state banking in the United States, during which states issued monies and exchange rates between state currencies were flexible (see Friedman and Schwartz.)[28] In principle, there exists an optimal rule for issuing national money, given that competition from other issuers exists. Not surprisingly, currency competition leads to at least a partial internalizing of the well-known negative externality (see Friedman)[29] imposed by overissue in the case of monopoly issue of currency, and imparts a greater degree of price stability to an international monetary system (see Girton and Roper).[30] Other considerations may well override the competitive one—particularly the debt financing motive in some instances—but the principle is a sound one meriting further theoretical and empirical work. Marc Miles, using a constant elasticity of substitution (CES) production framework, estimated the elasticity of substitution between U.S. and Canadian dollars and found it *greater* during floating than during fixed periods, significantly different from zero, but not infinite. (From 1960 to 1975, the elasticity of substitution was estimated to be 5.4.)[31]

---

*See Chapter 8 of this book for further treatment of this issue.

EXCHANGE RATES AND THE RELATIVE PRICE
OF TRADED GOODS

The minimum monetary model discussed here makes no distinction between traded and nontraded goods: domestic prices of all goods are simply assumed to be kept in line with international prices. This assumption does not hinge upon arbitrage in goods, but rather upon the idea of the long run neutrality of nominal magnitudes, namely the exchange rate and the money stock, in a monetary system. However, in the short run adjustment period to, for example, an exchange depreciation, the relative price of traded goods will rise, and consequently there will be not only liquidity effects as outlined in the minimum monetary model, but also substitution effects along the lines of the elasticity approach. The role of such substitution effects between traded and nontraded goods during the adjustment period to monetary shocks is stressed in a monetary framework in a number of papers that build upon the so-called Australian or Swan-Salter model.[32] This model is, once again, one of a small open economy that produces two composite goods, a traded one (exports and imports) and a nontraded one. In addition, individuals hold domestic money as their sole asset. Exchange depreciation thus has a liquidity effect, increasing the demand for money, and also a substitution effect, as individuals substitute traded goods for nontraded ones. Both effects work towards improving the balance of payments. However, as money flows in during the adjustment period these effects diminish and the system returns to its initial equilibrium. Consequently, real effects due to substitution take place only during the transitional adjustment process, while in the long run there are none. These transitional real effects are highlighted in Dornbusch, while the adjustment process itself has been dealt with by P. D. Jonson and H. Kierzkowski graphically and by Connolly and Taylor algebraically.[33]

A SHORT GUIDE TO EMPIRICAL STUDIES

A masterful survey by S. P. Magee of empirical work on the monetary approach to an open economy appeared in 1976, and one by M. Kreinen and L. Officer is in preparation.[34] Consequently we need touch upon only a few studies that an interested reader might consult. The considerable amount of empirical work done to date in the area and the rapid rate of appearance of new statistical tests is testimony to the strong empirical thrust of the monetary approach. It is unfortunate that some early reviewers, such as G. Haberler, either neglect the first empirical studies altogether or, as does Marina Von Neuman Whitman, incorrectly dismiss them as "the estimation of an accounting identity rather than a true behavioral relationship," in an otherwise excellent, well-balanced review.[35] (For an empirical rejection of the view that empirical studies of the monetary approach are estimating only an accounting identity, see Putnam and Wilford.)[36] For, as stressed by Rudolf Rhomberg and H. R. Heller in the introduction to the recent International Monetary Fund (IMF) volume, the possibility of empirical measurement of monetary and balance of payments aggregates fostered in part the development of the monetary framework.*

Here is a short list of selected empirical studies. (Full references are contained in the bibliography.)

1. Surveys:
   Magee
   Kreinen and Officer
2. Case studies:
   - Fixed exchange rate periods:
       Australia: Zecher
       Canada: Cox and Wilford
       Canada: Cox
       Germany: Kouri
       Germany: Porter
       Honduras: Wilford and Wilford
       Jamaica: Beals and Collery
       Japan: Bean
       Mexico: Wilford and Zecher
       Mexico: Wilford
       Mexico: Blejer
       Spain: Guitian
       Sweden: Genberg
       United Kingdom: Jonson
       Venezuela: Khan
       Eight European countries: Putnam and Wilford
   - Flexible exchange rate periods:
       Germany: Frenkel
       United States–United Kingdom: Putnam and Woodbury
   - Mixed exchange rate periods:
       Brazil: Connolly and da Silveira
       Canada: Girton and Roper
       England: Bilson

---

*In Rhomberg and Heller's terms: "In view of the availability of these two sets of data (monetary statistics and balance of payments accounts) in a large number of countries for which other statistical information was scarce, the thought naturally presented itself to develop a framework that could take full advantage of this data base." Regarding the IMF studies in that volume, on one hand, it would be too generous to credit the IMF with the empirical, back-of-the-envelope discovery of the monetary approach. On the other, it would be unfair not to note their numerous empirical studies regarding money in an open economy. Further, J. J. Polak's early theoretical essay and the IMF's actual lending practice stress the importance of domestic credit restraint to the state of the balance of payments.[37]

3. Cross section studies:
   - Capital flows offsetting monetary policy (4 countries):
     Kouri and Porter
   - Monetary approach to devaluation (18 countries):
     Connolly and Taylor
   - Exchange rate determination with rational expectations
     (34 countries):
     Bilson
   - Exchange market pressure model (5 countries):
     Sargen
   - Balance-of-payments determination (39 countries):
     Aghevli and Khan

NOTES

1. David Hume, "Of the Balance of Trade," in *Essays, Moral, Political, and Literary* (1752), Essay V, Part II, reprinted in *International Trade Theory: Hume to Ohlin*, ed. W. R. Allen (New York: Random House, 1965), p. 34.

2. Ibid., p. 36.

3. See, for instance, Donald McClosky and J. Richard Zecher, "How the Gold Standard Worked 1880-1913," in Jacob Frenkel and Harry G. Johnson, *The Monetary Approach to the Balance of Payments* (Toronto: The University of Toronto Press, 1976).

4. Hume, op. cit., p. 36. See Paul Samuelson, "An Exact Hume-Ricardo-Marshall Model of International Trade," *Journal of International Economics* 1 (February 1971) for further discussion of this matter.

5. Hume, op. cit., p. 36.

6. See both J. A. Frenkel and Harry G. Johnson, "The Monetary Approach to the Balance of Payments: Essential Concepts and Historical Origins," in J. A. Frenkel and H. G. Johnson, eds., *The Monetary Approach to the Balance of Payments* (Toronto: The University of Toronto Press, 1976); and Bluford H. Putnam, "David Hume and the Monetary Approach to the Balance of Payments," Mimeographed, 1976, for a discussion of Hume's writings on the balance of payments and on this point in particular.

7. See L. Girton and D. Roper, "A Monetary Model of Exchange Market Pressure Applied to the Post-War Canadian Experiences," *American Economic Review* 60 (September 1977): 537–48.

8. Standing as two landmarks in the theoretical development of the monetary approach to the open economy are Robert A. Mundell, *International Economics* (New York: Macmillan, 1969); and Robert A. Mundell, *Monetary Theory* (Pacific Palisades: Goodyear, 1971). Frenkel and Johnson's *The Monetary Approach to the Balance of Payments*, op. cit., contains a good number of key theoretical articles on the monetary approach, such as R. Dornbusch, "Devaluation, Money and Non-Traded Goods," *American Economic Review* 61 (December 1973): 871–80. In addition, it has a stimulating set of empirical studies. See also Harry G. Johnson, "The Monetary Approach to Balance of Payments Theory," in M. Connolly and A. Swoboda, eds., *International Trade and Money* (London: Allen and Unwin, 1973).

9. The following works are pertinent references: Milton Friedman, "The Optimum Quantity of Money," in *The Optimum Quantity of Money and Other Essays* (Chicago: Aldine, 1969); Milton Friedman, *A Program for Monetary Stability* (New York: Fordham University Press, 1960); and Milton Friedman and A. Schwartz, *A Monetary History of the United States 1867-1960*, National Bureau of Economic Research (Princeton: Princeton University Press, 1963).

10. Harry G. Johnson, "The Monetary Approach to the Balance of Payments: A Non-technical Guide," *Journal of International Economics* 7 (August 1977): 263.

11. Mundell, *Monetary Theory*, op. cit.

12. Gustav Cassel, "The Present Situation of the Foreign Exchanges," *The Economic Journal* (March 1916): 62-65.

13. J. M. Keynes, "Theory of Money and the Exchanges," in J. M. Keynes, *Monetary Reform* (London: Macmillan, 1924), p. 111.

14. H. Genberg, "Aspects of the Monetary Approach to Balance of Payments Theory: An Empirical Study of Sweden," in Frenkel and Johnson, op. cit., pp. 198-326; P. Isard, "How Far Can We Push the Law of One Price," *American Economic Review* 65 (December 1977): 942-48; D. McClosky and R. Zecher, "How the Gold Standard Worked, 1880-1913," in Frenkel and Johnson, op. cit.; R. M. Dunn, "Flexible Exchange Rates and Oligopoly Pricing: A Study of Canadian Markets," *Journal of Political Economy* 78 (January 1970): 146-51; Michael Bordo and E. Choudri, "The Behavior of the Prices of Traded and Non-traded Goods: The Canadian Cases 1962-74," Mimeographed, 1977; and M. Connolly and J. da Silveira, "An Application of the Girton-Roper Monetary Models of Exchange Market Pressure to Postwar Brazil," Mimeographed, 1978.

15. Girton and Roper, op. cit.

16. M. Connolly and D. Taylor, "Testing the Monetary Approach to Devaluation in Developing Countries," *Journal of Political Economy* 84 (August 1976): 849-59.

17. Connolly and da Silveira, op. cit.

18. R. Barro, "A Simple Flexible Exchange Rate Model with Uncertainty and Rational Expectations," Mimeographed, November 1975.

19. John Bilson, "A Simple Long-Run Model of Exchange Determination," Mimeo-graphed, 1977; and John Bilson, "Rational Expectations and the Exchange Rate," in J. A. Frenkel and H. G. Johnson, eds., *The Economics of Exchange Rates: Selected Studies* (Reading, Mass.: Addison Wesley, 1978). See also this book, Chapter 6.

20. See J. Frenkel, "A Monetary Approach to the Exchange Rate: Doctrinal Aspects and Empirical Evidence," *Scandinavian Journal of Economics* 78 (1976): 200-24; and J. Frenkel, "The Forward Exchange Rate, Expectations and the Demand for Money: The German Hyperinflation," *American Economic Review* 65 (September 1977): 653-69.

21. R. Dornbusch, "Exchange Rate Dynamics," *Journal of Political Economy* 84 (December 1976): 1161-76.

22. Irving Fisher, *The Theory of Interest* (New York, 1930).

23. See, for example, M. Whitman, "Global Monetarism and the Monetary Approach to the Balance of Payments," *Brookings Papers on Economic Activity* 3 (1975): 491-556.

24. P. Kouri and M. Porter, "International Capital Flows and Portfolio Equilibriums," *Journal of Political Economy* 82 (May/June 1974): 443-67.

25. A. Swoboda, "Equilibrium, Quasi-Equilibrium, and Macroeconomic Policy Under Fixed Exchange Rates," *Quarterly Journal of Economics* 86 (February 1972): 162-71.

26. See R. Boyer, "Currency Mobility and Balance of Payments Adjustment" (Chapter 13, this book); R. Boyer, "Nickels and Dimes," Federal Reserve Board of Governors manuscript; L. Girton and D. Roper, "Theory and Implications of Currency Substitution," *International Financial Discussion Paper* (Washington, D.C.: Federal Reserve Board of Governors, May 1976); G. Calvo and C. Rodriguez, "A Model of Exchange Rate Determination Under Currency Substitution and Rational Expectations," *Journal of Political Economy* 85 (June 1977): 617-25; and D. King, B. H. Putnam, and D. S. Wilford, "A Currency Portfolio Approach to Exchange Rate Determination: Exchange Rate Stability and the Independence of Monetary Policy" (Chapter 14, this book).

27. B. Klein, "Competing Monies: A Comment," *Journal of Money Credit and Banking* 6 (November 1975): 513-19; and G. Tullock, "Competing Monies," *Journal of Money Credit and Banking* 6 (November 1973): 491-97.

28. Friedman and Schwartz, op. cit.

29. Friedman, *A Program for Monetary Stability*, op. cit.

30. Girton and Roper, "Theory and Implications," op. cit.

31. Marc Miles, "Currency Substitution, Flexible Exchange Rates, and Monetary Independence," *American Economic Review* 68 (June 1978): 428–36; and Marc Miles, "Currency Substitution: Perspective, Implications, and Empirical Evidence" (Chapter 12, this book).

32. W. E. Salter, "Internal and External Balances: The Role of Price and Expenditure Effects," *The Economic Record* 35 (1952).

33. R. Dornbusch, "Real and Monetary Aspects of the Effects of Exchange Rate Changes," in R. Z. Aliber, ed., *National Monetary Policies and the International Financial System* (Chicago: University of Chicago Press, 1974); P. D. Jonson and H. Kierzkowski, "The Balance of Payments: An Analytic Exercise," *The Manchester School of Economic and Social Studies* 43 (June 1975): 105–33; M. Connolly and D. Taylor, "Adjustment to Devaluation with Money and Non-Traded Goods," *Journal of International Economics* 6 (August 1976): 289–98.

34. S. P. Magee, "The Empirical Evidence on the Monetary Approach to the Balance of Payments and Exchange Rates," *American Economic Review Papers and Proceedings* 66 (May 1976): 163–70; and M. Kreinen and L. Officer, "Survey of Empirical Evidence on the Monetary Approach to Open Economies," *Princeton Studies on International Finance* (Princeton: Princeton University Press, 1978).

35. G. Haberler, "The Monetary Approach to the Balance of Payments by Frenkel and Johnson," review in *Journal of Economic Literature* 14 (December 1976): 1324–28; and Whitman, op. cit.

36. B. H. Putnam and D. S. Wilford, "Monetary Equilibrium and International Reserve Flows: An Empirical Treatment of the Money Supply Identity Issue," Mimeographed, 1977.

37. R. Rhomberg and H. R. Heller, "Introductory Survey," *The Monetary Approach to the Balance of Payments* (Washington, D.C.: International Monetary Fund), pp. 6, 1–14; and J. J. Polak, "Monetary Analysis of Income Formation and Payments Problems," in IMF, *The Monetary Approach*, op. cit., pp. 15–64.

Robert E. Keleher

2

OF MONEY AND PRICES:
SOME HISTORICAL PERSPECTIVES

INTRODUCTION

The monetary approach to exchange rates and the balance of payments is a framework for analyzing open economies within a larger world economy. That is, this approach views the world aggregate as a system of smaller integrated open economies. Recent elaborations of this view have established that different models must be employed in analyzing the small, open economy (SOE) as distinct from the larger, closed aggregate. Moreover, different exchange rate regimes call for the use of alternative frameworks for examining individual small, open economies. Thus, in examining the relationship between money and prices, the monetary approach indicates that three fundamental cases exist that must be clearly distinguished from one another. Accordingly, the relationship between money and prices that has been delineated by the monetary approach for these three cases—the closed economy, the SOE under fixed exchange rates, and the SOE under flexible exchange rates—will be briefly outlined.

Relationship between money and prices in the case of the closed economy is well known. In this case, all the familiar propositions of the conventional monetarist-Patinkin position hold. That is, any increase in the nominal money stock such that actual money balances exceed desired money balances will cause prices to rise. Price level changes, then, serve as the adjusting mechanism to equilibrate discrepancies between actual and desired real money balances. Thus, the quantity theory of money—in the sense of causality running from the stock of money to prices—applies to the case of the closed economy. Advocates of the monetary approach contend that the only purely closed economy is the world economy and, consequently, it is held that the quantity theory applies to the world economy.

In the case of the SOE under a fixed exchange rate regime (where all goods are tradable),* any increase in the nominal money stock such that actual money balances exceed desired money balances cannot increase prices, since tradable good prices are determined in world markets and given exogenously to the SOE. In this case, a balance of payments deficit is created, which, itself, causes the excess supply of money to contract as these excess balances are traded for foreign goods and/or securities. This contraction will continue until actual and desired monetary balances are equated. In this case, then, the quantity theory of money (in the sense described above) does not apply, since prices are invariant with respect to changes in the domestic money supply.

In the case of the SOE under a flexible exchange rate regime, any increase in the nominal money stock such that actual money balances exceed desired money balances will cause an increase in prices via a fall in the exchange rate. This combination of exchange depreciation and price level increase serves as the adjustment mechanism that equilibrates discrepancies between actual and desired real money balances. According to the monetary approach, this depreciation is equivalent to domestic monetary contraction, in that both depreciation and contraction of the money supply bring about temporary real balance effects that operate to bring desired real money balances into equality with actual real money balances. The quantity theory of money, then, applies to this case, since changes in money will precede changes in the price level.

A contribution of the monetary approach is the careful and explicit delineation of these alternative frameworks by which to analyze relations between money and prices. Depending on the relevant circumstances, then, causality may or may not run from money to prices. However, the explicit recognition of these alternative frameworks and their implications for relations between money and prices are by no means revolutionary. Rather, all of the frameworks outlined above and the distinctions among them were well recognized by earlier generations of economists.† The purpose of this study, then, is to demonstrate that all of the essential elements of the various frameworks set out above, as well as their important implications relating to money and prices, were well recognized by earlier generations of economists.‡ Of these three frameworks, the convertible

---

*The various cases are presented here so as to delineate their fundamental differences. Although the cases are admittedly oversimplified, the basic contentions presented here would apply if complicating factors such as the addition of nontradable goods were added to the discussion.

†A good deal of confusion in interpreting historical monetary controversies relates to the fact that some of the authors failed to spell out explicitly the implicit assumptions and contexts of their theoretical formulations. This relates not only to obscurities relating to convertible versus inconvertible currencies but (as will be indicated below) to small, open economies versus large, closed economies as well.

‡ A secondary purpose of the study is to gain an improved understanding of the historical monetary controversies themselves, both by clearly spelling out the specific frameworks

currency (fixed exchange rate) model of the SOE frequently has been misrepresented by historical interpreters. Among contemporary economists, it is the least understood of the three models and its historical development, unlike that of the other frameworks, has not been adequately documented. Consequently, in this study, emphasis will be given to the fixed exchange rate model of the SOE. Throughout the study, however, it will be shown that various authors clearly recognized the other frameworks and their important (and differing) implications for relations between money and prices.

THE MONETARY APPROACH: HISTORICAL PERSPECTIVES

Some Preliminary Considerations

In discussing the chronological development of the monetary approach, attention will, in general, be given to major monetary writers in English thought, beginning with David Hume.[1] Although some important contributions to this development were made prior to Hume—notably by Isaac Gervaise—these contributions were either subsequently ignored or considered incomplete because of various inconsistencies or errors.* In addition to Hume, particular attention will be given to Adam Smith, David Ricardo, Thomas Tooke (and the Banking School), J. S. Mill, Knut Wicksell, and J. L. Laughlin.

However, before discussing the models employed by these early contributors, a brief discussion of some technical considerations relevant to the analyses of money and prices by economists in the eighteenth and early nineteenth centuries is in order. First, these early classical writers were intimately familiar with the operational aspects of the working of the gold standard. One of these aspects was the fact that under a convertible currency, exchange rates were not absolutely fixed but rather, as modus operandi, varied between relatively narrow bands (between gold import and export points). Secondly, there were no reliable general price indices available to the classical economists.† Consequently, in their discussions relating to money and prices, indirect proxies were frequently employed.[3]

---

employed by the participating authors and by describing the contexts or circumstances in which the authors wrote.

   *Although Hume may not have been the first English writer to set out elements of the fixed exchange rate framework, he set out a consistent, complete model and was by far the most well-known (and widely read) writer prior to Smith recognized by subsequent contributors. In emphasizing the chronological development of the fixed exchange rate model, it seems logical to start with Hume, since it is well known that subsequent contributors were familiar with Hume (but not with Gervaise).[2]

   †As Jacob Viner has ably pointed out:

   Hume wrote before the first attempt in England, that of Evelyn in 1798, to measure price levels by means of statistical averages. Even after 1798, the lead-

To the classical economists, a convenient proxy involved the price of bullion.* That is, the product of the currency price of gold (a fixed rate of exchange when currency is convertible) and the price of goods in terms of gold (determined in world markets for tradable commodities) was employed, albeit implicitly, as a proxy for the level of commodity prices. During periods when currency was convertible, then, the level of domestic prices could vary for one of two reasons: because of changes in the world price of commodities in terms of gold or because of variations in the exchanges between the gold points. During normal periods and within moderate time frames, changes in the former factor were not observed because of large outstanding world stocks of gold (relative to current production possibilities of gold). The latter, although it could be affected by banking and monetary policies, could vary only within relatively narrow bounds. Consequently, sizable amounts of inflation in any single country were regarded as impossible as long as convertibility was maintained. Nonetheless, because of high price elasticities related both to supplies (demands) of foreign exchange at gold export (import) points and to foreign demand (and supply) of tradable products, slight movements in prices could have large influences on commodity and asset flows and thereby could serve as the modus operandi of the system.[6] These considerations have important implications for the interpretation of the classical economists such as Hume to which we will now turn.

David Hume

Most interpretations of Hume recognize his natural distribution of specie hypothesis, in which world money is distributed by means of an automatic mechanism according to the relative demands for money balances. That is, the quantity of specie in any one country is a function of real factors normally associated with the demand for money, such as the volume of transactions, population, income, and productivity. On this point, there is virtual consensus. However, certain important implications of this framework for the individual small, open economy have received emphasis in only a few of these interpretations. First, for

---

ing economists until the time of Jevons either revealed no acquaintance with the notion of representing, by means of statistical averages, either a level of prices, or changes in such level, or found it unacceptable for various reasons. . . . While a number of crude index numbers were constructed during the first half of the Nineteenth Century, none of the classical economists . . . would have anything to do with them.[4]

*Torrens, for example, explicitly asserted that "an increase in the quantity and fall in the value of gold, in relation to commodities, is the same thing as an increase in the quantity and fall in the value of the currency in relation to commodities—is the same thing as a rise of prices."[5]

example, Hume's natural distribution hypothesis implied that money would be distributed *in proportion* to these real variables. Hume indicated that, in each country, money would automatically seek a natural "level" equal to that in other countries:* "It does not seem that money any more than water can be raised or lowered anywhere much beyond the level it has in places where communication is open, but that it must rise and fall in proportion to the goods and labor contained in each state."[7] This equality of level, as Viner has shown, related to *prices* and not to absolute quantities of money:

> The equality of level which Hume posited was not between absolute quantities of money but between the proportions of quantities of money to quantities of commodities, i.e., prices. . . .[8]

Thus, an implication of the natural distribution hypothesis for the SOE is the natural equalization of prices between it and other countries or, in short, the automatic (and exogenous) determination of prices.[10] Another implication of the natural distribution hypothesis relevant to the SOE is that the quantity of money in such an economy is a *dependent* variable, not subject to discretionary manipulation.[11] For this reason, suppositions of large, exogenous changes of the domestic money supply of the SOE are acceptable only for pedagogical purposes and not for practical examinations of the international monetary adjustment mechanism.[12] Most interpreters of Hume would have little difficulty with these propositions.

However, discussions of the adjustment mechanism—the price-specie-flow mechanism—have produced sharp differences in the interpretation of Hume. Specifically, many interpreters of Hume contend that the price-specie-flow mechanism works such that monetary adjustment proceeds by divergent movements in national price levels.[13] That is, it is contended by these interpreters that variations in the price level serve as the adjustment mechanism.[14] If this were the case, the view would contradict the law of one price, except in long-run equilibrium.[15] On rereading Hume, we prefer to adopt an alternative interpretation of the adjustment mechanism.[16]

According to this alternative interpretation, Hume endorsed the law of one price. He essentially outlined a model of price equalization, which he explicitly stated would make it impossible for the value of money to vary between provinces of the same kingdom. He states, for example:

> How is the balance kept in the provinces of every kingdom among themselves, but by the force of this principle, *which makes it impossible for money to lose its level*, and either to rise or sink beyond the proportion of the labour and commodities which are in each province.[17] [emphasis added]

---

*Hume indicated that "Wherever I speak of the level of money, I mean always its proportional level to the commodities, labour, industry, and skill, which is in the several states."[9]

And further:

> What happens in small portions of mankind, must take place in greater. . . . any man who travels over Europe at this day, may see, by the price of commodities, that money, in spite of the absurd jealousy of princes and states, has brought itself nearly to a level; and that the difference between one kingdom and another is not greater in this respect, than it is often between different provinces of the same kingdom.[18]

Hume repeatedly emphasized the rapid workings of price equalization in his writings.[19] This was particularly apparent after his correspondence with James Oswald (which predated the publication "Of the Balance of Trade"), where he explicitly recognized that prices in an SOE are not necessarily related to changes in the quantity of money but are tied to foreign (world) prices.* Hume, then, held that no important price level differences between countries would in practice be observable.[22] This recognition of the law of one price implied that Hume recognized, albeit implicitly, a high degree of price elasticity for tradable commodities and, hence, that *slight* price movements were the modus operandi of the system.

Since Hume recognized that money in an SOE is a dependent variable and not subject to discretionary manipulation (by virtue of his natural distribution hypothesis), he held that any excessive quantity of money could not long persist in a single country. Hume stressed that internal creation of bank credit in one country would result in offsetting outflows of gold rather than in domestic inflation.[23] That is, a trade deficit rather than single-country inflation would result. Accordingly, Hume's supposition of an enormous and exogenous alteration of the quantity of money in an SOE can only be viewed as a pedagogical device.[24]

An implication of Hume's position, then, is that the quantity theory of money—in the sense of causality running from money to prices—does not apply to the SOE. Yet Hume recognized its applicability to a closed economy:

---

*Oswald, after reviewing a preliminary manuscript of Hume's essay, "Of the Balance of Trade," explicitly pointed out that in an SOE, prices were tied to foreign (world) prices rather than to alterations in the quantity of money:

> The increased quantity of money would not necessarily increase the price of all labour and commodities; because the increased quantity, not being confined to the home labour and commodities, might, and certainly would, be sent to purchase both from foreign countries, which importation, unless obstructed by arbitrary and absurd laws, would keep down the price of commodities to the level of foreign countries. . . .[20]

Hume's response indicated that he agreed with Oswald's position and incorporated it into his subsequent analysis of the adjustment mechanism.[21]

If we consider any one Kingdom *by itself* . . . the prices of commodities are always proportioned to the plenty of money. . . .[25] [emphasis added]

Hume, then, not only outlined the fundamental model of the SOE under fixed exchange rates but also described the relationship between money and prices in a closed economy. Two of the three cases described above, then, were recognized by Hume.

Adam Smith

Smith was eminently familiar with the writings of Hume and always wrote, as did Hume, in the context of convertible currency.[26] Consequently, Smith endorsed most of the positions relevant to the convertible framework that were set out by Hume. For example, Smith clearly viewed money as a dependent variable:

> The quantity of money . . . must in every country naturally increase as the value of the annual produce increases. The value of the consumable goods annually circulated within the society being greater will require a greater quantity of money to circulate them. A part of the increased produce, therefore, will naturally be employed in purchasing, wherever it is to be had, the additional quantity of gold and silver necessary for circulating the rest. The increase of those metals will in this case be the effect, not the cause, of the public prosperity.[27]

Moreover, Smith explicitly denied the possibility of overissue. That is, Smith contended in a number of passages that the quantity of convertible paper added to the currency is always offset by an equal and direct outflow of specie; or, in short, that "paper money merely changes the form rather than the total of the money supply."[28] The following passage is particularly noteworthy:

> The increase of paper money, it has been said, by augmenting the quantity, and consequently diminishing the value of the whole currency, necessarily augments the money price of commodities. But as the quantity of gold and silver, which is taken from the currency, is always equal to the quantity of paper which is added to it, paper money does not necessarily increase the quantity of the whole currency. From the beginning of the last century to the present time, provisions never were cheaper in Scotland than in 1759, though, from the circulation of ten and five shilling bank notes, there was then more paper money in the country than at present. The proportion between the price of provisions in Scotland and that in England is the same now as before the great multiplication of banking companies in Scotland. Corn is, upon most occasions, fully as cheap in England as

> in France; though there is a great deal of paper money in England, and scarce any in France.[29]

In this denial of overissue, Smith indicates that an increase in convertible paper money will not affect prices and, consequently, will not alter the value of money. An implication of this position, then, is the endorsement of the law of one price. In discussing this passage, for example, J. W. Angell rightly notes that Smith's doctrine of offsetting specie flows "must necessarily presuppose fixity of prices, for the time being at least. It conceives of the 'channel of circulation' as being confined within rigid price walls. . . ."[30] This interpretation is further supported by noting that Smith, in his elaboration of the specie-flow mechanism, clearly placed emphasis on direct specie outflows (or "overflows," as Smith put it) and related import purchases, whereas he never stressed divergent price level movements as an adjustment mechanism in the *Wealth of Nations*.[31]

Another implication of Smith's view of offsetting specie flows is that the quantity theory of money (in the sense of changes in money preceding changes in prices) does not apply to the SOE under a convertible currency regime. This implication was explicitly voiced by Angell, who, in discussing Smith's views on this topic, noted that "Smith adopts what seems to be the exact antithesis of the quantity theory view."[32] Smith, of course, in outlining this position was referring to the open economy. Yet in discussions relating to a closed-world framework, he explicitly adopted a quantity theory view. For example, at one point, in commenting on the world value of the precious metals, he stated that:

> The discovery of abundant mines of America seems to have been the sole cause of this diminution (1570-1640) in the value of silver in proportion to that of corn. . . . the increase of the supply had, it seems, so far exceeded that of the demand, that the value of that metal sunk considerably.[33]

That Smith recognized the differing relationship between money and prices in the closed, as opposed to the open, framework is particularly evident in his discussion of specie flows. In one passage, for example, Smith was very careful to make a clear distinction between specie inflows in a single country due to increases in its demand for specie as opposed to autonomous increases in world specie supplies (from new world discoveries of gold and silver mines). Smith clearly showed that specie inflows caused by increases in the domestic demand for specie were not inflationary, since they merely represented a redistribution of world specie supplies, whereas inflows due to new gold and silver discoveries were inflationary. Hence, increases in the domestic money supply (world supplies constant) do not affect prices whereas increases in the world money supply do affect prices; the quantity theory applies to the closed world economy but does not apply to the small, open economy.[34]

Smith, then, like Hume, understood the relationship between money and prices in the context of the SOE under fixed exchange rates, and how this relationship is altered in the closed world framework. Two of the three cases described above, then, were recognized by both Hume and Smith.

David Ricardo

The essentials of the relationship between money and prices in both the case of the SOE on fixed exchange rates and the model of the closed economy, then, were formulated by Hume and Smith. These two authors, it should be noted, wrote during periods when convertible currencies existed and, consequently, had little reason to examine the inconvertible case. The convertible currency model of Hume and Smith was well recognized and endorsed by early bullionist writers. Viner indicates that during the period of early bullionist writings the bullionists "always explained the mode of operation of a metallic standard as if, under given conditions in the world at large, it dictated to a country adhering to it a specific quantity of currency and a specific range of commodity prices."[35] John Wheatley, for example, explicitly endorsed the natural distribution hypothesis and emphasized specie flows as opposed to price movements in describing the adjustment process.[36] Moreover, many of these bullionist writers also recognized basic elements of the closed framework. Wheatley, for instance, noted that whereas single country inflation was impossible under a convertible currency, "universally" high prices could be caused by an excessive amount of "world currency."[37]

The major contribution of the bullionists to the evolution of English monetary thought was the formulation of a model of inconvertible currency. It may be noted here, however, that in view of the fact that they adopted the previously cited convertible and closed models of Hume and Smith, the bullionists were the first group of English economists to recognize all three of the models outlined above (convertible, inconvertible, and closed models). In discussing the bullionists, we will concentrate on the most famous member of the group, David Ricardo.

Although Ricardo may not have been the original architect of the theories he endorsed, they emerged in their most lucid form from his pen.* He presented articulate versions of all three models described above. With regard to the model of the SOE under a convertible currency, Ricardo explicitly endorsed Hume's natural distribution hypothesis:

> Gold and silver, having been chosen for the general medium of circulation, they are, by the competition of commerce, distributed in such

---

*In concluding his classic essay, "The High Price of Bullion," Ricardo himself explicitly indicated that he was well aware that he had "not added to the stock of information with which the public has been enlightened by many able writers on the same important subject."[41]

proportions amongst the different countries of the world as to accommodate themselves to the natural traffic which would take place if no such metals existed and the trade between countries were purely a trade of barter.[38]

In addition to supporting this central theme, Ricardo also explicitly endorsed its important corollaries. Specifically, he indicated that under convertibility "the circulation could never be overfull," in that any excessive increase of such a currency would result in an offsetting outflow of specie via the balance of payments rather than affecting its purchasing power.[39] Moreover, Ricardo clearly indicated that, when convertible, money acted as a dependent variable and always and everywhere maintained equal value with other convertible currencies.[40] Accordingly, Ricardo supported the law of one price and indicated that the quantity theory of money did not apply to single countries under convertible currency regimes.[42]

The quantity theory, however, was strongly supported by Ricardo in the context of an inconvertible currency. Indeed, the examination of the inconvertible currency system in Great Britain during the period 1797 to 1821 constituted the major contribution of the bullionists (who included Ricardo and Henry Thornton). In examining this inconvertible currency system, Ricardo (and the other bullionists) demonstrated that the abandonment of the metallic standard removed the constraint of redemption from domestic monetary expansion. As was not the case with a convertible currency, sudden, exogenous changes in the money supply were possible with an inconvertible currency. (Money was no longer viewed as a dependent variable.) Ricardo and the other bullionists showed that any excessive monetary expansion would necessarily lead to both exchange depreciation and commodity price increases (including the price of bullion). In *The Bullion Report*, for example, it was noted that

a general rise of all prices, a rise in the market price of gold, and a fall in the foreign exchanges , will be the effect of an excessive quantity of circulating medium in a country which has adopted a currency not exportable to other countries, or not convertible at will into a coin which is exportable.[43]

Causal relations, then, were seen as running from changes in money to changes in prices. As such, the Ricardian bullionist model of an inconvertible currency system was rightly viewed as a restated formulation of the quantity theory of money. Ricardo, therefore, held that the quantity theory applied to the SOE on an inconvertible but not on a convertible currency regime.

In examining the relationship between money and prices in Great Britain, Ricardo was led to distinguish between domestic and external sources of inflation. In so doing, he indicated that he understood well the distinction between the open and the closed economies. His analysis indicated that while a currency was convertible any domestic alteration of the quantity of money in a single, open economy would not be inflationary but rather would involve a redistribution of given quantities of the world stock of precious metals. That is, other things being equal, an increase (decrease) in a country's share of the world stock of specie would result if that country's wealth increased (decreased), whereas a decrease (increase) in that share would result with a substantial increase (decrease) in bank note issue.[44] Neither of these alternatives would alter the level of domestic prices as long as world conditions remained unchanged.

On the other hand, Ricardo realized that an increase in the quantity of *world* money would lead to an increase in the price level. That is, he recognized the relationship between money and prices—the quantity theory—in the closed (world) framework:

> If the quantity of gold and silver *in the world* employed as money were exceedingly small, or abundantly great, it would not in the least affect the proportions in which they would be divided among the different nations—the variation in their quantity would have produced no other effect than to make the commodities for which they were exchanged comparatively dear or cheap.[45] [emphasis added]

Ricardo indicated his awareness of the workings of the quantity theory in the closed world framework in another way. He showed that even under a convertible currency, if all countries increased their note issue simultaneously (and in proportion) the total world money supply would increase, causing prices to rise in all countries without any single country necessarily experiencing reserve drains:

> ... if the circulation of England were ten millions, that of France five millions, that of Holland four millions, etc., whilst they kept their proportions, though the currency of each country were doubled or tripled, neither country would be conscious of an excess of currency. The prices of commodities would everywhere rise, on account of the increase of currency, but there would be no exportation of money from either. But if these proportions be destroyed by England alone doubling her currency, while that of France, Holland, etc., continued as before, we should then be conscious of an excess in our currency, and for the same reason the other countries would feel a deficiency in theirs, and part of our excess would be exported until the proportions of ten, five, four, etc., were again established.[46]

In the particular case in which all countries expand their monetary stocks simultaneously, then, convertibility does not serve as a check to either monetary overexpansion or inflation.* Finally, Ricardo was well aware of the significance of

---

*This insight had important implications for the currency-banking school debate; see below. It indicated that banks could affect prices either under inconvertibility or under convertibility if all banks adopted similar policies.

taking into account the size of an economy when examining the relationship between money and prices. In one passage, for example, he indicated that if England were a large enough economy, an English note expansion could influence the world money supply and, hence, not be totally offset by specie drains.[47] In this case, then, a single country's monetary expansion could affect prices, at least to some extent.

In analyzing the relationship between money and prices, then, Ricardo and the other bullionists had a thorough understanding of the distinctions among the alternative monetary frameworks that are essential for such investigations. They demonstrated that, whereas the quantity theory did not apply to the SOE under a convertible currency regime, it did apply both to large, closed economies and to the SOE under inconvertible currency arrangements.* Ricardo and the other bullionists, then, were the first English writers to understand all three of the frameworks set out above. Their analysis laid the foundations for later writers, including those of both the currency and the banking schools. It is to these writers that we turn now.

Tooke and the Banking School

The writings of Ricardo and the other bullionists served as the foundation from which the positions of both the currency and the banking schools evolved. The analyses of all three of these groups, for example, "took place within the common assumption of the desirability of metallic convertibility."[48] Although the currency and banking schools evolved from the same source and both supported convertibility, they adopted many positions that were diametrically opposed to one another.[50] An important reason that these contrary positions evolved from the same source is related to the fact that these views were based on Ricardian doctrine applicable, albeit implicitly, to differing contexts. An understanding of the currency-banking controversy, then, requires a thorough familiarity with the alternative frameworks employed in Ricardian analysis.

For example, one contention of Ricardo (and the other bullionists) was that convertibility in and of itself was sufficient to prevent any substantial over-issuance of bank notes by a single country and, therefore, sufficient to prevent

---

*The Bullion Report, for example, stated that for an inconvertible currency,

> An increase in the quantity of the local (inconvertible) currency of a particular country, will raise prices in that country exactly in the same manner as an increase in the general supply of precious metals raises prices all over the world. By means of the increase of quantity, the value of a given portion of that circulating medium, in exchange for other commodities, is lowered; in other words, the money prices of all other commodities are raised, and that of bullion with the rest.[49]

single-country inflation.[51] Convertibility, then, served as a mechanism for monetary (and inflation) control for the SOE. This Ricardian position was endorsed by banking school writers, such as Thomas Tooke, J. Fullarton, James Wilson, and J. W. Gilbart. However, as was shown above, Ricardo also demonstrated that if all countries expanded their note issues simultaneously, overexpansion and inflation would occur despite convertibility. Convertibility, then, was not necessarily a guaranteed safeguard against monetary overexpansion and inflation once it was recognized that there is less check to monetary overexpansion by countries or banks when they act in unison than when they act alone.[52] Ricardo had demonstrated, then, that different principles may apply when an analyst shifts emphasis from the context of the individual unit acting alone to the context of an aggregation of these units acting in unison. Different contexts, therefore, require different analytical frameworks. The currency school writers, such as Robert Torrens, Lord Overstone, and George Norman, concluded that, when viewed from the perspective of an aggregate of countries or banks as opposed to a single unit, some form of control over banking and monetary policy in addition to convertibility was necessary.[53] The currency school writers, then, reached their conclusions by carrying out their analysis, albeit implicitly, within the context of a larger, more aggregative framework, whereas the banking school writers were always concerned with the actions of an individual country or bank.* Both schools, nonetheless, evolved from the Ricardian bullionist framework.

This section will demonstrate that banking school writers recognized all three of the monetary frameworks spelled out above. Moreover, it will be shown that an understanding of these three frameworks easily clarifies various issues of the currency-banking school controversy. Although comparisons between the two

---

*This contention is further supported by recognizing a related episode of the period. That is, another reason for alternative positions evolving from Ricardian doctrine relates to the controversy regarding the particular banking institutions responsible for overissue during the period of restriction. Since country bank notes were convertible into more widely circulating Bank of England notes, the quantity of notes issued in the various provinces or regions of the country was viewed as being governed by a natural distribution hypothesis (analogous to specie distribution in various countries). Accordingly, the bullionists contended that regional country banks could not overissue and, hence, were not responsible for the rapid rate of note expansion during the period of restriction.[54] On the other hand, Bank of England notes were not convertible during this period and as a consequence were overissued. Therefore, bullionists placed responsibility for overissuance on the Bank of England.[55] However, Ricardo recognized that if all banks, including the Bank of England, expanded notes simultaneously, then convertibility would not serve as a constraint to country bank note issue. Hence, banking and monetary controls were necessary. The view that the Bank of England and the country banks acting together would issue to excess even under convertibility was "adopted by the currency school as one of the elements in their reply to the banking school doctrine that overissue was impossible under convertibility."[56] Implicitly, then, the currency school was employing the entire banking system as a frame of reference, whereas the banking school was focusing on the individual bank.

positions will be made, emphasis will be given to banking school writers, since these authors not only have been misunderstood but had a broader comprehension of the essentials of all three monetary frameworks.* In addition, attention will be focused on the most well-known contributor to banking school doctrine, Thomas Tooke.

Banking school writers, and particularly Tooke, clearly recognized the fixed exchange rate model of the SOE, as well as its important implications. In addition, these writers were, in general, careful to emphasize the context to which their doctrines applied. Normally, their analysis pertained to the small individual country (or the small individual bank).[57] These writers emphasized that in a small, open environment, the quantity of a convertible currency was determined by (and passively adapted to) the demands or needs of the public.[58] Any amount in excess of these demands would be immediately traded for other goods or securities. Accordingly, following not only Hume, Smith, and Ricardo but the views of country bankers as well, the banking school writers contended that overissue of a convertible currency was impossible because of offsetting flows of specie (or in the case of the country banks, the offsetting flows of Bank of England notes).†
Tooke, for example, indicated that

> in the case both of the Bank of England and of the country banks, if it were conceivable, which it hardly is, that any addition, beyond the amount of notes required for specific purposes, could be forced into the hands of the public, there is an operation constantly going on which would almost instantaneously reduce the amount within the limits of these purposes. . . . The advance by a bank issuing only convertible paper does not . . . cause, necessarily, any increase in the circulation. . . . [An] increase of the outstanding circulation would be the effect of increased transactions and prices and not the cause of them. . . .[60] ‡

Secondly, banking school writers—and especially Tooke—recognized, albeit implicitly, the law of one price (and, consequently, the workings of arbitrage). Tooke, being an empiricist, was familiar with price data for at least the period 1792 to

---

*Although the currency school, in general, came to dominate British monetary thought, it never achieved a dominant position on the continent, where the banking school received more support.[59]

†Currency school writers contended that overissuance under convertibility could occur at least in the short run and be of a magnitude large enough to threaten convertibility.[62] It was implicit in their writings that to bring this about, all banks would act in unison.[63]

‡Fullerton contends:

What Mr. Tooke, and those who hold similar opinions, contend for is, that, by the very constitution of a convertible currency, it can never be issued in larger quantities than are required for use and, therefore, can never be redundant.[64]

1856. Most of the data used by Tooke pertained to tradable goods.[61] Tooke analyzed these data and, on the basis of his empirical studies, indicated that prices apparently were independently determined in external international markets and not related to changes in the domestic money supply, even in the short run.[65] This conclusion was in accordance with banker opinion (with which Tooke was familiar) as to the international adjustment mechanism.[66]

The important implication of this, of course, was that the quantity theory of money (in the sense of causality running from changes in money to changes in prices) was not applicable to the individual SOE under a convertible currency. The contention that the quantity theory did not apply to this case was explicitly and repeatedly noted by Tooke:

> In point of fact and historically, as far as my researches have gone, in every single instance of a rise or fall in prices, the rise or fall has preceded and, therefore, could not be the effect of an enlargement or contraction of the bank circulation.[67]

> I believe that the amount of the circulating medium is the effect and not the cause of variations in prices.[68]

> The prices of commodities do not depend upon the quantity of money indicated by the amount of bank notes, nor upon the amount of the whole of the circulating medium, but that, on the contrary, the amount of the circulating medium is the consequence of prices.[69]

In testimony before the Parliamentary Committee on Banks of Issue in 1840 (which he later published in *History of Prices*), Tooke voiced this opinion repeatedly in responses to questions by the committee.* Instead of supporting the quantity theory in the case of the SOE, Tooke (and other banking school writers)

---

*This is exemplified by Tooke's answers to the following two questions by the committee:

Question 3303 (by committee): "Suppose . . . the quantity of the precious metals in the world to remain constant, and that the number of deposits in bankers' hands available to the purchase and sale of commodities is doubled, trebled, and so on, will the price of commodities vary in proportion to that increase of deposits in bankers' hands?" *Tooke's Response:* "Not in the slightest degree."

Question 3621 (by committee): "Are the Committee, then, to understand, that so long as the paper is convertible into specie, you cannot attribute any effect whatever upon prices to the variations in the amount of the bank notes in circulation?" *Tooke's Response:* "I am perfectly satisfied that no alteration in the prices can be traced in any way to the amount of the circulation."[72]

endorsed a reverse causation hypothesis. That is, in accordance with their demand-determined view, they inverted the chain of cause and effect of the quantity theorists and argued that increases in the quantity of money were determined by increases in prices and incomes rather than the reverse.[70] Moreover, "They were extremely careful to confine this proposition to the case of money convertible into specie and, hence, to a case where the arbitrage necessary to preserve the relevant price structure was possible."[71] Furthermore, it is evident in numerous passages that Tooke and other banking school writers emphasized this view to be especially pertinent to small, open economic units.[73] Being particularly relevant to such units, the theory was wholeheartedly accepted by bankers who, by their very nature, deal with money in an open economic environment.*

This banking school view was vigorously criticized by writers of the currency school, who supported the quantity theory, even in the context of the small, open economy with a convertible currency. That is, currency school writers contended that monetary overexpansion was possible in the case of the SOE with a convertible currency and, in describing adjustments to such an overexpansion, placed emphasis on changes in relative price levels rather than on monetary flows.[74] In criticizing writers of the banking school on this issue, currency school writers frequently tried to demonstrate the supposed fallacy of the banking school position by referring to examples of the quantity theory in very large or closed economies. That is, they essentially assumed that an increase in the money supply in a single SOE had an inflationary effect that was analogous to a monetary increase in a large, closed economy.[76] For example, Torrens, in his criticism of Tooke, essentially argued that large increases in the world gold stock and subsequent European inflation demonstrated the fallacy of the banking school position.[77]

The banking school authors, however, had been careful to indicate that their views were applicable to the SOE but not necessarily to the large or closed economy. They clearly recognized a distinction between the large, closed economy and the SOE. Tooke, Fullarton, and Wilson, for example, carefully distinguished between changes in a country's money supply resulting from domestic sources and changes in the money supply due to increases in the world gold stock and, hence, world money supply.[78] These authors clearly indicated that increases

---

*The views of the banking school writers were supported by all of the bankers who testified before various parliamentary committees on the subject. These bankers indicated that (in the words of Fullarton) "The amount of their issues is exclusively regulated by the extent of local dealings and expenditure in their respective Districts, fluctuating with the fluctuations of production and price, and that they neither can increase their issues beyond the limits which the range of such deals and expenditure prescribe, without the certainty of having their notes immediately returned to them nor diminish them, but at an almost equal certainty of the vacancy being filled up from some other source."[75] It is no coincidence, then, that bankers have traditionally been skeptical of the quantity theory of money; they have always operated in the context of an open environment (always constrained from expanding loans and deposits by leakages—as in an open economy).

in the domestic money supply that reflected increases in the world money supply were inflationary whereas increases in the domestic money supply arising from redistribution of the existing world supply (due, for example, to a favorable exchange) would not be inflationary.[79] * That is, domestic (one country) inflation was impossible so long as the currency remained convertible.

Wilson, for example, after demonstrating that Torrens equated an increase in the domestic money supply (due to domestic sources) to an increase in the world money supply, responded in the following manner:

> That this ingenious and accomplished economist should have stated these as two "analogous propositions" is the most striking evidence with which we have yet met of the utter confusion which prevails in men's minds of the very real nature of currency and capital . . . some have an idea that in every case of an influx of bullion, a similar effect should be experienced locally that is produced generally by an increase of metals from the mines. The difference is very essential. In the case of an ordinary influx of gold into this country, caused by a favorable state of the exchanges, the general quantity of gold is not changed, nor its relation in value to other commodities: A new distribution of it is all that takes place. To those who received larger quantities of metal from South America . . . in consequence of the increased productiveness of the mines, the additional quantity . . . would soon increase prices generally in proportion to the new supplies of the metals.
>
> But in the case of an influx of bullion, owing to a favorable exchange, the case is widely different. . . . We find that in practice, neither circulation nor prices increase under such circumstances. . . .[81]

After explicitly quoting these comments of Wilson, Tooke clearly voiced his agreement with this view:

> I quite agree with Mr. Wilson in his opinion . . . of the difference of the effects on prices between an influx of gold caused by an increase of metals from the mines, and the influx caused by a favorable exchange. . . .[82]

Moreover, Tooke demonstrated his recognition of the distinction between domestic and world monetary expansion in numerous other passages. In his testimony before the Parliamentary Committee on Banks of Issue in 1840, for example, Tooke made it clear that when referring to the case of the SOE, he was assuming

---

*Fullarton, for example, "went out of his way to make it clear that he did not deny the broad effects on prices of changes in the supply of the precious metals."[80]

that the world money supply was held constant. That is, he made note of the differences between the effects on prices of world monetary variations and the effects on prices of variations in the domestic currency, world money held constant.[83] Subsequent questions by the committee were explicitly prefaced by assuming that world money supplies be held constant.* Banking school writers, then, recognized the distinction between the SOE and the large, closed economy and the important implications of this distinction for analyzing causal relations between money and prices. Moreover, banking school writers presented empirical evidence to substantiate their contentions relating to the SOE, whereas the divergent price level adjustment mechanism endorsed by currency school writers never received empirical support.[84] These currency school writers, albeit implicitly, took as the premise for their analysis a larger, more aggregative framework. This is evident not only in their discussion of relations between money and prices but, as pointed out above, in their discussion of the possibility of convertible note overissue.[85]

In addition to their recognition of the distinction between the closed model and the case of the SOE on fixed exchange rates, banking school writers were aware of the inconvertible currency framework. Both Tooke and Fullarton, for example, contrasted an inconvertible with a convertible currency, noting that expansion of an inconvertible currency would have an important impact on prices.[87] Their view of the inconvertible case, then, was essentially a restatement of the bullionist position. Banking school writers, therefore, recognized that the quantity theory would hold in both the case of an inconvertible currency and the case of the closed economy.

In sum, banking school authors recognized all three of the models discussed above. These authors were, in general, practical men who not only were familiar with a good deal of empirical data but understood the views and opinions of bankers. Accordingly, their analysis emphasized the operation of the single, small economic unit in an open environment and indicated that the quantity theory, although valid in other contexts, did not apply to this context. When these alternative theoretical frameworks were not clearly delineated, a good deal of confusion about interpretation resulted.[88] It is for this very reason that many subsequent economists have denigrated the writings of the banking school.

J. S. Mill

When one discusses the development of these principles of monetary theory, J. S. Mill looms as an important figure, because he was so widely read even if for

---

*At one point in the testimony, Tooke indicated that he recognized the importance of country size. That is, he indicated that if a country's note issue increased to the extent that the single country specie outflow was large enough to affect world specie values, then prices of commodities in that particular country might still be affected. This, however, could not occur if the relevant economy was small.[86]

no other reason. It has been established, for example, that during the latter half of the nineteenth century, Mill's *Principles of Political Economy* was "the undisputed bible of economists. . . . As late as 1900, Mill's work was still the basic textbook in elementary courses in both British and American universities."[89] This observation, together with the fact that Mill endorsed a good many of the banking school propositions, then, makes Mill important in describing the evolution of these monetary principles.

Mill was familiar with the writings of banking school authors such as Tooke and Fullarton and, in fact, supported the banking school position against the Act of 1844.[90] He explicitly supported various propositions of the banking school writers. For example, in addition to explicitly recognizing the natural distribution of specie hypothesis, Mill pointed out that in the normal "quiescent state," the overissue of a convertible currency was impossible, since it would lead to the outflow of specie via the balance of payments.[91] Specifically, Mill noted that in normal circumstances alterations in convertible note issue can have no impact on prices, and that

> there can be no addition, at the discretion of bankers, to the general circulating medium: Any increase of their issues either comes back to them, or remains idle in the hands of the public, and *no rise takes place in prices.*[92] [emphasis added]

Mill explicitly quoted passages from both Tooke and Fullarton in which these banking school authors forcefully stated that because the volume of convertible note issue was determined by demand, it could not possibly increase prices in the SOE.[93] Mill also noted that the unanimous opinion of country bankers examined before various parliamentary committees was in accord with this view.[94] After presenting these views of the banking school, Mill stated that this doctrine appeared to him to be "incontrovertible." He went on to say:

> I give complete credence to the assertion of the country bankers very clearly and correctly condensed . . . [by] Mr. Fullarton. I am convinced that they cannot possibly increase their issue of notes in any other circumstances than those which are there stated. I believe, also, that the theory, grounded by Mr. Fullarton upon this fact, contains a large portion of truth, and is far nearer to being the expression of the whole truth than any form whatever of the currency theory.[95]

In endorsing the view that any expansion of convertible note issue could not affect prices in an SOE, Mill supported, albeit implicitly, the law of one price. He explicitly endorsed it in another passage:

> As soon as the price of cloth is lower in England than in Germany, it will begin to be exported, and the price of cloth in Germany will

fall to what it is in England. . . . By the fall, however, of cloth in England, cloth will fall in Germany also. . . . By the rise of linen in Germany, linen must rise in England also. . . .[96]

In view of these considerations, Mill must be viewed as endorsing the view that, in the case of the SOE with a convertible currency, the quantity theory (in the sense of causality running from money to prices) does not hold. Yet Mill clearly recognized that theory's validity in the case of the large, closed economy. Specifically, Mill described how an increase in the world money supply would have a proportional effect on world prices.[97] Moreover, Mill discussed at length the working of an inconvertible paper currency. He devoted an entire chapter to that discussion in his *Principles.*[98] Mill indicated that, although a convertible currency could not be issued to excess, an inconvertible currency could be overissued and would consequently have a definite inflationary impact, an observation supporting the quantity theory.[99] In short, Mill clearly recognized all three of the fundamental frameworks outlined above. In spite of this recognition, however, in certain passages Mill appeared to lend some support to contrary views, from the currency school.[100] His views with respect to the currency and banking schools, then, were not wholly consistent. Overall, however, his views supported the position of the banking school. Despite these apparent inconsistencies, Mill's support of the banking school principles had important implications. Since Mill's works were so widely read, his endorsement of the banking school served to propagate important elements of that view to make them readily available to later generations of economists.

K. Wicksell

Although Wicksell was not an English economist, he was very familiar with the English authors discussed above. As a consequence, his ideas on monetary theory were, in large part, an extension and propagation of these views. Moreover, Wicksell's writings were available in English in the twentieth century and have been said to have importantly influenced subsequent British and American economists. Wicksell, therefore, represents an important element in any discussion of the evolution of English monetary thought.

In any examination of Wicksell's writings, it is evident that Wicksell fully recognized the important contributions to monetary theory made by the authors discussed above, particularly Ricardo, the banking school writers, and J. S. Mill. These authors are quoted extensively throughout Wicksell's discussions of monetary theory.[101] It is evident, moreover, that from his studies of these earlier authors Wicksell acquired a thorough comprehension of the fundamental frameworks outlined in the present study, as well as an understanding of how the development of these frameworks evolved over time.* As a consequence, he supported the propositions related to the SOE under a convertible currency presented by the authors cited above. His interpretation of these propositions is entirely consistent with the explanations presented in the present study. Moreover, Wicksell stressed that when these considerations pertained specifically to a small, open framework, they should not be applied to other contexts.[103] Consider one of these propositions: there is no doubt that Wicksell understood the law of one price and its important implications. In Wicksell's writings, lucid and forceful statements of this law are presented in several passages:

> No matter how eagerly the products of one country may be demanded by another country . . . no appreciable difference of prices can persist when there is a free interchange of goods.[104]

> If [the obligation to redeem bank notes in metal] exists, . . . then naturally a powerful brake is applied to the banks, simply because commodity prices in such a country can no longer rise materially above the price level in all other countries having the same metal as a measure of value.[105]

Elsewhere, Wicksell contended that if two countries conduct free trade and are divided only by a land boundary, then:

> If these countries were both living under a specie regime, there could not possibly exist different prices of the same commodity on both sides of the frontier; and if we suppose, which of course is not exactly true, that the level of prices in the interior of each country is materially the same as in the boundary districts, there could be no difference of prices at all between them . . . difference(s) of prices in the two countries . . . would be theoretically impossible and practically confined between very narrow limits.[106]

In stressing the validity of the law of one price, Wicksell explicitly recognized its implication that divergent relative price levels could *not* serve as an international adjustment mechanism under a convertible currency regime. He indicated that prices were determined exogenously by direct and rapid arbitrage links that were

---

*In addition to understanding the fundamental ideas presented by Ricardo, banking school writers, and Mill, Wicksell also recognized various subtle arguments of these authors. For example, Wicksell recognized the distinction made by Ricardo between the behavior of an individual economic unit and the behavior of a universal set of these units acting in unison. That is, Wicksell had a thorough understanding of the subtle distinctions between an open and a closed economy.[102]

independent of specie movements.[107] These observations regarding the law of one price have the important implication that the quantity theory of money (in the sense of causality) does not apply to the single SOE under a convertible currency regime. Wicksell recognized well this contention when he demonstrated not only that international adjustments could take place without divergent price level movements but also that domestic prices were determined by international factors independent of domestic monetary considerations.[108]

The distinction between convertible and inconvertible monetary systems and the important implications of this distinction were also recognized by Wicksell. That is, he stated that whereas overissuance and, therefore, single-country inflation were possible under an inconvertible monetary regime, they were not possible under convertibility.[109] The quantity theory, then, although not applicable to the SOE under convertibility, applied to the SOE under an inconvertible monetary system. Finally, Wicksell clearly understood the importance of recognizing the open vis-a-vis the closed economic framework. He explicitly noted in several passages that the only truly closed economy is the world economy.[110] Although he recognized that convertibility ensured the impossibility of single-country inflation, Wicksell restated the Ricardian position that if all countries pursued monetary expansion simultaneously (and, therefore, increased the world money supply), inflation could result despite convertibility.[111] The quantity theory, then, was viewed as applicable to the closed economy.

J. L. Laughlin

Another author who was an important figure in discussions of the evolution of the above frameworks was Laughlin. Laughlin understood well the fundamentals of all three of the frameworks cited above.[112] His understanding of the SOE under a convertible currency was thorough and comprehensive, and his discussion of that model and its important implications was among the most forceful and lucid to be found in the writings of any of the authors discussed here.

Laughlin indicated that the volume of money in an SOE with a convertible currency was demand-determined (endogenous) and noted that a convertible note issue could not be overissued.[113] Consequently, for such an economy he argued that the money stock could not be treated as an exogenous, controllable variable. Any discussion beginning with the assumption of an exogenous change in the money stock (all other things being equal), therefore, was viewed by Laughlin as a fallacious argument.[114]

Laughlin explicitly and repeatedly endorsed the law of one price. For example, in one passage, he noted that

> the action of the international markets, with telegraphic quotations from every part of the world, precludes the supposition that gold prices could in general remain on a higher level in one country than in

another (cost of carriage apart) even for a brief time, because, in order to gain the profit, merchants would seize the opportunity to send goods to the markets where prices are high.[115]

Moreover, Laughlin explained the implications of that law for relations between money and prices. In particular, he explicitly recognized that for the SOE with a convertible currency, prices are determined exogenously in world markets by the rapid workings of arbitrage and not by the domestic money stock.

> A rise in the price of any commodity due to local causes (such as deficient harvests, war, etc.) is *instantly* met by importations from other countries; indeed the actual event is more often discounted by shipments of goods. . . . The competition between trading countries, as between different parts of the same country, being exceedingly keen, merchants in the leading centres would send the goods themselves to the spot where high prices existed, and by a quick increase of the supply of goods they would reduce prices in the country whose level was artificially high. . . . prices would *at once* fall by competition of goods with goods to a normal international level (allowing for differences due to costs of carriage). . . . In fact, it has become clear, by the logic of events, that the shipments of gold between commercial countries have little or nothing to do with the level of prices of merchandise in any one country.[116]

Accordingly, Laughlin noted that divergent price levels could not be part of the international monetary adjustment mechanism for this type of economy, since such a mechanism would contradict the law of one price.[117] In stating these views, Laughlin made it clear that he was essentially endorsing the view of the banking school writers on this issue and opposing that of the currency school.[118] Unlike some other authors holding similar views, Laughlin very explicitly recognized the implications of this position for the quantity theory of money. In particular, Laughlin—following the views of the banking school—stated repeatedly and forcefully that the quantity theory did not apply to the SOE under a convertible monetary regime.[119]

In addition to examining the relations between money and prices for the SOE with a convertible currency, Laughlin also analyzed those relations for the case of an inconvertible currency. He noted that, in this case, the quantity theory was quite valid.[120]

Laughlin also recognized the distinction between the closed and the open economies and the important implications for money and prices of this distinction. He noted, for example, that for an individual country an inflow of gold reflecting an increase in the world gold stock (and, hence, world money supply) would cause an increase in prices, whereas a gold inflow reflecting a single country's favorable balance of payments (and, hence, manifesting a redistribution of the existing world stock of gold) would not affect the level of prices in that country.[121] Moreover, he explicitly noted that under a convertible monetary regime, an increase in the domestic money supply could affect the domestic price level only if it were large enough to affect world prices.[122] Hence, the quantity theory was valid in the closed world economy and not applicable to the SOE with a convertible currency.

In sum, Laughlin recognized well all three of the frameworks described above, as he demonstrated in the following noteworthy passage:

> If my previous reasoning has been correct, prices would not rise merely from an increase in the media of exchange [of the SOE]; . . . prices could not rise unless there were a serious fall throughout the world in the value of gold—which, owing to its great stock, is quite unlikely to occur in any ordinary period of time. But it is as plain as a pikestaff that a rise of general prices may be brought about by a device that would lower the value of the standard, such as a debasement of the coinage, or any legislative operations which might transfer the standard to a cheaper metal, or which might establish an inconvertible paper as a standard on a depreciating level.[123]

CONCLUSIONS

A contribution of the modern monetary approach has been the careful delineation of three basic monetary models. In this study, after a brief outline of the relationship between money and prices for these monetary models, the historical evolution of the models in English monetary thought was described. This description indicated that all three frameworks and the important distinctions among them were well recognized by earlier generations of economists and, in fact, were clearly delineated in the early nineteenth century by the bullionist writers. Prominent English economists, then, understood the three models and their important distinctions from the early 1800s until well into the 1900s. After that, however, the model of the SOE under a convertible currency and its companion principle—the law of one price—apparently either were forgotten or fell into disfavor until their recent revival in the modern monetary approach. While the reason for this lapse is somewhat enigmatic, some suggestions have been offered in the literature.

One reason for the temporary demise of this model was the endorsement of the currency school version of the international adjustment mechanism under a convertible currency regime given by prominent economists, such as Irving Fisher, J. M. Keynes, A. C. Pigou, and Gustav Cassel. In general, the writings of these authors supported the currency school view that divergent movements in general price levels constituted the adjustment mechanism of a fixed exchange rate (or convertible currency) system—a position that directly contradicted the law of one price. Indeed, this view led these writers to argue that fixed exchange rates and price stability were incompatible.[124]

Another reason for the demise of the fixed exchange rate model of the SOE was the emphasis given by various Harvard neoclassicists (such as Taussig, Viner, Beach, and Williams) to exceptions to the law of one price. As J. G. Witte and B. Henneberry have indicated, this emphasis apparently went unchallenged at the time and, consequently, contributed to the disfavor of the model.[125]

A third reason for the model's temporary demise was the emergence of the macroeconomic analysis of closed systems. That is, the development and analysis of closed models such as the Keynesian and later monetarist models directed the attention of the profession away from the analysis of open economic models. Moreover, by the early twentieth century, the U.S. economy had developed to the extent that, as a first approximation, it was treated as a closed economy.

For these (and probably other) reasons, then, the model of the SOE under a convertible currency and its companion principle—the law of one price—were disregarded after the early twentieth century. It was not until recent detailed analyses of currency devaluation and, consequently, the resurrection of the monetary approach that the model has again found support among economists.

NOTES

1. For contributions by non-English writers, see F. J. De Jong, *Development of Monetary Theory in the Netherlands* (Rotterdam: Rotterdam University Press, 1973); Robert V. Eagly, "The Swedish and English Bullionist Controversies," in *Events, Ideology, and Economic Theory*, ed. Robert V. Eagly (Detroit: Wayne State University Press, 1968); Robert V. Eagly, *The Swedish Bullionist Controversy* (Philadelphia: American Philosophical Society, 1971); and Thomas T. Sekine, "The Discovery of International Monetary Equilibrium by Vanderlint, Cantillon, Gervaise, and Hume," *Economia Internazionale* 26, no. 2 (1973).

2. See, for example, Sekine, op. cit.; J. Frenkel and H. G. Johnson, "The Monetary Approach to the Balance of Payments: Essential Concepts and Historical Origins," in *The Monetary Approach to the Balance of Payments*, ed. J. Frenkel and Harry G. Johnson (Toronto: University of Toronto Press, 1976), p. 37; J. W. Angell, *The Theory of International Prices* (New York: Augustus Kelley, 1965), p. 26 fn, p. 32; I. Gervaise, *The System or Theory of the Trade of the World* (Baltimore: Johns Hopkins University Press, 1954); and J. M. Letiche, "Isaac Gervaise on the International Mechanism of Adjustment," *Journal of Political Economy* 60 (1952).

3. See, for example, Jacob Viner, *Studies in the Theory of International Trade* (New York: Augustus Kelley, 1965), p. 127; O. St. Clair, *A Key to Ricardo* (New York: Kelley and Millman, 1957), p. 298; D. P. O'Brien, *The Classical Economists* (Oxford: Clarendon Press, 1975), pp. 148-49; Johan Myhrman, "Experiences of Flexible Exchange Rates in Earlier Periods: Theories, Evidence, and a New View," *Scandinavian Journal of Economics* 78, no. 2 (1976): 171; and Eagly, "The Swedish and English Bullionist Controversies," op. cit., p. 26.

4. Viner, op. cit., pp. 312-13.

5. L. Robbins, *Robert Torrens and the Evolution of Classical Economics* (London: Macmillan, 1958), p. 125. See also J. L. Laughlin, *The Principles of Money* (New York: Charles Scribner's Sons, 1903), p. 417.

6. See Viner, op. cit., p. 333; Robert V. Eagly, "Adam Smith and the Specie-Flow Doctrine," *Scottish Journal of Political Economy* 17 (February 1970): 64; L. Girton and D. Roper, "J. Laurence Laughlin and the Quantity Theory of Money," International Finance Discussion Papers #103, March 1977, Board of Governors of the Federal Reserve System, p. 14.

7. D. Hume, "Hume to Montesquieu," April 10, 1749, in *Writings on Economics*, ed. Eugene Rotwein (Freeport, N.Y.: Books for Libraries Press, 1955) (reprinted 1972), p. 189.

8. Viner, op. cit., p. 313 fn. See also Charles E. Staley, "Hume and Viner on the International Adjustment Mechanism," *History of Political Economy* 8, no. 2 (Summer 1976): 255.

9. D. Hume, "Of the Balance of Trade," in *Writings*, op. cit., p. 66 fn.

10. Hume was explicit that these considerations were subject to the allowance for transportation costs. See Hume, "Of the Balance of Trade," p. 66 fn. See also Viner, op. cit., p. 314.

11. See Barbara Henneberry and James G. Witte, "Variable Gold Parities from a Classical Viewpoint: Hume Versus the Monetarists," unpublished manuscript, Indiana University, November 1974, p. 1. See also Viner, op. cit., p. 376.

12. See Girton and Roper, op. cit., pp. 21, 23.

13. For a critique of this view, see J. G. Witte and B. Henneberry, "A Monetary-Real Approach to Balance-of-Payments Theory: Old-New Synthesis for Old-New Problems," unpublished manuscript, Indiana University, April 1977, p. 2.

14. See, for example, Arnold Collery, *International Adjustment, Open Economies, and the Quantity Theory of Money*, Princeton Studies in International Finance no. 28 (June 1971), p. 26; Harry G. Johnson, "The Monetary Approach to Balance of Payments Theory," *Journal of Financial and Quantitative Analysis* (March 1972): 1555; Harry G. Johnson, "Money, Balance of Payments Theory and the International Monetary Problem," *Essays in International Finance*, International Finance Section, Department of Economics, Princeton University, no. 124, November 1977, p. 5. This view is also implicit in the contention of some contemporary monetarists that fixed exchange rates and price level stability are incompatible. (See Henneberry and Witte, op. cit., p. 7.)

15. See Witte and Henneberry, op. cit., p. 2.

16. This view has been given elsewhere. See, for example, Henneberry and Witte, op. cit.

17. D. Hume, "Of the Balance of Trade," in *Writings*, op. cit., p. 65. See also D. Hume, "Of Money," in *Writings*, op. cit., p. 35. It will be remembered that this equality of level related to prices and not to absolute quantities of money. The view that Hume endorsed the law of one price has also been voiced by Viner. See Viner, op. cit., pp. 316, 317, 319.

18. This hypothesis of Hume—that price differences were no greater between countries than within countries—was empirically supported more than 200 years later by both Genberg, and McCloskey and Zecher. See A. H. Genberg, "Aspects of the Monetary Approach to Balance of Payments Theory," in *The Monetary Approach to the Balance of Payments*, op. cit.; and D. N. McCloskey and J. R. Zecher, "How the Gold Standard Worked, 1880-1913," in *The Monetary Approach to the Balance of Payments*, op. cit., p. 63.

19. See, for example, Hume, "Of the Balance of Trade," op. cit., pp. 63, 69, 72; D. Hume, "Hume to Montesquieu," in *Writings*, op. cit., p. 188; and D. Hume, "Hume to Oswald," in *Writings*, op. cit., p. 197.

20. James Oswald, "Oswald to Hume," in *Writings*, op. cit., pp. 191-92.

21. David Hume, "Hume to Oswald," in *Writings*, op. cit., p. 197.

22. Hume repeatedly recognized the existence of transportation costs and, hence, the possibility of price differences for nontradables. See, for example, Hume, "Of the Balance of Trade," op. cit., p. 66 fn.

23. See Henneberry and Witte, op. cit., p. 2. Also see, for example, Hume, "Of the Balance of Trade," op. cit., pp. 68-70, 72; and Hume, "Hume to Oswald," op. cit., p. 198.

24. See Hume, "Of the Balance of Trade," op. cit., pp. 62-63. See also Girton and Roper, op. cit., p. 23.

25. D. Hume, "Of Money," in *Writings*, op. cit., p. 33.

26. Angell, op. cit., p. 38; J. Hollander, "The Development of the Theory of Money from Adam Smith to David Ricardo," *Quarterly Journal of Economics* (1911): 435; and O'Brien, op. cit., p. 151.

27. A. Smith, *An Inquiry into the Nature and Causes of the Wealth of Nations* (New York: Random House, 1937), pp. 323–24. See also p. 188.

28. Douglas Vickers, "Adam Smith and the Status of the Theory of Money," in *Essays on Adam Smith*, ed. A. Skinner and T. Wilson (Oxford: Clarendon Press, 1975), p. 498.

29. Smith, op. cit., pp. 308–09. See also ibid., pp. 277–78, 284.

30. Angell, op. cit., p. 34. Laughlin also explicitly interpreted Smith in this manner. See, for example, Laughlin, op. cit., p. 238.

31. See, for example, A. I. Bloomfield, "Adam Smith and the Theory of International Trade," in *Essays on Adam Smith*, op. cit., p. 480; O'Brien, op. cit., p. 146; and Vickers, op. cit., p. 484. Although Smith mentioned prices in an earlier description of the adjustment mechanism, he ended that description by emphasizing that prices in different countries will stay in line with one another. See A. Smith, *Lectures on Justice, Police, Revenue and Arms* (New York: Kelley and Millman, 1956), p. 197.

32. Angell, op. cit., p. 34. See also, for example, Laughlin, op. cit., p. 238.

33. Smith, *Wealth of Nations*, op. cit., p. 191.

34. See ibid., p. 188. See also Frank Petrella, "Adam Smith's Rejection of Hume's Price-Specie-Flow Mechanism: A Minor Mystery Resolved," *Southern Economic Journal* (January 1968): 372.

35. Viner, op. cit., p. 205.

36. Hollander, op. cit., p. 465.

37. Ibid., p. 465.

38. David Ricardo, *The Works and Correspondence*, ed. Piero Sraffa (London: Cambridge University Press, 1951), vol. 1, p. 137. See also vol. 3, p. 52.

39. Ibid., vol. 3, pp. 90–92, 57, 64 fn.

40. Ibid., vol. 3, pp. 52, 53, 56.

41. Ibid., vol. 3, p. 99.

42. For evidence that Ricardo supported the law of one price, see Viner, op. cit., p. 315, and Ricardo, op. cit., vol. 9, p. 285. Ricardo recognized that intercountry price differences might exist for some goods, but either he emphasized that these goods were nontradables or the context indicates that this is what he meant. See Viner, op. cit., pp. 315, 323. See, for example, Ricardo, op. cit., vol. 3, pp. 56–57, 64 fn., 90, and vol. 6 (letter to Malthus), p. 90. See also Angell, op. cit., p. 59, where he states, "With respect to metallic currencies, Ricardo emphatically denies that there is any proportional relationship between money and prices."

43. *Report from the Select Committee on the High Price of Bullion*, reprinted in *The Paper Pound of 1797-1821: The Bullion Report*, ed. Edwin Cannan (New York: Augustus Kelley, 1969), p. 17. See also Ricardo, op. cit., vol. 3, pp. 91–92.

44. See, for example, Ricardo, op. cit., vol. 3, pp. 53, 57.

45. Ricardo, op. cit., vol. 3, p. 53.

46. Ibid., pp. 56–57. See also ibid., pp. 218–19. This interpretation of Ricardo was given by K. Wicksell. See, for example, K. Wicksell, *Interest and Prices* (New York: Augustus Kelley, 1965), pp. 81–82; and K. Wicksell, *Lectures on Political Economy*, vol. 2, "Money" (New York: Augustus Kelley, 1971).

47. Ricardo, op. cit., vol. 3, p. 57 fn.

48. Robbins, op. cit., p. 122.

49. *Report from the Select Committee*, op. cit., p. 16.

50. Various analyses of the controversies between the currency and banking schools are given elsewhere. See, for example, Viner, op. cit., and F. W. Fetter, *Development of British Monetary Orthodoxy, 1797-1875* (Cambridge, Mass.: Harvard University Press, 1965).

51. See, for example, Robbins, op. cit., pp. 100, 123; and O'Brien, op. cit., p. 153.

52. Viner, op. cit., p. 240.

53. See, for example, ibid., p. 223.

54. Viner, op. cit., p. 235.

55. Fetter, op. cit., p. 36; and Ricardo, op. cit., vol. 3, pp. 87, 88.

56. Viner, op. cit., p. 240.

57. See, for example, M. Daugherty, "The Currency-Banking Controversy: Parts I and II," *Southern Economic Journal* 9: 151.

58. See, for example, Daugherty, op. cit., p. 150, and D. E. W. Laidler, "Thomas Tooke on Monetary Reform," *Essays on Money and Inflation*, ed. D. E. W. Laidler (Chicago: University of Chicago Press, 1975), p. 214.

59. See D. E. W. Laidler and A. R. Nobay, "International Aspects of Inflation: A Survey," in *Recent Issues in International Monetary Economics*, ed. E. Claasen and P. Salin (New York: North-Holland, 1976), p. 301 fn.

60. Thomas Tooke, *A History of Prices* (New York: Adelphi, 1928), vol. 4, pp. 185, 192, 194.

61. See, for example, T. E. Gregory, "Introduction," Tooke, op. cit., pp. 13-14. It should be noted that the prices employed by Tooke were individual commodity prices and not index numbers.

62. See, for example, Laidler, op. cit., p. 214; Robbins, op. cit., p. 126; and K. Wicksell, *Interest and Prices*, op. cit., p. 83.

63. See Viner, op. cit., p. 240.

64. J. Fullarton, *On the Regulation of Currencies* (1844), p. 58, as quoted in Robbins, op. cit.

65. See, for example, Viner, op. cit., p. 223 fn.; F. Machlup, "Summary of the Discussion on Frenkel," *Recent Issues in International Monetary Economics*, op. cit., p. 50; and Daugherty, op. cit., p. 151.

66. See, for example, Fetter, op. cit., p. 228.

67. Tooke, op. cit., p. 652. From J. S. Mill, *Principles of Political Economy* (London: Longmans, Green, 1926), p. 652. See also Gregory, op. cit., pp. 76, 81.

68. Tooke, op. cit., vol. 4, p. 462. See also ibid., vol. 1, p. 149.

69. Tooke, *An Inquiry into the Currency Principle*, pp. 123-24. From Robbins, op. cit., p. 124. See also O'Brien, op. cit., p. 158, and Daugherty, op. cit., p. 149.

70. See, for example, Gregory, op. cit., p. 81; O'Brien, op. cit., p. 158; and Tooke, op. cit., vol. 4, p. 462.

71. Laidler and Nobay, op. cit., p. 301.

72. Tooke, *History of Prices*, op. cit., vol. 4, pp. 463, 470.

73. See, for example, Tooke, *History of Prices*, vol. 3, p. 191.

74. See, for example, Fetter, op. cit., p. 226, and Daugherty, op. cit., p. 146.

75. Fullarton, op. cit., p. 85, quoted by Mill, op. cit., p. 653. See also Wicksell, op. cit., p. 84; and Tooke, op. cit., vol. 4, p. 232, where he indicates that these bankers also contended that they could not influence prices.

76. See Tooke, *History of Prices*, vol. 4, p. 207.

77. Robert Torrens, *Principles and Practical Operation of Sir Robert Peel's Act of 1844* (3d ed.; London: Longmans, 1858), p. 190, quoted in Robbins, op. cit., p. 124.

78. See Fetter, op. cit., p. 190.

79. See Tooke, *History of Prices*, vol. 4, p. 206.

80. Robbins, op. cit., p. 125.

81. James Wilson, *On Capital, Currency, and Banking*, pp. 85, 87, quoted in Tooke, *History of Prices*, vol. 4, p. 208.

82. Tooke, *History of Prices*, vol. 4, p. 209.

83. Ibid., p. 462.

84. See, for example, Tooke, op. cit., vol. 3, p. 66; Wicksell, *Lectures on Political Economy*, op. cit., vol. 2, p. 173; and Fetter, op. cit., p. 227.

85. See, for example, Viner, op. cit., p. 240.

86. Tooke, op. cit., pp. 462-63.

87. See, for example, Daugherty, op. cit., p. 150; and Tooke, op. cit., vol. 4, p. 463.

88. See, for example, Fetter, op. cit., p. 191; and Wicksell, *Interest and Prices*, op. cit., p. 85.

89. M. Blaug, *Economic Theory in Retrospect* (Homewood, Ill.: Irwin, 1968), p. 180.

90. See, for example, Fetter, op. cit., p. 226.

91. See, for example, Mill, op. cit., Book 3, Chapters 13, 22.

92. Mill, ibid., p. 654. See also Wicksell, *Interest and Prices*, op. cit., p. 86; and Wicksell, *Lectures on Political Economy*, op. cit., vol. 2, p. 174, where Wicksell notes that "Mill considered that Tooke's view of the innocuousness of the banks as regards price movements was quite correct in normal, tranquil times. . . ."

93. Mill, op. cit., pp. 652–53.

94. Ibid.

95. Ibid., p. 653.

96. Ibid., p. 622 fn.

97. Ibid., p. 630.

98. Ibid., Book 3, Chapter 13.

99. With respect to Mill's analysis of an inconvertible currency, he essentially reproduced the basic arguments of Ricardo. See, for example, Blaug, op. cit., p. 200.

100. See, for example, Fetter, op. cit., p. 226. In particular, he mentions price level adjustment as the adjustment mechanism in some passages.

101. See Wicksell's *Interest and Prices*, op. cit., and *Lectures on Political Economy*, op. cit., vol. 2. See also Laidler and Nobay, op. cit., p. 301.

102. See, for example, Wicksell, *Interest and Prices*, op. cit., pp. 81, 82, 85; and Wicksell, *Lectures*, op. cit., p. 171.

103. See, for example, Wicksell, *Interest and Prices*, op. cit., p. 85.

104. Wicksell, *Lectures on Political Economy*, p. 159.

105. Wicksell, *Lectures on Political Economy*, op. cit., vol. 2, p. 171. See also ibid., p. 177.

106. Wicksell, "International Freights and Prices," *Quarterly Journal of Economics* 32 (1918): 405. See also Laidler and Nobay, op. cit., p. 301.

107. See Wicksell, *Interest and Prices*, op. cit., pp. 157–58. See also Viner, op. ctt., p. 305.

108. Wicksell, *Lectures on Political Economy*, op. cit., vol. 2, p. 177; and Wicksell, *Interest and Prices*, op. cit., pp. 157–58.

109. See Wicksell, *Lectures on Political Economy*, op. cit., p. 171.

110. See, for example, Wicksell, *Interest and Prices*, op. cit., pp. 82, 85, 157.

111. Wicksell, op. cit., pp. 81–82; and Wicksell, *Lectures on Political Economy*, op. cit., p. 171.

112. An excellent analysis of Laughlin and his monetary writings was recently presented by Girton and Roper. See Girton and Roper, op. cit. This section does not attempt to expand upon the Girton and Roper paper but rather attempts to place Laughlin among other authors in an evolutionary framework.

113. Laughlin, op. cit., pp. 409, 417; and Girton and Roper, op. cit., p. 15.

114. See, for example, Girton and Roper, op. cit., pp. 13, 15, 23.

115. Laughlin, op. cit., p. 369.

116. Laughlin, op. cit., pp. 380–82. See also, for example, Laughlin, op. cit., pp. 252, 371–72, 375, 377, 379–82, 388, 417.

117. See, for example, ibid., p. 379. See also Girton and Roper, op. cit., p. 24.

118. See, for example, Laughlin, op. cit., pp. 257, 264, 268–69.

119. See, for example, ibid., pp. 247, 263, 371. See also Girton and Roper, op. cit., pp. 13, 21.

120. See, for example, Laughlin, op. cit., pp. 247–48, 285, 314, 400, 407, 510–14, 528–31. See also Girton and Roper, op. cit., pp. 13, 21.

121. See, for example, Laughlin, op. cit., pp. 103, 379, 388–89, 393, 417. See also Girton and Roper, p. 21.

122. See Laughlin, op. cit., pp. 135–37, 388; and Girton and Roper, op. cit., pp. 14, 15.

123. Laughlin, op. cit., p. 393.

124. See, for example, G. Cassel, *Theory of Social Economy* (New York: Augustus Kelley, 1967), p. 522; I. Fisher, *The Purchasing Power of Money* (New York: Macmillan, 1911), p. 172; J. M. Keynes, *Monetary Reform* (New York: Harcourt Brace, 1924), p. 173; A. C. Pigou, *Industrial Fluctuations*, 2d ed. (New York: Augustus Kelley, 1967), p. 303.

125. See Witte and Henneberry, op. cit., p. 2.

Donald S. Kemp

3

A MONETARY VIEW OF
THE BALANCE OF PAYMENTS

In surveying the body of research dealing with the balance of payments, two major shortcomings are immediately apparent.[1] First, there are no widely accepted theories of the balance of payments which simultaneously incorporate both the current and capital account. The great majority of models used in payments theory consider either the capital account or the current account separately. Second, there have been very few attempts to include even the fundamentals of portfolio choice theory in balance-of-payments models. This is particularly surprising in view of the essentially monetary nature of payments theory.

This article presents an approach to payments theory which addresses both of these shortcomings. Since this essentially involves an extension of the rudiments of monetary theory to the area of the balance of payments, it is henceforth referred to as a monetary view of the balance of payments (MBOP).*

AN OVERVIEW OF THE THEORY

The MBOP may be summarized by the proposition that the transactions recorded in balance-of-payments (BOP) statistics reflect aggregate portfolio

This study was published in the St. Louis Federal Reserve Bank *Review*, April 1975, pp. 14–22.

*The theoretical foundation of this approach to payments theory may be found in Robert A. Mundell, *Monetary Theory: Inflation, Interest, and Growth in the World Economy* (Pacific Palisades, California: Goodyear, 1971). The formal model, presented later in this article, draws extensively on work done at the University of Chicago Workshop in International Economics and the analysis presented in Harry G. Johnson, "The Monetary Approach to Balance-of-Payments Theory," *Further Essays in Monetary Economics* (Cambridge, decisions by both foreign and domestic economic units. Under a system of fixed exchange rates, such as the gold standard or the type of arrangement set up in 1944 at Bretton Woods, overall net surpluses (deficits) in the trade and capital accounts are viewed as flows associated with either an excess demand for money on the part of domestic (foreign) economic units or an excess supply of money in foreign economies (the domestic economy). Consequently, in analyzing the rate of change of international reserves (the money account) the monetary approach focuses on the determinants of the excess demand for or supply of money.* According to this view, surpluses (deficits) in the money account measure the rate at which money balances are being accumulated (reduced) domestically. That is, a BOP flow is one of the mechanisms by which actual money balances are adjusted to their desired levels.

Suppose, for example, there is an autonomous increase in the money supply of country j, which leads to an increase in the demand for goods, services, and securities in that country. Under a system of fixed exchange rates, any such increase in domestic demand will result in a tendency for prices of domestic real and financial assets in country j to rise, in the short run, relative to those in foreign markets. Economic units in country j will react by decreasing their demands for domestic real and financial assets in favor of foreign assets, while domestic suppliers of these assets will seek to sell more at home and less abroad. At the same time, foreign economic units will decrease their demands for the assets of country j and foreign suppliers will attempt to sell more of their own assets in country j. All of these factors work in favor of an increase in imports and a decrease in exports in country j. The resultant deterioration of the BOP reflects the exchange of money balances for real and financial assets by economic units of country j. The foreign recipients of these money balances will convert them into their own currencies at their respective central banks. These foreign central banks will then present the balances to the central bank in country j in return for international reserves. Since international reserves are one of the components of a country's monetary base,[2] the effect of this transaction will be a decrease in the money supply of country j towards its level prior to the autonomous increase and an increase in the money supplies of its surplus trading partners.

Under a system of freely floating exchange rates, the required adjustment of money balances is accomplished through movements in the exchange rate. Under

Massachusetts: Harvard University Press, 1973), pp. 229–49. This article is essentially a synthesis and extension of these previous works.

*The overall net balance in the trade and capital accounts will henceforth be referred to as the money account. This reflects the fact that all transactions recorded below the line in this account have a direct impact on a nation's money supply. Under a pure gold standard, changes in official gold holdings are the only item below the line in this account. Under a Bretton Woods type system changes in official holdings of gold, SDRs, and foreign exchange and changes in the reserve position at the IMF are all included below the line in the money account.

such a system the BOP (on a money account basis) equals zero by definition and there are no intercountry movements of international reserves. As such, required adjustments in money balances cannot be accommodated through balance-of-payments flows. In this case the adjustment of actual money balances to their desired levels is accomplished by changes in domestic prices and exchange rates (which change concomitantly with and accommodate the required movement in domestic price levels).

The above approach is in sharp contrast with what amounts to the current conventional wisdom of payments theory; namely, the elasticities and absorption approaches. Implicit in both of these approaches is the assumption that either there are no monetary consequences associated with the BOP, or that to the extent the potential for such consequences exists, they can be and are absorbed (sterilized) by domestic monetary authorities.[3]

The MBOP regards all BOP deficits and surpluses and movements in floating exchange rates as phases in a stock adjustment which are the result of a disparity between the demand for and supply of money. This approach asserts that, under a system of fixed exchange rates, there are inflows (outflows) of international reserves associated with BOP surpluses (deficits) and that these flows cannot be sterilized in the long run. Furthermore, because of the impact of these reserve flows on a country's monetary base, they will result in variations in the supply of money relative to the demand for it and thus have an equilibrating impact on the level of money balances and the BOP. According to this view, the only way to obtain persistent deficits or surpluses is to construct a model in which the need for stock adjustments is being continuously recreated.

The only solutions to these reserve flows are processes which facilitate the return of actual money balances to their desired levels. This adjustment can be accomplished either automatically, through inflows or outflows of international reserves, or through appropriate actions by the domestic monetary authorities which change some other component of the monetary base by the same amount. Under a system of freely floating exchange rates the adjustment is also accomplished either automatically by changes in domestic price levels and the concomitant changes in the exchange rate, or again by the appropriate actions on the part of the monetary authorities. The only other potentially successful policy actions available are those which, in the end, have the same effect on money balances as those just mentioned.

SOME FUNDAMENTAL PROPOSITIONS

In order to facilitate the development of a model later in this article, there are some fundamental propositions associated with the MBOP that should be discussed.

1) The MBOP maintains that the transactions recorded in the balance of payments are essentially a reflection of monetary phenomena. As such, it places

emphasis on the direct influence of an excess demand for or supply of money on the BOP.

Implicit in this approach is the assumption that the demand for and supply of money are stable functions of a limited number of variables. The MBOP does not imply that changes in the money supply are the only factors which affect the BOP. It nevertheless does say that the primary channel by which changes in any real variable affect the BOP is through their effects on the demand for or supply of money.[4] Thus, any analysis of the impact of a policy or other change must begin with an analysis of how this change generates a divergence between actual and desired money balances or affects such a divergence that already exists.

2) In the analysis presented in this article, the crucial BOP concept is that which captures all transactions reflecting the adjustment of actual money balances to their desired levels. That is, the only transactions considered below the line are those which have an influence on domestic and foreign monetary bases and thus on domestic and foreign money supplies.[5]

The analysis presented here does not attempt to provide a theory of the individual subaccounts; it merely lumps the individual components (goods, services, transfers, short- and long-term capital) into a single category—"items above the line." This approach recognizes that an excess supply of or demand for money may be cleared through the markets for either goods, services, or securities.[6] Furthermore, if the BOP is viewed within this framework, the pitfalls of placing emphasis on any particular subaccount are obvious. For example, the effects on aggregate economic activity of a deficit in the merchandise trade account could be neutralized by a surplus in one of the capital accounts. In this case, any negative aggregate demand effects resulting from an increase in imports of goods would be offset by an inflow of capital and thus an increase in investment demand. The two effects would offset each other and aggregate money balances would be unchanged.

3) The MBOP relies on the assumption of an efficient world market for goods, services, and securities.* Under a system of fixed exchange rates, the price of any good or service in one country relative to its price in any other country can change only in the short run. Likewise, the rate of return on any asset can differ from the rate of return on assets of comparable risk and maturity in any other country only in the short run. It follows that in the long run price levels and interest rates in all countries must move rigidly in line with one another. In fact, in a fixed exchange rate regime it is the attempts to arbitrage intercountry price and interest rate differentials that are the driving force leading to the reduction or

---

*While it is acknowledged that there are some goods that are not traded internationally, there are limits to relative price changes between these nontraded goods and other (traded) goods. The higher the elasticities of substitution between these two classes of goods in both production and consumption, the smaller the scope for relative price changes and the more direct the international price interdependence.

accumulation of money balances and a concomitant temporary BOP deficit or surplus.

Under a system of freely floating exchange rates, price levels may move at different rates between countries. However, the impact of these differential rates of change on individual relative prices between countries is offset by opposite movements in exchange rates. The same arbitrage opportunities that lead to reserve flows under fixed rates lead to exchange rate adjustments that exactly compensate for differential price level changes between countries.

4) The MBOP is a theory of an automatic adjustment process. According to this theory, any BOP disequilibrium or exchange rate movement reflects a disparity between actual and desired money balances and will automatically correct itself. While the adjustment process is different under different exchange rate regimes, the implication is that the process is automatic and that its effects cannot be neutralized in the long run. Any BOP imbalance or exchange rate change is a phase in the automatic adjustment process and attempts to counter these processes merely increase the forces which give rise to the adjustment ultimately required for a return to equilibrium.

5) The MBOP is concerned primarily with the long run. The approach recognizes that short-run analysis is often complicated by the fact that the postulated adjustment behavior is incomplete in the short run. For example, the adjustment of actual money balances to their desired levels does not occur instantaneously, but rather requires the passage of time. As another example, it is possible that the monetary authorities may attempt to neutralize the impact of international reserve flows on their respective money supplies in the short run.[7] However, the MBOP asserts that governments cannot follow such policies in the long run. This seems reasonable because, in the long run, success in neutralizing the effects of international reserve flows implies that the governments of some (surplus) countries are willing to trade investment and consumption goods for foreign currency balances. The accumulation of these balances by surplus country governments represents a nonmarket induced transfer of wealth away from domestic to foreign consumers. For whatever reason, it is unrealistic to suppose that a government would pursue such policies in the long run.

6) An implication of this theory is that, under a system of fixed exchange rates, domestic monetary policy does not control a country's money supply. Excessive monetary expansion (contraction), via expansion (contraction) of some controllable component of the monetary base, will result in an outflow (inflow) of international reserves (an uncontrollable component of the monetary base) and a tendency for the money supply to return to its former level.* The resulting BOP deficit (surplus) is only a reflection of these uncontrollable international reserve

---

*While this is true for most countries, it is not necessarily the case for the reserve currency country. The special case of a reserve currency country will be discussed in the next section.

outflows (inflows). Through this process, the inflationary or deflationary impact of domestic monetary policy is mitigated with respect to the domestic economy and is imposed on the rest of the world via inter-country flows of international reserves. At the same time, however, the domestic economy is subject to the influence of inflationary or deflationary monetary actions taken in other countries.

Under a system of freely floating exchange rates, the domestic monetary authorities retain dominant control over the money supply, while the interaction of domestic and foreign monetary policies determines the exchange rate rather than the BOP (which is now zero by definition). In this case, a country neither imports nor exports international reserves. As a result, the domestic economy is subjected to the full consequences of inflationary or deflationary domestic monetary policies and is insulated from the effects of monetary actions taken in other countries.

7) Another feature of the MBOP is that it provides a framework within which one is able to assess the differential impact of monetary disturbances which occur in a world in which there is at least one reserve currency country (RCC) as opposed to those occurring in a world with no RCCs. An RCC is a country whose currency is held by others as a form of international reserves. It is this special status afforded to the currency of the RCC which leads to a slightly altered adjustment process for the world and the RCC itself.

THE SPECIAL CASE OF A
RESERVE CURRENCY COUNTRY

Because international reserves and reserve currencies exist only under a system of fixed exchange rates, the following analysis applies only to that case. For all non-RCCs, expansionary (contractionary) monetary policies are offset by a BOP deficit (surplus) and the resulting contraction (expansion) of the international reserve component of the monetary base. However, for an RCC this need not be the case. An expansionary (contractionary) monetary policy in the RCC may have no effect on its BOP as defined in this article. However, the RCC's trading partners will always experience a BOP surplus (deficit) and an inflow (outflow) of international reserves as a result of such RCC policies.* The reason for this is that the RCC currency is held by foreign central banks as a form of international reserves. While non-RCC monetary authorities are not willing to accumulate large balances denominated in other non-RCC currencies, they are willing to accumulate large balances denominated in the RCC currency. Because these balances are themselves a type of international reserves, non-RCC monetary authorities may

---

*Recall that the BOP concept used in this article is the balance in the money account. That is, the only items recorded below the line are those that affect the domestic money supply.

not be inclined to present them to the RCC authorities in exchange for other international reserves.

However, to the extent that the RCC loses no international reserves as a result of an increase in other components of its monetary base, it does experience an accumulation of liquid liabilities to foreign official holders.* As these liabilities of the RCC are regarded as assets by foreign official holders, their accumulation represents an inflow of international reserves and a BOP surplus for RCC trading partners.

The how and why of all of this can be brought out by reference to the balance sheets of the world's monetary authorities. While the following analysis applies to the case of expansionary monetary policy in the RCC, it is equally applicable to the analysis of contractionary monetary policy. In addition, in order to simplify the analysis we will assume that foreign central banks invest *all* of their RCC currency holdings in government securities issued by the RCC. However, we fully recognize that this need not be the case. Non-RCC central banks can and frequently do invest their RCC currency holdings in other assets or simply allow them to accumulate as deposits at the RCC central bank. Whatever the non-RCC authorities decide to do, however, all that is crucial for our analysis to hold is that they do not accumulate deposits at the RCC central bank.

Table 3.1 indicates what happens to the monetary bases of all countries as a result of an attempt by the RCC monetary authorities to increase the domestic money supply in the face of a fixed demand for money. Tier (A) illustrates that the initial impact of such an undertaking is to increase the monetary base of the RCC only. Tier (B) illustrates what happens to the respective monetary bases as a result of the forthcoming intercountry reserve flows. Non-RCCs accumulate international reserves (R) in the form of deposits denominated in the RCC currency held at the RCC central bank. As long as these R are held in this form, the RCC monetary base decreases towards its initial level and the non-RCC monetary bases increase, just as in the case of a world in which there are no RCCs.

Since the non-RCCs view these reserve currency balances as R, they are willing to accumulate them in the same manner that they accumulate other R. However, these R differ from others in one significant aspect—namely, they can be invested in government securities issued by the RCC. When non-RCCs choose to do this, the effects are as illustrated in tier (C). When non-RCC monetary authorities purchase RCC government securities, the OL entry in the RCC balance sheet is drawn down. This has the effect of increasing the monetary base of the RCC without causing a decrease in the monetary bases of the non-RCCs. The net

---

*While the accumulations or reductions of the holdings of liabilities do not affect the RCC balance of payments as defined in this article, they do affect some RCC balance-of-payments concepts. For example, such transactions would affect the Official Settlements Balance in the United States.

TABLE 3.1

Monetary Authorities Balance Sheet

Tier	RCC Monetary Authority's Balance Sheet		Collective Balance Sheet for all Non-RCC Monetary Authorities	
(A)	R (O) D (+) —OL (O)	DR (+) C (O)	R (O) D(O) —OL (O)	DR (O) C (O)
(B)	R (O) D (O) —OL (+)	DR (—) C (O)	R (+) D (O) —OL (O)	DR (+) C (O)
(C)	R (O) D (O) —OL (—)	DR (+) C (O)	R (O) D (O) OL (O)	DR (O) C (O)
(NET)	R (O) D (+) —OL (O)	DR(+) C (O)	R (+) D (O) —OL (O)	DR (+) C (O)

Note: R = official holdings of international reserves.

D = domestic credit; this consists of central bank holdings of securities, discounts and advances, and float.

—OL = other liabilities of the monetary authorities (including foreign deposits at Federal Reserve Banks). These items conventionally appear on the source side of the base as a negative item. They are subtracted from other items in calculating the source base.

C = currency held by the public.

DR = reserves of the domestic banking community.

*See Albert E. Burger, *The Money Supply Process* (Belmont, California: Wadsworth, 1971), p. 38.

Source: Compiled by the author.

effect of all of this is that the monetary bases of all countries have increased (as shown in the NET tier).

In view of the above analysis, a world in which there exists at least one RCC differs significantly from a world in which there are no RCCs. In a world with

RCCs, BOP deficits and surpluses may by themselves decrease and increase the level of R in the world and in individual countries. In a world with no RCCs, BOP deficits and surpluses result in a redistribution of an existing stock of R among countries, but produce no change in the overall level. As a result, in a world with RCCs, the world and each individual non-RCC will ordinarily experience much more difficulty in controlling its money supply. Thus, the existence of RCCs compounds the problems of money stock control which are already inherent in any system of fixed exchange rates.

In addition, this analysis implies that the inflationary or deflationary impact of RCC monetary policy is spread over the entire world. Unlike the case of a non-RCC, however, there may be no mitigation of the impact on the domestic economy since the RCC may neither gain nor lose reserves. As a result, prices in the RCC could change by the same amount as they would under a system of freely floating exchange rates. What's worse, however, is that the rest of the world will gain or lose international reserves and bear the same price level impact as the RCC. Thus, the potential for large BOP surpluses and deficits and for world wide inflations and deflations are greater under a fixed exchange rate system with RCCs than under any other system considered in this article.

A MONETARY MODEL OF THE BALANCE OF PAYMENTS

Now that the essential features of the MBOP have been spelled out, let us turn to the derivation of a model in which these features are expressed by a set of equations.* First, the model is derived for a non-RCC under a system of fixed exchange rates. Second, the same model is applied to the case of an RCC under fixed exchange rates. Finally, the model is applied to the case of freely floating exchange rates.

The common elements in each of these models are stable money demand and money supply functions.† The money supply function for each country may be stated as

$$MS_j = a_j [R_j + D_j] \tag{1}$$

where: MS_j = money supply in country j

---

*In order to simplify the presentation, many of the steps in the derivation of the model have been bypassed in the text. For the interested reader, a more thorough presentation of the model is provided in an appendix, which is available from the Federal Reserve Bank of St. Louis upon request.

†For an analysis of the development of the money supply function employed in this article, see Jerry L. Jordan, "Elements of Money Stock Determination," St. Louis Federal Reserve Bank *Review* (October 1969), pp. 10–19.

a_j = money multiplier in country j

R_j = official holdings of international reserves in country j; hereafter referred to as the international component of the monetary base

D_j = all other components of the monetary base in country j; hereafter referred to as the domestically controlled component of the monetary base

$D_j + R_j = MB_j$ = monetary base in country j

The demand for money in each country is assumed to be a function of real income, the nominal rate of interest, and prices.

$$MD_j = f_j[y_j, r, P] \tag{2}$$

where:

MD_j = demand for money in country j

P = price index in the world and thus in country j*

y_j = real income in country j

r = nominal rate of interest in the world and thus in country j

In accordance with the general monetarist framework of the model, country j is in equilibrium if and only if the growth of the supply of money equals the growth of the demand for money. We are able to specify the conditions necessary for fulfilling this requirement by expressing equations (1) and (2) in terms of rates of change and then equating the resulting expressions. This procedure allows us to derive an expression for the rate of growth of international reserves in country j.†

$$\frac{R_j}{MB_j} g_{R_j} = g_p + a_j g_{y_j} + \beta_j g_r - \frac{D_j}{MB_j} g_{D_j} \tag{3}$$

where:

a_j = income elasticity of demand for money in country j

β_j = interest rate elasticity of demand for money in country j

---

*This reflects the assumption that under a system of fixed exchange rates, a country's price level and interest rates move in line with the world price level and interest rates. However, in the case of freely floating exchange rates the assumption regarding the price level is no longer valid. As such, the money demand function must be specified somewhat differently in that case.

†Henceforth in this article $g_x = d\ln x/dt$. That is, g_x is the expression for the continuous rate of growth of variable x.

We are able to derive an expression for the growth rate of world prices $[g_p]$ by summing the expressions for the growth rates of the demand for and supply of money over all countries and equating the resultant expressions.

$$g_p = \sum_{i=1}^{N} w_i g_{MS_i} - \sum_{i=1}^{N} w_i [a_i g_{y_i} + \beta_i g_r] \tag{4}$$

where:　$w_i = \dfrac{MS_i}{\sum\limits_{i=1}^{N} MS_i}$　= 　weights calculated on the basis of money supplies converted by exchange rates to equivalent units of currency j.

FIXED EXCHANGE RATES IN A WORLD WITH NO RCCs

Recall that by definition $g_{R_j} = (1/R_j)(dR_j/dt)$. Under a system of fixed exchange rates in a world in which there are no reserve currency countries, dR_j/dt is the expression for the balance of payments in the money account. It represents the rate at which country j is either gaining or losing international reserves during a given time period (t). With this in mind, and upon making some simplifying assumptions regarding the interest and income elasticities of demand for money, we are able to substitute expression (4) into expression (3) and get an expression for the balance of payments in country j.*

$$\frac{1}{MB_j}BOP_j = [\sum_{i=1}^{N} w_i g_{MS_i} - \frac{D_j}{MB_j}g_{D_j}] + [g_{y_j} - \sum_{i=1}^{N} w_i g_{y_i}] \tag{5}$$

Expression (5) is essentially an embodiment of the features of the price specie flow mechanism, which operates under a system of fixed exchange rates in a world in which there are no reserve currency countries.* That is, expression (5) states that the BOP is a function of:

---

*We have assumed that $a_i = 1$ for all i and that $\beta_j = \sum_{i=1}^{N} w_i \beta_i$. Neither of these assumptions is crucial to the analysis at hand. They are invoked here mainly to simplify the presentation. The assumption that $a_i = 1$ is interpreted as assuming that the income elasticity of demand for money is unity in all countries. Assuming that $\sum_{i=1}^{N} w_i \beta_i = \beta_j$ means that the interest elasticity of demand for money in country j is equal to a weighted average of the interest elasticities of demand for money in all countries. A more restrictive implication of this assumption would be that the interest elasticities are equal in all countries.

†The price specie flow mechanism is an attempt to explain international gold flows under the gold standard. It is associated primarily with the work of David Hume in the 18th century. However, in our case the BOP includes more than just gold flows. It includes flows of all international reserves–gold, SDR's, foreign exchange, and reserve positions at the IMF.

1) the rate of growth of real income in country j relative to the average rate of growth of real income for all countries, and

2) the rate of growth of the domestically controlled component of the monetary base in country j relative to an average rate of money growth for the whole world.

FIXED EXCHANGE RATE IN A WORLD
WITH AT LEAST ONE RCC

In a world in which there is at least one RCC, expression (5) it is still an appropriate representation of the forces giving rise to BOP flows in non-RCCs. However, for an RCC there may be no international reserve flows associated with the BOP accounts; in which case $g_{R_j} = 0$. In the case of an RCC, excessive expansion (contraction) of the domestically controlled component of the monetary base need not lead to an offsetting contraction (expansion) of the international reserve component. At the same time, however, excessive expansion (contraction) of the domestically controlled component of the monetary base in the RCC will lead to an accumulation (reduction) of international reserves in all other countries. As mentioned previously, we will assume that these international reserves will be held in the form of securities issued by the RCC government to non-RCC official holders. For the RCC, it is the net accumulation or reduction of such liabilities that is determined by monetary actions in our model. This process can be captured in our model by setting $g_{R_{RCC}} = 0$ (where the RCC is the jth country) and replacing the term $\Sigma_{i=1}^{N} w_i g_{MB_j}$ in expression (5) with a more detailed formulation of the factors contributing to the growth of the money supply in all countries.

$$
\frac{1}{MB_w} BOL_{RCC} = [\sum_{i=1}^{N} w_i \frac{D_i}{MB_i} g_{D_i} - \frac{D_{RCC}}{MB_{RCC}} g_{d_{RCC}}]
$$
$$
+ [g_{y_{RCC}} - \sum_{i=1}^{N} w_i g_{y_i}]
$$

(6)

where: MB_w = the sum of the monetary bases of all countries in the world.

BOL_{RCC} = the net accumulation of claims against the RCC by foreign official institutions during time period (t).*

---

*For the United States this BOP concept closely resembles the balance on liabilities to foreign official holders. However, this account is distinctly different from the BOP concept utilized in equation (5). Equation (5) explains the balance in the money account, whereas the BOP concept used in equation (6) has no relation to the money supply.

This expression states that the change in the level of the liabilities of the RCC to foreign office holders that results from domestic monetary policy in the RCC is determined by the following:

1) the rate of growth of the domestically controlled component of the monetary base in the RCC relative to a weighted average of its rate of growth in all countries.

2) the rate of growth of real income in the RCC relative to a weighted average of the rates of growth of real income in all countries.

FREELY FLOATING EXCHANGE RATES

For the case of freely floating exchange rates, two modifications of the model are necessary. First, the model must be adapted to reflect the fact that there are no international reserve flows, so that the growth rate of a country's money supply is determined solely by domestic monetary policy $[g_{p_j}]$. Second, the money demand function must be modified to reflect the fact that the rate of price level change in one country may differ from the rate prevailing in the rest of the world.

Upon incorporating both of these modifications into the model, we are able to derive an expression for the determination of movements in the exchange rate.

$$g_{E_j} = [g_{MS_{ROW}} - g_{MS_j}] + [g_{y_j} - g_{y_{ROW}}] \tag{7}$$

where: $E_j = \dfrac{P_{ROW}}{P_j}$ = the price of currency j in terms of foreign currencies.

$P_{ROW} = \sum\limits_{i=1}^{N-1} h_t P_1$ = the price level in the rest of the world; that is, a weighted average of the price levels in all other countries.

$h_i = \dfrac{y_i}{\sum\limits_{i=1}^{N-1} y_i}$ = weights calculated on the basis of real GNP

P_j = price level in country j.

This expression states that the exchange value of currency j in terms of foreign currencies is determined by the rate of growth of the money supply and real income in country j relative to the rate of growth of the money supply and real income respectively in the rest of the world. As such, it implies that currency depreciations are the result of excessive monetary growth. It therefore supports the proposition that inflation causes depreciation of the domestic currency rather than vice versa.

SUMMARY AND CONCLUSIONS

The MBOP may be summarized by the proposition that the transactions recorded in balance-of-payments statistics reflect aggregate portfolio decisions by both foreign and domestic economic units. The framework presented in this article suggests some important policy considerations that cannot be addressed within the framework which characterizes most of the currently accepted body of payments theory.

The analysis presented here casts the balance of payments in the role of an automatic adjustment mechanism. Balance-of-payments deficits and surpluses, or movements in freely floating exchange rates, are viewed as being simultaneously both the result of a divergence between actual and desired money balances and a mechanism by which such a divergence is corrected. As such, persistent balance-of-payments deficits (surpluses) or depreciations (appreciations) of the foreign exchange value of a currency reflect a continual re-creation of a situation in which excessive monetary expansion in the country in question is greater (less) than the worldwide average. Furthermore, the only solution to such international disturbances are policies which facilitate the equalization of actual and desired money balances.

The futility of tariff and non-tariff barriers to trade which attempt to alter balance-of-payments flows or exchange rate movements becomes readily apparent when one views them within the framework presented above. Suppose, for example, that an import tariff is imposed with the aim of reducing a balance-of-payments deficit in the money account. According to the MBOP, international reserve flows will assure that the balance-of-payments deficit disappears in the long run whether the tariff is imposed or not. That is, even if the tariff were not imposed, the excess money balances, and therefore the deficit, would disappear as a result of the outflow of international reserves. However, if the tariff is imposed, relative prices will be artificially altered from the levels consistent with the most efficient allocation of resources and maximum gains from trade. Furthermore, the situation is no better if the tariff is imposed in retaliation against restrictive trade practices on the part of other nations. In this case, all that the tariff accomplishes is to further distort relative prices and further reduce the welfare of all nations.

Another advantage of the MBOP is that it enables one to clearly evaluate the relative desirability of different exchange rate regimes in terms of their promotion of autonomy of domestic monetary policy and domestic as well as worldwide price stability. Under a system of freely floating exchange rates a country retains dominant control over its money growth, incurs the full consequences of its domestic monetary policy, and is not subject to the effects of inflationary or deflationary monetary policies undertaken in other countries. Under a system of fixed exchange rates in a world in which there are no reserve currency countries, a country loses control of its rate of money growth, has the domestic impact of its monetary policy mitigated, and is subject to the effects of monetary policies pursued by other countries. Under a system of fixed exchange rates in a world in which there is at least one reserve currency country, we have the potential for the worst of both of the above systems. While the impact of expansionary (contractionary) monetary policies in the reserve currency country is imposed on the rest of the world, there may be no mitigation of their domestic impact. As a result, the entire world is prone towards large changes in its money supply which are initiated by actions taken in the reserve currency country. This conclusion appears to be consistent with the inflationary experiences of the western world which began in the late 1960s.

Finally, if the balance of payments is viewed within the MBOP framework, the pitfalls of placing emphasis on any particular BOP subaccount are obvious. A deficit (surplus) in any one account need not have any effect on domestic aggregate economic activity if its impact on money balances is offset by a surplus (deficit) in another account.

This point is especially significant in view of the large merchandise trade deficits that many oil consuming countries have been experiencing. The analysis presented in this article indicates that the impact of these deficits on money balances, and therefore on aggregate economic activity in the deficit countries, will be substantially reduced as a result of large inflows of capital from OPEC members. Of course this does not mean that oil consuming countries are no worse off now than they were prior to the fourfold increase in oil prices. The MBOP merely states that the impact on GNP will be mitigated through subsequent inflows of capital. The distribution of a given GNP between the residents of oil consuming and oil producing countries however, is altered in favor of the oil producers.

NOTES

1. For a lucid analysis of the current state of payments theory, see Anne O. Krueger, "Balance-of-Payments Theory," *The Journal of Economic Literature* 17 (March 1969): 1-26.

2. For a detailed discussion and analysis of the concept of the monetary base, see Leonall C. Andersen and Jerry L. Jordan, "The Monetary Base–Explanation and Analytical Use," Federal Reserve Bank of St. Louis *Review* 50, 8 (August 1968): 7-11.

3. The elasticity and absorption approaches are theories of the trade account alone and they neglect the issue of capital flows. For a discussion of the essentials of the elasticities approach, see Joan Robinson, "The Foreign Exchanges," in *Readings in the Theory of International Trade*, Committee of the American Economic Association (Philadelphia: Blakiston, 1949), pp. 83-103. For a discussion of the absorption approach, see Sidney S. Alexander, "Effects of a Devaluation on a Trade Balance," in *Readings in International Economics*, Committee of the American Economic Association (Homewood, Ill.: Richard D. Irwin, 1968), pp. 359-73. For a discussion of the differences between the monetarists' approach and both the elasticities and absorption approaches to payments theory, see Harry G. Johnson, "The Monetary Approach to Balance-of-Payments Theory," in *Further Essays in Monetary Economics* (Cambridge, Mass.: Harvard University Press, 1973), pp. 229-49.

4. For an analysis of the BOP effects of changes in a real variable (a change in tariff) within a monetarist's framework, see Michael Mussa, "A Monetary Approach to Balance-of-Payments Analysis," *Journal of Money, Credit and Banking* 6 (August 1974): 333-51.

5. For a review of balance-of-payments concepts and their meaning, see John Pippenger, "Balance-of-Payments Deficits Measurement and Interpretation," Federal Reserve Bank of St. Louis *Review* 55 (November 1973): 6-14. For a discussion of which transactions to include below the line, see the second explanatory note in this article.

6. This is not to say the MBOP framework would not be useful in analyzing individual subaccounts. However, such analysis would require a rigorous specification of the channels of monetary influence. For a survey and analysis of the literature pertaining to these channels, see Roger W. Spencer, "Channels of Monetary Influence: A Survey," Federal Reserve Bank of St. Louis *Review* 56 (November 1974): 8-26. For an example of how this framework could be applied to the analysis of the capital account alone, see Pentti J. K. Kouri and Michael G. Porter, "International Capital Flows and Portfolio Equilibrium," *Journal of Political Economy* 82 (May/June 1974): 443-67.

7. For an analysis of West German attempts to neutralize the effects of reserve flows, see Manfred Willms, "Controlling Money in an Open Economy: The German Case," Federal Reserve Bank of St. Louis *Review* 53, 4 (April 1971): 10-27.

Bluford H. Putnam
D. Sykes Wilford

4

MONEY, INCOME, AND
CAUSALITY IN THE
UNITED STATES AND
THE UNITED KINGDOM

Christopher Sims has presented an innovative statistical technique to determine the direction of causality, then applied this methodology to money and
nominal income in the United States. He concluded: "The main empirical finding
is that the hypothesis that causality is unidirectional from money to income agrees
with the postwar U.S. data, whereas the hypothesis that causality is unidirectional
from income to money is rejected."[1] In a more recent paper in the *American Economic Review*, David Williams, C. A. E. Goodhart and D. H. Gowland applied
Sims' statistical methodology to the United Kingdom and concluded: "We found
for the U.K. some evidence of unidirectional causality running from nominal
incomes to money but also some evidence of unidirectional causality running
from money to prices. Taken together, this evidence suggests, perhaps, a more
complicated causal relationship between money and incomes in which both are
determined simultaneously."[2] Furthermore, Williams, Goodhart and Gowland
suggest some general possibilities for the differences between the United States
and the United Kingdom, and they are careful to note that: "Because of the various differences in context the finding that in the United Kingdom the relationship
between money and income appears different from that found by Sims for the
United States in no way casts any doubt on the validity of Sims' own results."[3]

The purpose of this note is to present a concise model which draws together
the findings of Sims for the United States and of Williams, Goodhart and Gowland

The authors wish to thank the *American Economic Review* for permission to reprint
this study, which appeared in Volume 68 (June 1978), pp. 423-27. Also, the authors are
indebted to David T. King, J. Ernest Tanner, Walton T. Wilford, and J. Richard Zecher for
their comments on earlier versions of this paper.

for the United Kingdom. To accomplish this, a fixed exchange rate system is modeled in which one country, the United States, serves as the primary reserve currency country, while other countries, the United Kingdom in this case, hold a substantial portion of their international reserves denominated in terms of the reserve currency.* Particular attention is paid to the asymmetrical nature of the system and the empirical results of Sims and Williams, Goodhart and Gowland.

The model is couched in a world in which asset reallocations are viewed as adjustments toward maintaining general equilibrium. This equilibrium is based on a stable set of preferences regarding the structure of individual portfolios, broadly defined in terms of holdings of real consumption goods, real interest bearing financial assets, real money balances, and leisure time. The assumption of equilibrium conditions in all markets allows attention to focus directly on the money market to isolate the process of portfolio adjustment in international markets. As in similar models based on the monetary approach to the balance of payments, three equations are specified for each country: a money demand function, a money supply identity, and the condition of monetary equilibrium.[4] The difference between the reserve currency country and all other countries lies in the money supply identity. To follow through the consequences of the differences, the case of the reserve currency country is presented first, and then the case for other countries.

THE RESERVE CURRENCY COUNTRY

The model of the reserve currency country contains three straightforward equations. For simplicity, money demand depends on permanent real income and the price level:

$$M^d(A) = k(A)P(A)Y(A) \tag{1}$$

where the letter 'A' stands for the reserve currency country,

$$
\begin{array}{ll}
k & = \text{constant} \\
P & = \text{price level} \\
Y & = \text{permanent real income} \\
\text{and} \quad M^d & = \text{quantity of money demanded.}
\end{array}
$$

The reserve currency country's central bank has the power to determine the nominal money stock. Thus,

$$M^S = M. \tag{2}$$

---

*One may note that for the Commonwealth countries the British pound acted as a reserve currency. However, the pound's relative world influence vis-a-vis the U.S. dollar was small during the Bretton Woods period.

This money supply equation does not ignore the fact that the reserve currency country operates in the context of international markets (i.e., is an open economy). Equation (2) implies that the domestic money stock of the reserve currency country need not be responsive to its balance of payments. When money flows from the reserve currency country to the rest of the world, that money eventually is purchased by foreign central banks, due to their agreement to buy and sell currency at a fixed price. However, foreign central banks do not hold the major portion of their international reserves in noninterest-bearing form when an alternative exists. In this case, the foreign central banks purchase government securities from the reserve currency country.* Under these conditions, a balance of payments deficit results in an outflow of government securities, but not of money. Thus, the central bank of the reserve currency country maintains control over the nominal money stock. Furthermore, the reserve currency country is the only country with the power to create international reserves, thereby enabling it to remain independent of external influences.

Finally, the model is closed with the condition of monetary equilibrium:

$$M^d = M^s. \tag{3}$$

Solving this system for the price level and converting to growth terms yields:

$$g(P(A)) = g(M(A)) - g(Y(A)) \tag{4}$$

where $g(X) = (dX/dt)/X$, for $X = P, M$, and Y.

Growth of the price level is determined by the growth of the money supply relative to permanent real income growth. If permanent real income is growing at a stable rate and is, for the most part, independent of monetary disturbances, then changes in nominal income are caused primarily by changes in the supply of

---

*During the Bretton Woods period, when a particular central bank received dollars, which it held as international reserves, a portion of these dollars, that which was not needed for governmental transactions demand, were used to buy U.S. government securities. That is, the dollars returned to the United States, and instead of holding currency, foreign central banks held U.S. government securities. Thus, one may equate the flow of a dollar from a foreign central bank to the United States, not to a loss of international reserves for the United States, but to a securities account transaction between the authorities of the United States and the foreign central bank. As such, this transaction would be counted in the U.S. official settlements balance, since U.S. liabilities to foreign official agencies are affected. But, the money supply of the United States is not necessarily affected. For a more detailed explanation of this point see Donald S. Kemp, Chapter 3 of this book, as well as Lance Girton and D. W. Henderson, "Financial Capital Movements and Central Bank Behavior in a Two Country, Short-Run Portfolio Balance Model," *Journal of Monetary Economics* 2 (January 1976): 33–61; or A. K. Swoboda, "Gold, Dollars, Eurodollars, and the World Money Stock under Fixed Exchange Rates," *American Economic Review* 68 (September 1978).

money—the result which Sims obtained for the United States. The essential point is that it is not necessary to postulate that the United States is a closed economy to explain Sims' results. During the Bretton Woods period, the dollar played a leading role in world economic activity. However, by serving as the reserve currency country, the United States maintained control over its domestic money supply.

THE REST OF THE WORLD

The asymmetrical properties of the international monetary system become apparent when examining the non-reserve currency case. For simplicity, the money demand function is unchanged from the preceding analysis:

$$M^d(j) = k(j)P(j)Y(j) \tag{5}$$

where the letter 'j' stands for any non-reserve currency country.

With respect to the money supply identity, however, there are major differences between the reserve currency country and other countries. In the process of maintaining fixed exchange rates, central banks will incur inflows and outflows of reserve currency assets (i.e., international reserves). Because their monetary base depends on the asset portfolio of the central bank, the balance of payments will directly affect the domestic money supply. That is:

$$M^s(j) = aH = a(R + D) \tag{6}$$

where a = the money multiplier

H = high-powered money, or the monetary base

R = international reserve assets (liabilities of the reserve currency country)

and D = domestic assets held by the central bank.

Dividing high-powered money, which makes up the bulk of the liability side of the central bank's portfolio, into international reserves and domestic assets from the asset side of the portfolio, introduces the effects of the balance of payments directly into the money supply identity.[5] This formulation of high-powered money allows one to focus directly upon the sources of high-powered money, foreign or domestic.

The condition of monetary equilibrium completes the model:

$$M^s(j) = M^d(j). \tag{7}$$

Solving the system for the international reserve flow and converting to growth terms yields:

$$\frac{R}{H}g(R) = g(p(j)) + g(Y(j)) - g(a) - \frac{D}{H}g(D). \tag{8}$$

In this monetary approach to the balance of payments, the non-reserve currency country's prices are determined on unified world markets and are given exogenously to the domestic economy. The balance of payments reflects attempts by individuals to maintain equilibrium money balances as they adjust their expenditures and receipts. The endogeneity of the international reserve flow thereby implies the endogeneity of the money supply, leading to the conclusion that the non-reserve currency country's monetary authorities cannot determine the domestic money stock.

Two asymmetrical properties of the international system are now apparent. First, the reserve currency country can control its money supply, while other countries cannot. Secondly, the reserve currency country can influence its price level, while other countries must accept prices as determined on unified world markets. This holds true even though the reserve currency country participates in rising price level. Nominal income increases, and there is an inflow of international reserves as individuals seek to maintain equilibrium money balances. The balance of payments surplus reestablishes monetary equilibrium by expanding the supply of money to meet demand. Now suppose that from a position of equilibrium a non-reserve currency country attempts to raise its nominal money supply. As individuals reduce their excess money balances, the central bank experiences an outflow of international reserves due to residents' increased expenditures on foreign goods and assets. The loss of international reserves impacts directly on the monetary base, and the money supply moves back toward its initial level. International reserve flows equilibrate money supply to money demand as determined primarily by permanent real income and the price level. With prices determined on unified world markets and permanent real income not directly affected by the balance of payments, then essentially, nominal income and the money supply are simultaneously determined—a conclusion supported by the empirical findings of Williams, Goodhart and Gowland for the United Kingdom.*

SUMMARY

A fixed exchange rate system in which one country serves as the reserve currency country has important asymmetrical properties. Indeed, only the reserve

---

*The reader should note that the empirical technique employed by both Sims and Williams, Goodhart and Gowland can only indicate causality when leads and lags exist among the variables studied. For clarity, no attempt has been made to specify these leads and lags mathematically, but as the preceding paragraph indicates, there is a clear presumption as to their existence and direction.

currency country can control its money supply. From this property, several implications concerning the direction of causality follow directly. Control of the money supply results in the ability to influence the price level, and thus nominal income in the reserve currency country. Hence, Sims found that causality flows from money to nominal income in the United States. Furthermore, changes in prices and nominal incomes in the reserve currency country will simultaneously affect conditions in world markets. Individuals in other countries, reacting to these changes, adjust their portfolios. This adjustment process prompts simultaneous changes in prices, nominal income, and the money stock in non-reserve currency countries. Thus, Williams, Goodhart and Gowland found that in the United Kingdom neither money nor nominal income cause each other.

Both Sims' and Williams, Goodhart and Gowland's investigations covered the Bretton Woods period, during which the world was essentially operating on a dollar standard. Given a model highlighting the asymmetrical properties of such an international monetary system, the apparently inconsistent findings by Sims for the United States and Williams, Goodhart and Gowland's for the United Kingdom are, instead, entirely compatible.

NOTES

1. C. A. Sims, "Money, Income, and Causality," *American Economic Review* 62 (September 1972): 590.

2. D. Williams, C. A. E. Goodhart, and D. H. Gowland, "Money, Income and Causality: The U.K. Experience," *American Economic Review* 66 (June 1976): 423.

3. Ibid., p. 417.

4. There are several articles that summarize the essentials of the monetary approach to the balance of payments. For particular references see H. G. Johnson, *Further Essays in Monetary Economics* (Cambridge, Mass.: Harvard University Press, 1973), pp. 229–49; H. G. Johnson, "Elasticity, Absorption, Keynesian Multiplier, Keynesian Policy, and Monetary Approaches to Devaluation Theory: A Simple Geometric Exposition," *American Economic Review* 66 (June 1976): 448–52; D. S. Kemp, "A Monetary View of the Balance of Payments," Federal Reserve Bank of St. Louis *Review* 57 (April 1975): 14–22; B. H. Putnam, "Non-traded Goods and the Monetary Approach to the Balance of Payments," Federal Reserve Bank of New York Research Paper #7714, 1976; J. Frenkel and C. A. Rodriguez, "Portfolio Equilibrium and the Balance of Payments: A Monetary Approach," *American Economic Review* 65 (September 1975): 674–88; J. Frenkel and H. G. Johnson, "The Monetary Approach to the Balance of Payments: Essential Concepts and Origins," in *The Monetary Approach to the Balance of Payments*, ed. Jacob Frenkel and Harry G. Johnson (Toronto: University of Toronto Press, 1976), pp. 21–45; D. S. Wilford, *Monetary Policy and the Open Economy: Mexico's Experience* (New York: Praeger, 1977); J. R. Zecher, "Monetary Equilibrium and International Reserve Flows in Australia," *Journal of Finance* 29 (December 1974): 1523–30.

5. A detailed explanation of this view of the money supply process can be found in Zecher, op. cit.; Kemp, op. cit.; or L. Andersen and J. Jordan, "The Monetary Base: Explanation and Analytical Use," Federal Reserve Bank of St. Louis *Review* 50, 8 (August 1968): 7–11.

Bluford H. Putnam
D. Sykes Wilford

5

INTERNATIONAL RESERVE FLOWS: SEEMINGLY UNRELATED REGRESSIONS

INTRODUCTION

Much of the recent literature dealing with the balance of payments has centered around the monetary approach to the balance of payments. This new body of literature developed by, among others, Mundell, Komiya, Johnson, and Zecher[1] views the balance of payments as the result of adjustments in a country's stock of money, while traditional approaches to the balance of payments emphasize adjustments in the current account. An international reserve flow or a payments imbalance is viewed as the mechanism which ensures that the stock of money in a country adjusts to its desired level. That is, international reserve flows are determined by the excess demand or supply of money within a particular country. The monetary approach therefore focuses on the money market for a particular country within the context of a large world.

A number of papers have discussed the usefulness of this approach, and recently some empirical analyses have been undertaken.[2] Most of these discussions are based upon the central set of assumptions that prices and interest rates are determined in world goods, services, and capital markets which are well integrated, thus implying that a small country's domestic price on goods, services, and capital is exogenously determined. The additional assumptions of fixed

The authors wish to thank *Weltwirtschaftliches Archiv* for permission to reprint this study, which appeared in volume 114 (Summer 1978): 211–226. Also, the authors wish to thank J. Richard Zecher, W. Michael Cox, Walton T. Wilford, M. A. Akhtar, David T. King, and Hubertus Muller-Groeling for their generous discussions of this topic.

exchange rates and full employment allow these authors to solve for an international reserve flow equation.* Another factor which the empirical studies have in common is that individual country cases are examined. Although world factors are taken into account through various devices, simultaneous empirical analysis of various countries' reserve flows has not been performed.

This paper extends the empirical analysis of international reserve flows in two ways. First, the study incorporates the interrelationship of several countries' reserve flow equations by utilizing the seemingly unrelated regressions technique. Certain points, heretofore not fully developed in the literature,[3] suggest that these individual countries' international reserve flows are related through various world markets (goods and capital) and institutional arrangements (Bretton Woods) such that shocks to the world system may impact groups of countries simultaneously. We employ seemingly unrelated regression analysis to a group of European countries which are closely tied through capital markets as well as through political constraints for the period 1952-71.[4]

Secondly, in addition to estimating equations specified solely with the domestic price level and interest rate as proxies for the world price level and interest rate, the purchasing power parity and interest rate parity assumptions are integrated directly into the reduced form tests. Thus, U.S. prices and interest rates, also serving as proxies for world variables, are substituted for domestic variables. This approach allows us to comment directly on certain basic differences between the monetary approach and alternative theories.†

The analysis upholds the hypothesis that there exists a high degree of integration in capital and goods markets. Empirical results conform to the a priori notions of the monetary approach. And use of the seemingly unrelated regression technique greatly improves the efficiency of our parametric estimates, supporting the hypothesis that balance of payments disturbances are, as would be anticipated, often related.

THE BASIC MODEL

The monetary approach to the balance of payments model can be developed in five basic steps utilizing three assumptions. Following Johnson and Zecher,[5] for the jth country, the three structural equations are:

---

*The assumption of full employment can easily be relaxed without disturbing the model. One need only assume that reserve flows do not have an impact upon current period real output.

†This paper is not designed to fully examine the differences among all competing theories of the balance of payments. The interested reader should refer to Donald S. Kemp (this book, Chapter 3), Harry G. Johnson, *Further Essays in Monetary Economics* (Cambridge, Mass.: Harvard University Press, 1973), and Harry G. Johnson, "The Monetary Approach to

$$M_j^d = P_j Y_j^{a_1} e^{u_j} / i_j^{a_2} \text{ *}$$
(1)

$$M_j^s = a_j H_j$$
(2)

$$M_j^s = M_j^d,$$
(3)

where M_j^d = the demand for money by country j,

M_j^s = the supply of money in country j,

P_j = the price level in country j,

i_j = the interest rate in country j,

Y_j = the level of output in country j,

u_j = a log normally distributed disturbance term for country j,

a_j = the money multiplier in country j, and

H_j = the stock of highpowered money in country j.

The three assumptions are

(a) the jth country's price level is world determined,

(b) the jth country's interest rate is world determined, and

(c) the jth country's balance of payments does not affect real output.

By examining the balance sheet of the monetary authorities it can be shown that

$$M_j^s = a_j(R_j + D_j) \text{ where}$$
(4)

R_j = the stock of international reserves held by authorities and

---

Balance-of-Payments Theory: A Diagrammatic Analysis," *The Manchester School of Economics and Social Studies* 43 (1975): 220–74; as well as S. P. Magee, "Empirical Evidence on the Monetary Approach to the Balance of Payments and Exchange Rates," *American Economic Review* 66 (May 1976): 163–70; or Marina v. N. Whitman, "Global Monetarism and the Monetary Approach to the Balance of Payments," *Brookings Papers on Economic Activity* no. 3 (1975): 491–536.

*This specification of the money demand function assumes no money illusion.

D_j = domestic credit*

Assuming a fixed exchange rate one may solve for an international reserve flow equation where the level of foreign reserves held by the monetary authorities is functionally related to excess demand for money over domestically supplied money. Combining equations (1), (3), and (4), placing them in growth terms and rearranging to name the growth in reserves as the dependent variable, one obtains the basic reserve flow equation:

$$(R_j/H_j)gR_j = a_1 gY_j - a_2 gi_j + gP_j - ga_j - (D_j/H_j)gD_j + u_j \tag{5}$$

where $gX_j = d \ln X_j/dt$ = the rate of growth in country j of X: X = R, Y, P, i, a, and D.

The first three terms on the right hand side of equation (5) determine the growth in money demand while the next two terms capture the growth in the relevant domestic money supply variables. Price and interest rate variables are both assumed to be world determined, thus the price level effect on reserves is positive and the interest rate effect is negative. The inverse relationship between the interest rate and international reserve flows follows from the demand for money specification yielding a result, as Johnson pointed out, which is somewhat contrary to traditional literature.[7] The relationship of the reserve flow equation implies that attempts to increase the domestic money supply above demand results in a balance of payments deficit since the equilibrium condition (money supply equals money demand) must be satisfied.

RELATED DISTURBANCES

Estimation of the reduced form reserve flow equation for the jth country represented by equation (5), with modifications, has constituted the extent of empirical investigation in the literature.† We do not contend that this is an improper methodology for analyzing an individual country reserve flow. However,

---

*Domestic credit consists to a large extent of the authorities' holdings of domestic assets (both public and private liabilities) minus domestic liabilities other than highpowered money. For most countries, changes in D are closely related to the monetization of treasury debt. See Akhtar, Putnam, and Wilford for a theoretical discussion of the relationship of the change in D to the operation of the United Kingdom's treasury.[6]

†Of course, there are variations on the theme; some taking particular model building approaches involving portfolio theory such as Kouri and Porter,[8] utilizing rational expectation such as Cox (this book, Chapter 6), or including exchange rate changes as did Girton and Roper. However, these variations have concentrated on a single small country.

participation in world markets allows information to be gained by examining each country in the context of a larger group. The reserve flow equation for the ith country may have an error which is related to the error of the jth country. Thus, if one is investigating the reserve flow equation of n different countries and

$$Eu_j^t u_{j+1}^t \neq 0$$

t = time and u_j^t = the error in the time t for the jth country, then a proper methodology for examining individual reserve flow equations would involve estimating the equations jointly as one set.

The rationale for the relation of errors among individual country reserve flow equations can be derived from many factors. First, it is evident that a principal relation which may not be captured in the independent variables of the individual equations is the effect of any shocks directly or indirectly derived from integrated financial systems. During the period of fixed exchange rates, domestic credit creation in the reserve currency country (i.e., the United States) had an impact on world international reserves and world money supply. Deviations in credit conditions in the reserve currency country may not be completely reflected in current world prices and interest rates but would still affect the balance of payments of many countries.* Second, real factors which tend to disrupt a major segment of world trade may also lead to correlation of the error terms of reserve flow equations. For instance, a dock strike in the United States or a drought in a major agricultural region of the world might cause shocks in several countries' reserve flows simultaneously.†

This study focuses upon eight European countries characterized by highly integrated traded goods markets and well-developed Euro-capital markets yielding sufficient conditions for the existence of correlation among reserve flow equation error terms. We argue that efficiency is increased through estimating the coefficients of the reserve flow equations in a stacked format utilizing a GLS procedure.‡ However, it must be noted that the gain in efficiency may be somewhat offset due to any correlation between the explanatory variables' matrices of the different countries.[9]

---

*For a further discussion of the role of the reserve currency country in a fixed exchange rate system see Swoboda, op. cit., Kemp, op. cit., and Putnam and Wilford, op. cit.

†A classic example of a simultaneous shock to the international payments system, which occurred outside of the sample period utilized here, was the fourfold increase in oil prices by OPEC in 1973.

‡As will be noted later, the increase in estimating efficiency is manifested in a reduction of the standard errors associated with the coefficients of the explantory variables. The seemingly unrelated regressions technique utilizes the information contained in the correlations of the error terms of the individual equations, and in re-estimating the equation system is able to reduce the portion of error attributed to the explanatory variables. Thus, with simultaneous exogenous shocks accounted for, at least in part, the efficiency of the estimates is enhanced.

EMPIRICAL RESULTS

The first set of regressions to be estimated is derived directly from equation (5). The set of eight equations is estimated for Austria, Belgium, Denmark, France, Germany, Italy, the Netherlands, and the United Kingdom, with the jth country's reserve flow regression equation of the form:

$$(R_j/H_j)gR_j = b_1 gY_j + b_2 gi_j + b_3 gP_j + b_4 ga_j + b_5(D_j/H_j)gD_j + u_j. \tag{6}$$

The second set of estimating equations utilizes the same procedure of estimation except that the jth country's price variable is replaced by the U.S. CPI as a proxy of the movement in world price levels. Thus, the jth country's reserve flow regression equation is of the form

$$(R_j/H_j)gR_j = b_1 gY_j + b_2 gi_j + b_3 gP_{us} + b_4 ga_j + b_5(D_j/H_j)gD_j + u_j. \tag{7}$$

Since the world is well integrated in the goods market one would, a priori, expect growth in prices to be very similar or, in a strict sense, equal. In an empirical sense, the use of a consistent proxy provides one with the opportunity to examine the consistency of the theory as well as the stability of the coefficients.

The third set of estimating equations explicitly adds the constraint that the interest rate variable is a proxy for the world rate; therefore, the U.S. interest rate is substituted into the second formulation, (7), for i_j. Thus, the reduced form for the jth equation is

$$(R_j/H_j)gR_j = b_1 gY_j + b_2 gi_{us} + b_3 gP_{us} + b_4 ga_j + b_5(D_j/H_j)gD_j + u_j. \tag{8}$$

This specification follows from the hypothesis that the world's financial markets ensure interest arbitrage such that movements in any interest rates (the U.S. rate specifically) reflect the underlying real factors which cause a portfolio holder to demand money.

A priori, for all individual country equations in each equation set, the anticipated coeffecent for the income variable, b_1, is close to positive unity. This interpretation rests on the role of real income as a determinant of the demand for money. Alternative theories, such as the elasticities or absorption approaches would postulate a negative coefficient for income. That is, a rise in income would increase imports and, ceteris paribus, result in a deterioration of the current account. These are primarily theories of the balance on current account, not theories of the combined current and capital accounts or the overall balance of payments, as is the case with the monetary approach. Hence, the direct comparability of the theories is limited without some assumptions concerning capital account behavior in the alternative models.

The sign of the estimated coefficient for the interest rate variable, b_2, should be negative for all equation sets. Again, this interpretation rests on the role of the interest rate in money demand as well as the assumption that world interest rates are linked together. That is, an increase in the world interest rate (or its proxy) implies a decrease in the demand for money and an outflow of international reserves. Conventional theory might argue that an increase in domestic interest rates relative to world interest rates would draw capital from the rest of the world, leading to a reserve inflow. Such an alternative hypothesis suggests a positive sign for b_2 in equations (6) and (7) which use domestic interest rates and a negative sign for equation (8) which uses the U.S. interest rate.*

From the point of view of the theory presented, the coefficient of the price level should be near positive unity. This assumes no domestic money illusion in the demand for money and unified world goods markets, such that world price equal domestic price changes. An alternative hypothesis would be that an increase in domestic prices, with world prices constant, would imply an increase in imports, a decline in exports, a reserve outflow, and a negative sign on the price level in equation (6), while positive in equations (7) and (8) which use U.S. prices.

If the monetary approach is to be supported by the empirical evidence, the price level and the interest rate in each country must serve as determinants of the demand for money and behave as if world goods and capital markets are well-integrated. This means that the price level should carry a positive sign and the interest rate a negative sign for each country and in each equation set, regardless of whether a domestic or world proxy is used to represent the relevant variable.†

Coefficients on the sources of domestic monetary influence, both ga and (D/H) gD, are expected to be negative unity. Non-monetary theories of the balance of payments tend to exclude these variables from the analysis, so no comparisons analogous to the ones given for the demand variables are available.‡

The annual data for the fixed exchange rate period 1952-1971 are from *International Financial Statistics*. Interest rates are comparable for all countries and the price variables are the individual çonsumer price indices. The real income

---

*Of course, a complete specification of the alternative approach is required for an empirical comparison, and this exercise is beyond the scope of this paper.

†Some variation in the size of the coefficient across countries and across equation sets is likely due to the stochastic process.

‡In the extreme case where the specified money demand function for a country fits perfectly with zero error in every observation period, equation (6) would also fit perfectly. Then, it would be precisely true that for a given demand for money, any percent change in domestic money (ga + (D/H)gD) would be offset by an opposite change in international reserves ((R/H)gR). In this case, if the domestic money variables, a and D, satisfy the statistical independence properties required by regression analysis, then their estimated coefficients would be precisely negative unity. On the other extreme, where no statistical relationship exists between money demand and the specified explanatory variables (Y, P, and i), then regression equation (6) might yield positive, negative, or even zero coefficients with respect to ga and (D/H)gD. Prior testing has indicated that the underlying money demand functions are relatively stable, but by no means perfect fits.

variable is nominal GNP deflated by the consumer price index. Money supplies are narrowly defined.

Tables 5.1, 5.2, and 5.3 report the regression results for the eight countries based upon equation forms (6), (7), and (8) respectively. Single equation estimation results (OLS) as well as seemingly unrelated regression (GLS) results are reported for each country. The summary statistics, meaningful for the OLS regressions only, indicated that auto-correlation was not a significant problem, thus averting the necessity of an iterative estimation procedure. All F-values were significant at the 0.05 level.* The R^2's are reported and all are in the .80 to .98 range which is relatively high, given that percentage change specifications are utilized. Summary statistics are not applicable for the seemingly unrelated regressions results, so that the contribution of this technique may be best measured by the consistent drop in the standard errors of the coefficients as reflected in the t-statistics movements. In general, the statistical results are encouraging.

One of the most important results from this exercise is the stability of the money demand coefficients (b_1, b_2, and b_3) as well as the money supply coefficients (b_4 and b_5) over the three separate specifications. In very few cases did the estimated coefficients move significantly when the U.S. price level and interest rate were substituted into the equations for respective domestic variables. The stability as well as the relative size and significance of the coefficients strongly support the integrated markets assumption of the monetary approach to the balance of payments.

The income elasticity of money demand, b_1, is significantly different from 0 and close to its hypothesized value of +1 in *all* cases except Denmark and then only when specification (8) is used. In most cases, especially with respect to specifications (6) and (7), the results for b_1 are not only as anticipated but strongly supported by strong t-statistic values. Since b_1 is the most important elasticity coefficient estimated in the policy sense and given that a stable money demand relationship is necessary to the use of the model for policy, these results are most positive.

The interest elasticity is consistent across all three specifications, being negative and relatively small in all cases, except Denmark. It is significant for the United Kingdom, Germany, France, and Austria and consistently insignificant for the other countries. This result is similar to findings by Zecher and Rutledge.[10] Akhtar notes that the role of the interest rate in a money demand function is not easily interpreted, since the former may influence the latter through either an own price effect or a cross price effect or both.[11] The use of the U.S. rate as a proxy in Table 5.3 yields results which are overall poorer, but still consistent with those in the other tables. In summary, our results on b_2 conform to a priori expectations of the integration of world capital markets.

---

*The $a = 0.05$ one tailed test is used in all discussions in this section unless otherwise noted.

TABLE 5.1

International Reserve Flows[a]: Domestic Prices and Interest Rates

Country j	Explanatory Variables						
	Real Income	Interest Rate	Price Level	Money Multiplier[b]	Domestic Credit	Type	R^2
Austria	0.76	-0.24	0.93	-0.50	-1.21	OLS	.92
	(5.66)	(-4.19)	(4.53)	(-2.95)	(-8.12)		
	0.69	-0.22	1.05	-0.60	-1.12	GLS	
	(6.07)	(-5.01)	(6.73)	(-5.05)	(-10.35)		
Belgium	0.69	-0.15	0.85	-0.83	-1.08	OLS	.88
	(4.02)	(-2.22)	(1.99)	(-2.34)	(-10.06)		
	0.68	-0.01	0.73	-0.75	-1.11	GLS	
	(4.22)	(-1.76)	(1.80)	(-2.33)	(-11.19)		
Denmark	0.71	-0.27	1.18	-0.99	-0.98	OLS	.91
	(3.58)	(-1.33)	(4.98)	(-4.20)	(-8.93)		
	0.69	-0.12	1.10	-0.99	-0.99	GLS	
	(4.02)	(-0.70)	(5.25)	(-4.89)	(-10.36)		
France	1.22	-0.37	0.17	-0.43	-0.95	OLS	.88
	(5.91)	(-3.98)	(1.10)	(-1.34)	(-9.29)		
	1.32	-0.38	0.15	-0.62	-1.00	GLS	
	(7.45)	(-4.67)	(1.16)	(-2.31)	(-11.57)		
Germany	0.83	-0.04	1.05	-0.54	-1.08	OLS	.98
	(8.34)	(-3.09)	(3.43)	(-3.62)	(-18.07)		
	0.84	-0.05	1.12	-0.54	-1.08	GLS	
	(9.70)	(-4.01)	(4.26)	(-4.67)	(-22.83)		
Italy	1.05	-0.09	1.12	-0.49	-0.82	OLS	.82
	(5.18)	(-1.06)	(2.53)	(-6.22)	(-6.98)		
	1.02	-0.13	1.21	—0.46	-0.83	GLS	
	(5.81)	(-1.88)	(3.17)	(-6.51)	(-8.14)		
Netherlands	0.56	-0.13	0.88	0.52	-1.13	OLS	.97
	(3.69)	(-1.91)	(3.03)	(-3.45)	(-24.51)		
	0.61	-0.06	0.70	-0.59	-1.13	GLS	
	(5.83)	(-1.20)	(3.61)	(-5.80)	(-35.44)		
United Kingdom	0.91	-0.12	0.30	-0.34	-0.82	OLS	.94
	(5.60	(-2.32)	(2.26)	(-4.45)	(-13.21)		
	0.91	-0.10	0.30	-0.32	-0.84	GLS	
	(6.20)	(-2.20)	(2.48)	(-5.24)	(-16.90)		

[a]Period: 1952-1971; reserves $(R_j/H_j)gR_j$.
[b]Calculated on basis of M1.
Note: t-statistics are in parentheses.
Source: International Financial Statistics (Washington, D.C.: International Monetary Fund).

TABLE 5.2

International Reserve Flows[a]: U.S. Prices and Domestic Interest Rates

Country j	Explanatory Variables						
	Real Income	Interest Rate	Price Level	Money Multiplier[b]	Domestic Credit	Type	R^2
Austria	0.76	-0.21	1.00	-0.71	-1.19	OLS	.84
	(3.53)	(-2.64)	(1.98)	(-2.99)	(-5.70)		
	0.69	-0.19	1.09	-0.77	-1.19	GLS	
	(3.62)	(-3.00)	(2.33)	(-4.05)	(-7.17)		
Belgium	0.81	-0.10	0.22	-0.49	-1.08	OLS	.84
	(4.39)	(-1.32	(0.49)	(-1.24)	(-8.81)		
	0.69	-0.05	0.37	-0.54	-1.04	GLS	
	(4.41)	(-0.94)	(1.00)	(-1.87)	(-11.47)		
Denmark	0.76	-0.03	1.24	-1.01	-0.96	OLS	.80
	(2.36)	(-0.09)	(1.91)	(-2.92)	(-5.94)		
	0.61	-0.04	1.18	-0.72	-0.88	GLS	
	(2.26)	(-0.15)	(1.93)	(-2.58)	(-6.71)		
France	1.24	-0.42	0.22	-0.43	-0.94	OLS	.87
	(5.48)	(-3.97)	(0.49)	(-1.28)	(-8.93)		
	1.22	-0.37	1.13	-0.43	-0.88	GLS	
	(6.38)	(-4.17)	(2.75)	(-1.58)	(-10.33)		
Germany	0.88	-0.05	0.85	-0.59	-1.05	OLS	.97
	(8.33)	(-3.44)	(2.86)	(-3.72)	(-16.69)		
	0.84	-0.04	0.89	-0.56	-1.07	GLS	
	(8.44)	(-3.14)	(3.09)	(-3.96)	(-19.26)		
Italy	1.15	-0.03	1.08	-0.52	-0.79	OLS	.80
	(5.95)	(-0.34)	(2.12)	(-6.13)	(-6.56)		
	1.03	-0.02	1.38	-0.45	-0.85	GLS	
	(6.14)	(-0.40)	(3.13)	(-7.31)	(-9.82)		
Netherlands	0.70	-0.13	1.00	-0.57	-1.07	OLS	.97
	(4.74)	(-1.54)	(2.12)	(-3.02)	(-20.39)		
	0.54	-0.09	1.29	-0.74	-1.08	GLS	
	(4.55)	(-1.48)	(3.37)	(-5.61)	(-29.20)		
United Kingdom	0.83	-0.12	0.59	-0.33	-0.79	OLS	.96
	(5.86)	(-2.78)	(3.35)	(-5.12)	(-14.62)		
	0.83	-0.01	0.58	-0.33	-0.80	GLS	
	(5.98)	(-2.61)	(3.33)	(-5.38)	(-15.43)		

[a]Period: 1952-1971; reserves $(R_j/H_j)gR_j$.
[b]Calculated on basis of M1.
Note: t-statistics are in parentheses.
Source: International Financial Statistics (Washington, D.C.: International Monetary Fund).

TABLE 5.3

International Reserve Flows[a]: U.S. Prices and Interest Rates

Country j	Explanatory Variables					Type	R^2
	Real Income	Interest Rate	Price Level	Money Multi-plier[b]	Domes-tic Credit		
Austria	0.64	−0.21	1.27	−0.81	−1.36	OLS	.80
	(2.71)	(−1.46)	(2.11)	(−2.93)	(−6.27)		
	0.60	−0.20	1.30	−0.78	−1.40	GLS	
	(3.25)	(−1.42)	(2.37)	(−4.77)	(−9.61)		
Belgium	0.78	−0.09	0.12	−0.23	−1.01	OLS	.84
	(4.22)	(−1.09)	(0.29)	(−0.75)	(−7.39)		
	0.56	−0.10	0.59	−0.41	−0.93	GLS	
	(4.54)	(−1.35)	(1.88)	(−2.49)	(−12.96)		
Denmark	0.73	0.17	1.06	−1.10	−0.99	OLS	.81
	(2.37)	(1.15)	(1.78)	(−4.03)	(−8.04)		
	0.40	0.17	1.33	−0.89	−0.96	GLS	
	(2.05)	(1.13)	(2.51)	(−5.46)	(−13.36)		
France	1.21	−0.34	−0.39	0.35	−0.78	OLS	.85
	(4.95)	(−3.34)	(−0.89)	(1.07)	(−7.06)		
	1.21	−0.03	−0.41	0.36	−0.78	GLS	
	(6.21)	(−3.45)	(−1.00)	(1.53)	(−9.59)		
Germany	0.76	−0.07	1.03	−0.23	−1.10	OLS	.95
	(5.78)	(−0.71)	(2.57)	(−1.49)	(−13.60)		
	0.72	−0.06	1.09	−0.27	−1.11	GLS	
	(6.49)	(−0.65)	(2.89)	(−2.45)	(−19.01)		
Italy	1.34	−0.24	1.38	−0.52	−0.91	OLS	.85
	(7.54)	(−2.53)	(3.12)	(−7.39)	(−8.83)		
	1.13	−0.22	1.67	−0.48	−0.90	GLS	
	(7.27)	(−2.40)	(4.29)	(−8.80)	(−11.44)		
Netherlands	0.74	−0.15	0.84	−0.50	−1.08	OLS	.97
	(5.18)	(−1.78)	(2.07)	(−2.96)	(−22.16)		
	0.58	−0.15	1.22	−0.64	−1.08	GLS	
	(4.83)	(−1.80)	(3.34)	(−4.73)	(−27.82)		
United Kingdom	0.89	−0.07	0.47	−0.30	−0.83	OLS	.93
	(5.28)	(−1.16)	(2.35)	(−3.95)	(−13.55)		
	0.85	−0.05	0.51	−0.31	−0.87	GLS	
	(5.27)	(−0.89)	(2.56)	(−4.42)	(−15.30)		

[a]Period: 1952–1971; reserves $(R_j/H_j)gR_j$.
[b]Calculated on basis of M1.
Note: t-statistics are in parentheses.
Source: International Financial Statistics (Washington, D.C.: International Monetary Fund).

The coefficient on prices, b_3, is close to +1 for all other countries except France and the United Kingdom. Overall, the results, both OLS and GLS, conform to the theoretical specification. France and Britain, interestingly, are two of the four countries which exhibit strong interest rate influence on reserve flows, and the inflationary expectations component of interest rate movements may be serving as a proxy for the actual price variable.

The sign of the money multiplier variable coefficient, b_4, in all cases conforms to expectations in both OLS and GLS estimates. The size of the estimated coefficient is different from -1 for most cases, although Denmark and Belgium produced estimates very close to minus unity. The relative stability of this variable for most countries over the period tested could explain the results. When examined in its role as a policy variable our results support the hypothesis that a tightening of monetary policy through reserve requirements, or any other money multiplier control variable, ceteris paribus, will lead to reserve inflows.

The other money supply variable, domestic credit, appears to have a stronger effect on reserves. The coefficient on growth in domestic credit (scaled by its share of highpowered money), b_5, is very close to its hypothesized value of -1 in all cases tested. The t-statistics in the GLS regression range upward to 35.44 in the case of the Netherlands for specification (6) in Table 5.1. Even the OLS results never yield a t-statistic on b_5 less than 5.70.

The performance of both OLS and GLS (seemingly unrelated) results for both the money demand and money supply variables with respect to coefficient size and sign (for most countries) lends credence to the monetary approach. Indeed, the stability of the estimated coefficients when moving from domestic to U.S. price and interest rate variables is impressive. The improved performance of the GLS estimation suggests that the equations are not only stable but are also related over time. In summary, the regression results confirm our a priori notions about the effect of domestic money demand and domestically supplied money on reserve flows, as well as about the validity of the assumptions concerning integrated world goods, services and capital markets.

CONCLUSION

The empirical evidence presented here and developed in the context of the monetary approach to the balance of payments provides useful insights into world monetary adjustment on two counts. First, the use of a seemingly unrelated regressions approach in estimating international reserve flows for eight European nations improved estimating efficiency vis-a-vis standard OLS techniques. This gain in efficiency resulted from a correlation among the error terms in the equation set; thus, factors which are not included in the fundamental determinants, but that jointly effect the balance of payments of a group of countries, are captured in the estimation procedure. Secondly, the use of three specifications of the international reserve flow equation allowed for the examination of assumptions of unified goods and asset markets. In particular, the substitution of the U.S. price level and U.S. interest rate for national price and interest rate variables did not substantially alter the estimation results. This is a particularly impressive result, because it depends so heavily on a high degree of integration in international goods and financial markets. In sum, the results strongly support the monetary approach views of world payments adjustment and, in addition, point to the usefulness of further research with theoretical and empirical attention to the interaction among countries in the context of highly integrated world markets.

NOTES

1. R. A. Mundell, *International Economics* (New York: Macmillan, 1968); Ryutaro Komiya, "Economic Growth and the Balance of Payments," *Journal of Political Economy* 77 (January-February 1969): 35–48; Harry G. Johnson, *Further Essays in Monetary Economics* (Cambridge, Mass.: Harvard University Press, 1973); and J. Richard Zecher, "Monetary Equilibrium and International Reserve Flows in Australia," *Journal of Finance* 29 (December 1974): 1523–30.

2. For a discussion of theoretical and empirical extensions of the basic money demand and supply relationships as they apply to reserve flows see W. Michael Cox (this book, Chapter 6); M. Connolly (this book, Chapter 1); Johnson, op. cit., pp. 229–49; J. Frenkel and Harry G. Johnson, eds., *The Monetary Approach to the Balance of Payments* (London: Allen and Unwin, 1976); Harry G. Johnson, "The Monetary Approach to Balance-of-Payments Theory: A Diagramatic Analysis," *The Manchester School of Economics and Social Studies* 43 (1975): 220–74; A. Swoboda, "Gold, Dollars, Euro-Dollars and the World Money Stock and Fixed Exchange Rates," *American Economic Review* 68 (September 1978); and Bluford H. Putnam and D. Sykes Wilford, "Money, Income and Causality in the U.S. and the U.K.: A Theoretical Explanation of Different Findings," *American Economic Review* 68 (June 1978): 423–27.

3. Two papers that have discussed this problem are D. Sykes Wilford and Walton T. Wilford, "Monetary Approach to Balance of Payments: On World Prices and the Reserve Flow Equation," *Weltwirtschaftliches Archiv* 113 (1977): 31–39; and L. Girton and Donald Roper, "A Monetary Model of Fixed and Flexible Exchange Rates Applied to the Post-War Canadian Experience," *American Economic Review* 67 (September 1977): 537–48.

4. This procedure follows from seminal work for grouping equations done by Arnold Zellner, "An Efficient Method of Estimating Seemingly Unrelated Regressions and Tests for Aggregation Bias," *Journal of the American Statistical Association* 57 (1962): 348–68; followed by N. C. Kakwani, "The Unbiasedness of Zellner's Seemingly Unrelated Equations Estimates," *Journal of the American Statistical Association* 62 (1967): 141–42; and Jan Kementa and R. F. Gilbert, "Small Sample Properties of Alternative Estimators of Seemingly Unrelated Regressions," *Journal of the American Statistical Association* 63 (1968): 1180–1200.

5. Johnson, *Further Essays in Monetary Economics*, pp. 229–49; and Zecher, op. cit.

6. M. A. Akhtar, B. H. Putnam, and D. S. Wilford, "Fiscal Constraints, Domestic Credit, and International Reserve Flows," *Journal of Money, Credit and Banking* 11 (1979).

7. Johnson, *Further Essays*, op. cit., p. 240.

8. Pentti J. K. Khouri and Michael G. Porter, "International Capital Flows and Portfolio Equilibrium," *Journal of Political Economy* 82 (May-June 1974): 443–67.

9. For a more complete discussion see Arnold Zellner and D. S. Huang, "Further Properties of Efficient Estimators for Seemingly Unrelated Regression Equations," *International Economic Review* 3 (1962): 300–13.

10. Zecher, op. cit.; and John Rutledge, "Balance of Payments and Money Demand," paper presented to the Southern Economic Association meetings, November 1975, New Orleans, La.

11. M. A. Akhtar, "Demand Functions for High-Powered Money in the United States," Mimeographed, Federal Reserve Bank of New York, 1977.

W. Michael Cox

6

SOME EMPIRICAL EVIDENCE ON AN INCOMPLETE INFORMATION MODEL OF THE MONETARY APPROACH TO THE BALANCE OF PAYMENTS

Typical models of the monetary approach to the balance of payments assume that the domestic price level continuously reflects worldwide monetary equilibrium. The implications of relaxing this assumption and instead allowing for a time delay in the flow of commodity price information across countries have been investigated by W. Michael Cox.[1] In such a setup the domestic price level may be either endogenous or exogenous depending on the strength of the interdependencies among national monetary policies. The purpose of the present study is to provide some simple tests of this hypothesis.

The study's first section gives a brief summary of the theoretical results. The remainder of the study contains the results and a discussion of the empirical testing of this hypothesis for Canada. Over the 1963-69 period, the chosen measure of monetary policy of Canada and the United States—open market operations—shows substantial correlation in monthly growth rates. The regressions indicate that, on a monthly basis, Canadian balance of payments phenomena can be explained significantly better in a framework that allows for a time delay in the flow of commodity price information across these countries, but also specifically takes into account the correlation between the monetary policies of the United States and Canada.[2]

The author would like to thank Richard Zecher and Ernest Tanner for their comments on an earlier draft of this study. Also, comments by Robert Barro have been of benefit on several occasions.

SUMMARY OF EARLIER RESULTS

A brief summary of the theoretical results is provided in this section. There is assumed to be an instantaneous global flow of information concerning interest rates, but a lag in the flow of all other types of information across countries. Specifically, the foreign price level, the level of foreign real income, and foreign monetary variables are available to the home economy with a one period lag. This asymmetry of information is rationalized by the view that financial asset markets are substantially more centralized than other types of markets. The formal model is summarized by the following set of equations:

Home Country

Home Money Demand:	$M_d = APy^{b_1} i^{-b_2} e^u$	(1)
Home Money Supply:	$M_s \equiv a[R + D]$	(2)
Home Monetary Equilibrium:	$M_d = M_s$	(3)
Home Commodity Demand:	$y^d = [P/E \cdot P^{o^e}]^\delta e^{k_d t + \xi_d}$	(4)
Home Commodity Supply:	$y^s = [P/E \cdot P^{o^e}]^\gamma e^{k_s t + \xi_s}$	(5)
Home Commodity Equilibrium:	$y^d = y^s$	(6)

Foreign Country

Foreign Money Demand:	$M^{o^d} = A^o P^o y^{o^{b_1}} i^{o^{-b_2}} e^{u^o}$	(7)
Foreign Money Supply:	$M^{o^s} \equiv a^o[R^o + D^o]$	(8)
Foreign Monetary Equilibrium:	$M^{o^d} = M^{o^s}$	(9)

Parity Conditions

Purchasing Power Parity:	$P = P^o \cdot E$	(10)
Interest Parity:*	$i = i^o$	(11)

---

*The more general interest parity condition is $i = i* + g_E^e$. However, in periods of fixed exchange rates with no expected devaluations (or unexpected devaluations) g_E^e equals zero. The interest parity condition could also be represented as $r = r*$ where the variable r represents the real rate of return on financial assets. This is formally equivalent to the above statement since the purchasing power parity condition (10) and rational expectations imply that $g_P^e = g_{P*}^e + g_E^e$ and by the Fisher relations, $i = r + g_P^e$, and $i* = r* + g_{P*}^e$.

The superscripts d and s represent demand and supply respectively. The superscript e denotes the "rational" expectation of a variable, and omicron denotes the foreign economy. The money stock (M), price level (P), level of real income (y), interest rate (i), exchange rate (E), level of domestic credit (D), international reserves (R), money multiplier (a), and high-powered money (H) are assumed to represent equilibrium values. The term g_x represents the growth in these variables; specifically $g_x = d \ln x/dt; x = M, y, i, P, E, R, a, D, (g_E = 0)$. The variable D represents the domestic monetary policy variable for Canada and D^0 represents that variable for the United States. More specifically, g_D and g_{D^o} represent open market purchases (+) and sales (-) by the home and foreign monetary authorities, respectively.*

For simplicity, the income elasticity (b_1) and interest elasticity (b_2) of money demand are assumed to be equal across countries. All random error terms, u, u^o, ξ_d, and ξ_s, are assumed to be serially independent, mutually uncorrelated, with a zero mean and constant variance in their differenced form $u' \equiv du$, $u^{o'} \equiv du^o$, $\xi_d' \equiv d\xi_d$, and $\xi_s' \equiv d\xi_s'$. Output (y^o) and the money multiplier (a^o) of the foreign economy are assumed to grow randomly about their trend rates $\bar{g}_{yo}$ and $\bar{g}_{ao}$, respectively. The output level of the foreign economy represents the full employment level of output with no allowance for speculation over space since the home economy's commodity market is by assumption insignificant compared to the foreign economy.† The final assumption is that the home economy's domestic credit expansion (g_D) and the foreign economy's domestic credit expansion (g_{D^o}) follow a bivariate normal distribution with known average growth rates (to date) $\bar{g}_D \equiv \mu$, $\bar{g}_{D^o} \equiv \mu^o$, known variances in the growth rates, σ^2 and σ^{o2}, respectively, and a known correlation in the growth rates, ρ.

Three alternative home-country reserve flow equations can be derived from the above model and set of assumptions. Two of these equations represent full current information specifications. These are

$$\frac{R}{H}g_R = g_p + b_1 g_y - b_2 g_i - g_a - \frac{D}{H}g_D + u', \tag{12}$$

and,

$$\frac{R}{H}g_R = b_1(g_y - g_{yo}) - (g_a - g_{ao}) - \frac{D}{H}g_D + \frac{D^o}{H^o}g_{D^o} + \tau. \tag{13}$$

---

*By definition the variable D measures other assets (other than international reserves) minus other liabilities of the central bank. An open market purchase increases D and thereby M since it increases the central banks asset portfolio.

†The full employment level of foreign output is assumed to be exogenous to the foreign money market. W. Michael Cox and Halbert White[4] have investigated the implications of relaxing this assumption and instead allowing output to be affected by unanticipated price disturbances.

The first of these equations is the familiar form of the monetary approach to the balance of payments developed by Harry G. Johnson.[3] The second full information reserve flow equation (13) is obtained by solving for g_{p0} from the foreign country monetary conditions (7) through (9), using (10) and (11).* Implicit in equation (12) is the assumption of worldwide monetary equilibrium. This assumption is made explicit in the form of equation (13).†

Under incomplete current information, however, the above model suggests that the appropriate reserve flow equation appears as

$$\frac{R}{H}g_R = b_1(g_y - \bar{g}_{y0}) - (g_a - \bar{g}_{a0}) + \frac{D^O}{H^O}(\mu^O - \rho\frac{\sigma^O}{\sigma}\mu) - (\frac{D}{H} - \frac{D^O}{H^O}\rho\frac{\sigma^O}{\sigma})g_D + \tau. \tag{14}$$

The central contrast between the full information reserve flow equations, (12) and (13), and the incomplete current information reserve flow equation (14) concerns the coefficient on the home country monetary policy variable g_D. Under full current information this coefficient has a hypothesized value of minus D/H (a value of minus unity for the variable $(D/H)g_D$), suggesting that domestic monetary policy is powerless to affect the domestic money stock. Under incomplete current information, however, the coefficient g_D appears as $(D/H - (D^O/H^O)\rho(\sigma^O/\sigma))$, suggesting that domestic monetary expansion may not lead to a dollar-for-dollar outflow of reserves, depending on the value of the history of summarized statistics ρ, σ^O, and σ. In short, this is true because the existence of a correlation between domestic monetary policy and foreign monetary policy destroys the exogeneity of home money demand to the home authorities' actions.

EMPIRICAL ESTIMATION

The purpose of this section is to report the results of some simple estimations of the alternative reserve flow equations. Canada was selected as the home country and the United States was chosen as a measure of the rest of the world (foreigners). This selection was made on the basis of country size, openness of the economies, and extent of financial market development. The period selected for study is January 1963 through December 1969, since during this period Canada's government was committed to maintaining fixed exchange rates. Over this period Canada's gross national product was roughly one-seventh that of the United States and its money supply one-twelfth that of the United States, so that Canada satisfies the small country assumptions needed for this study. This made possible the use of one country—the United States—as a measure of the rest of the world.

---

*The basic model referred to here is that described by Michael Connolly (this book, Chapter 1).

†A further assumption is that $(R^O/H^O)g_{R0}$ is zero. For the large country, by definition reserve flows constitute insignificant changes in the level of high-powered money.

All data are monthly observations, seasonally adjusted where applicable, with Canadian dollar statistics transferred into United States dollar statistics via the spot exchange rate. The narrow definition of money—currency plus demand deposits—was selected for the United States, and the broad definition—currency, demand deposits, and time deposits—was used for Canada. This provides a measure of comparable money supplies since Canadian demand and time deposits are highly substitutable. Permanent income series were constructed using a five-month declining weight average. The three-month treasury bill rate served as the interest rate series and the consumer price index served as the price series. Domestic credit was calculated as high-powered money less international reserves.

Tables 6.1 and 6.2 report the results of the full information reserve flow equations. The results for the standard reserve flow equation (12) indicate that, even on a monthly basis, the demand for money is sufficiently stable to yield the expected results. The estimated coefficients of g_P, g_y, g_a, and $(D/H) g_D$ are all within two standard deviations of their respective hypothesized values of $+1.0$, $+1.0$, -1.0, and -1.0. Estimation of the alternative full information reserve flow equation (13) suggests that, even on a monthly basis, monetary and real phenomena are transmitted across countries. That is, the variables g_{y^0}, g_{a^0}, and $(D^0/H^0) g_{D^0}$ provide a reasonably good proxy for the growth in prices in the home country. The R^2 and F-level of each full information equation are high, indicating that a substantial portion of the variance in reserve flows can be explained by either set of independent variables. The slightly lower R^2 and F-level experienced when moving from the standard full information specification (12) to the alternative full information specification (13) is to be expected, due to the introduction of an additional stochastic disturbance in (13).

These results seem to support a state of world as described by the full information monetary approach to the balance of payments. However, they are not inconsistent with a state of world where market participant behavior is based on expectations. Consider the two contrasting hypotheses: that economic behavior is based solely on known (realized) information; and that individuals behave on the basis of expectations. A statistical test yielding a high level of significance with known (realized) information as explanatory variables would seem to confirm the hypothesis that economic behavior is based solely on known data. However, the true hypothesis may be that individuals behave on the basis of expectations but form expectations accurately. Were this the case, however, one would expect some improvement when moving from the full information specifications to the specification where expectations play a role.[5]

For the analysis of reserve flows based on expectations, three types of information sets are considered:

1. Previous-twelve-month series: Here the relevant statistics, ρ, μ, μ^0, σ, and σ^0 are calculated each month from the data of the previous twelve months. In moving from month to month the most distant observation on g_D and on g_{D^0} is discarded and the most recent included. These statistics are reported in Table 6.3.

TABLE 6.1

Estimates of the Standard Full Information Reserve Flow Equation

(Dependent Variable: $\dfrac{R}{H} g_R$)

Estimated Coefficient of the Explanatory Variable							
g_p	g_y	g_i	g_a	$\dfrac{D}{H} g_D$	R^2	F-Level	D–W
.72	.75	−.01	−.80	−.90	.77	45.05	1.24
(2.08)	(4.03)	(−.06)	(−9.33)	(−14.54)			

Source: Compiled by the author with data from *International Financial Statistics* (Washington, D.C.: International Monetary Fund), various issues.

TABLE 6.2

Estimates of the Alternative Full Information Reserve Flow Equation

(Dependent Variable: $\frac{R}{H}g_R$)

	Estimated Coefficient of the Explanatory Variable					
$(g_y - g_{yo})$	$(g_a - g_{ao})$	$\frac{D^o}{H^o}g_{D^o}$	$\frac{D}{H}g_D$	R^2	F-Level	D–W
.64	-.81	.92	-.92	.74	39.73	1.42
(2.45)	(-9.00)	(5.44)	(-13.61)			

Source: Compiled by the author with data from *International Financial Statistics* (Washington, D.C.: International Monetary Fund), various issues.

9/13, for better fit. (comp)

TABLE 6.3

Correlation Between Monthly Rates of Domestic Credit Creation for Canada and United States: Previous-twelve-month Series

Year						Month						
	1	2	3	4	5	6	7	8	9	10	11	12
1964	.483	.466	.446	.452	.382	.184	-.306	-.328	-.623	-.420	-.111	-.129
1965	-.007	.081	.159	.182	.184	.137	.185	.244	.318	.448	.210	.269
1966	.284	.273	.203	.437	.377	.419	.433	.360	.280	.278	.280	.300
1967	.188	.186	.209	-.058	-.226	.109	.095	.198	.120	.199	.192	-.050
1968	.032	-.066	.342	.353	.520	.530	.435	.454	.523	.405	.538	.670
1969	.674	.654	.401	.183	.190	.118	.132	.159	.174	.055	-.140	-.162

Notes: These statistics correspond to the variable $\rho \equiv \text{cor}(g_D, g_{Do})$ where g_D represents a series of previous-twelve-month observations on Canadian rates of domestic credit creation and g_{Do} represents that variable for the United States. The variable g_D was calculated as $\log\left(\dfrac{D}{D_{-1}}\right)$ where D_{-1} represents the one period lagged value of Canadian domestic credit. Similarly for the United States.

Source: Compiled by the author with data from *International Financial Statistics* (Washington, D.C.: International Monetary Fund), various issues.

TABLE 6.4

Correlation Between Monthly Rates of Domestic Credit Creation for Canada and United States: Continuously Updated Series

Year	Month											
	1	2	3	4	5	6	7	8	9	10	11	12
1964	.483	.484	.466	.468	.461	.319	.303	.289	.251	.240	.270	.273
1965	.273	.271	.275	.275	.272	.239	.235	.251	.253	.256	.254	.259
1966	.266	.268	.260	.306	.296	.276	.276	.275	.268	.263	.263	.262
1967	.247	.249	.248	.244	.236	.241	.241	.240	.236	.241	.236	.205
1968	.208	.208	.227	.230	.249	.248	.240	.238	.236	.235	.250	.252
1969	.254	.253	.231	.196	.193	.188	.185	.184	.183	.176	.173	.169

Notes: These statistics correspond to the variable $\rho \equiv \mathrm{cor}(g_D \cdot g_{Do})$ where g_D represents a continuously updated series of observations on Canadian rates of domestic credit creation and g_{Do} represents that variable for the United States.

Source: Compiled by the author with data from *International Financial Statistics* (Washington, D.C.: International Monetary Fund), various issues.

TABLE 6.5

Estimates of the Incomplete Current Information Reserve Flow Equation

(Dependent Variable: $\dfrac{R}{H}g_R$)

	Estimated Coefficient of the Explanatory Variable						
Information Set	$(g_y - \bar{g}_{yo})$	$(g_a - \bar{g}_{ao})$	$\dfrac{D^0}{H^0}(\mu^o - \rho\dfrac{\sigma^o}{\sigma} - \mu)$	$(\dfrac{D}{H} - \dfrac{D^0}{H^0}\rho\dfrac{\sigma^0}{\sigma})g_D$	R^2	F	D-W
Previous twelve months	.96	-.91	1.39	-1.00	.83	64.97	1.83
	(4.44)	(-11.77)	(8.19)	(-17.51)			
Continuously updated	.87	-.87	.65	-.95	.75	43.32	1.38
	(3.42)	(-9.44)	(5.50)	(-14.20)			
Period average	.89	-.89	1.48	-.97	.83	66.42	1.27
	(4.15)	(-11.77)	(8.10)	(-17.72)			

Source: Compiled by the author with data from *International Financial Statistics* (Washington, D.C.: International Monetary Fund), various issues.

2. Continuously updated series: In this case the relevant statistics are updated each month on the basis of last month's observations on g_D and g_{Do}. Old information is never discarded. These statistics are reported in Table 6.4.

3. Period-average: Here, the statistics ρ, μ, μ^o, σ, and σ^o are calculated over the entire period and held constant at their respective values throughout the estimation period. The statistic ρ, for example, corresponds to the end-of-period value (.169) given in Table 6.4.*

In each case, the statistics are calculated giving equal weight to each period. The variables μ and μ^o measure the simple average of g_D and g_{Do}, σ and σ^o measure the unweighted standard deviations of g_D and g_{Do} from μ and μ^o, respectively, and ρ measures the simple correlation of g_D and g_{Do} over each of the information sets.

Estimation of the incomplete information reserve flow equation yields the results given in Table 6.5.† R^2's in each of the regression equations based on incomplete current information are higher than those of either full information specification. In addition, for two of the three information sets considered, the F-levels improve. The statistic

$$\frac{(SSR_Q - SSR_K)/(Q-K)}{SSE_Q/(n-Q)} \sim F_{Q-K,n-Q'}$$

where SSR_K = unexplained sum of squares in the full information specifications,

SSR_Q = unexplained sum of squares in the incomplete information specification,

SSE_Q = explained sum of squares in the incomplete information specification,

Q = the number of explanatory variables in the incomplete information specification,

K = the number of explanatory variables in the full information specification, and

n = the number of observations,

can be used to test the hypothesis at a given level of significance, that the incomplete information specification explains more of the variance in reserve flows than do the full information specifications. Calculation of this statistic for

---

*The period average values for the monthly observations on μ, μ^o, σ, and σ^o are .0025, .0065, .1686, and .0091, respectively. The calculated series for μ, μ^o, σ, and σ^o for the other two information sets are available upon request.

†Prior testing of the money demand equations for Canada and the United States revealed insignificantly different (at the 95 percent level) interest and income elasticities of money demand across the two countries.

each of the information sets considered and comparison against its critical value reveal that two of the three information sets yield (at the 99 percent level) a significantly better explanation of the variance in Canadian reserve flows than either full information specification.

Comparing individual explanatory variables across equations, one notices an improvement in the t-statistics in every case, and in all cases but one the coefficients move more toward their hypothesized values. Of particular interest is the coefficient on domestic credit growth. The results of Table 6.3 indicate that adapting the standard coefficient on domestic credit growth (D/H) with a term that accounts for the influence of expectations and monetary interdependencies, $(D^0/H^0)\rho(\sigma^0/\sigma)$, moves the estimated coefficient more toward its hypothesized value of minus unity for each of the information sets considered. In addition, for two of the three information sets considered the t-ratios show improvement.

Appearing consistently least significant in explanatory power is the expectations equation based on the continuously updated information set. Both the previous-twelve-months and period-average information sets yield a substantially better fit for the reserve flow equation. One possible explanation concerns the comparative costs and benefits of maintaining each of the information sets. The period-average information set would be the least costly to maintain since the relevant statistics, ρ, μ, μ^0, σ, and σ^0 are taken at their average values and no reaccumulation of the data is ever made. In terms of benefits, this set would yield fair predictive power as long as the joint distribution of monetary policies was not subject to frequent shifting. Greatest benefits would be likely to be associated with the previous-twelve-months information set. This set would predict the relevant statistics well in a world where the interdependencies among national monetary policies were stable or in one where they underwent constant structural changes. In terms of costs, maintenance of this information set would require periodic calculation of the relevant statistics over twelve data points, necessitating a small but positive accumulation cost. Highest cost would be associated with maintenance of the continuously updated set, since old information is never discarded and each period a calculation of the relevant statistics requires reaccumulation over all the data. In addition, the benefits of such a set would be inferior to those of the period-average set. For these reasons the previous-twelve-months and period-average methods represent more likely methods of accumulating the relevant information. The inferior explanatory power of the reserve flow equation based on the continuously updated information set would then be expected.

SUMMARY AND CONCLUSION

The findings suggest that incorporating expectations into the model of the monetary approach and simultaneously taking account of the correlation among monetary policies yields an improved explanation of monthly balance-of-payments phenomena of Canada. The source of this improvement lies in the ability of the expectations equation to explain monthly reserve flows under various degrees of expectations accuracy, while the full information reserve flow equations account for reserve flows when those expectations are correct.

This evidence supports the hypothesis that in the short run, monetary policy in the small open economy may not lead to offsetting adjustments in the balance of payments. Some short-run control of the domestic monetary base is implied. However, monetary policy is not available as a long run instrument of stabilization.

NOTES

1. W. Michael Cox, "An Incomplete Information Model of the Monetary Model of the Monetary Approach to the Balance of Payments," Mimeographed, University of Rochester, 1978.

2. For an analysis of Canadian monetary policy, see T. J. Courchene, *Money, Inflation, and the Bank of Canada* (Montreal: C. D. Howe Research Institute, 1976).

3. Harry G. Johnson, *Essays in Monetary Economics* (Cambridge, Mass.: Harvard University Press, 1973). Other references on the general theory of the monetary approach useful for this discussion are: J. R. Zecher, "Monetary Equilibrium and International Reserve Flows in Australia," *Journal of Finance* 29 (December 1974): 1323-30; Stephen Mager, "Empirical Evidence on the Monetary Approach to the Balance of Payments and Exchange Rates," *American Economic Review* 66 (May 1976): 163-70; Bluford H. Putnam and D. Sykes Wilford, "Money, Income, and Causality in the U.S. and the U.K.: A Theoretical Explanation of Different Findings," *American Economic Review* 68 (June 1978); and J. Frenkel and Harry G. Johnson, *The Monetary Approach to the Balance of Payments* (London: Allen and Unwin, 1976).

4. W. Michael Cox and Halbert White, "Unanticipated Money, Output and Prices in the Small Economy," Mimeographed, 1978.

5. Related literature to the questions raised in this section includes Robert Barro, "Rational Expectations and the Role of Monetary Policy," *Journal of Monetary Economics*, no. 1 (January 1976): 1-32; and Robert Lucas, "Some International Evidence on Output-Inflation Tradeoffs," *American Economic Review* 63 (June 1973): 326-34.

Walton T. Wilford   7

SOME OBSERVATIONS ON
THE MONETARY APPROACH
TO BALANCE OF PAYMENTS
AND THE THIRD WORLD

The initial theoretical work on the monetary approach to balance of payments, which was introduced by Harry G. Johnson and R. A. Mundell[1] and elaborated by a number of subsequent articles,[2] has provided the underpinnings for a growing literature on empirical applications as they relate to the developed industrial western economies.[3] More recently the approach has been utilized to explain the relationship between monetary policy and the balance of payments adjustments for the economies of a myriad of developing countries whose growth is especially closely linked to international trade. The past five years have witnessed a wealth of empirical studies that test the influence of domestic credit creation upon price movements.[4]

While the important policy directives that follow from the theoretical literature carry essentially the same relevance for both the developed western economies and Third World nations, the latter present unique structural characteristics, and this survey focuses upon the theoretical and empirical contributions of the monetary approach as they relate to the small, open developing country economies, which are especially vulnerable to the vicissitudes of the international economy. The first section presents a simple monetary model in which world price determination is introduced, and the second section undertakes some observations on the usefulness of the approach as it relates to Third World nations. Finally, some of the more recent empirical contributions on Third World applications of the monetary approach are reviewed.

THE THEORY OF THE MONETARY APPROACH

Several models on the monetary approach have been offered in the literature.[5] Although not all of the models explicitly view the adjustment process as a strictly monetary phenomenon, most of the literature makes three basic assumptions, including: country X is a price taker in world goods, services, and capital markets; country X maintains a fixed and stable exchange rate; and the balance of payments does not affect real output. Utilizing these assumptions and knowledge of the monetary authority balance sheet, one may derive the standard reserve flow equation as follows. The model is developed at this point since it allows the reader to refer back to a basic model when examining the various empirical results alluded to later in this study.

The monetary model may be defined in eight basic steps.[6] The stock of high-powered money is related to the money supply in the following identity:

$$M = a \cdot H \tag{1}$$

where M = money supply
      a = the money multiplier, and
      H = the stock of high-powered money.[7]

The monetary authority balance sheet appears as follows

Monetary Authority Balance Sheet

Assets	Liabilities
R	H
OA	OL

where R = international reserves
      OA = assets of monetary authority other than R, and
      OL = liabilities other than high-powered money.

OA consists of central bank rediscounts, government bonds, and private notes, while OL includes primarily treasury and bank deposits at the central bank. Therefore,

$$H = R + (OA - OL) = R + D \tag{2}$$

where $D = OA - OL$ = domestic credit.

Substituting equation (2) into (1) we derive a new money supply function

$$M = a \cdot (R + D). \tag{3}$$

Postulate a money demand equation in the form

$$M/P = Y^{a_1} e / i^{a_2} \tag{4}$$

where
- P = price index,
- Y = real income,
- i = market rate of interest,
- e = a stochastic disturbance term,
- a_1 = income elasticity of money demand, and
- a_2 = interest elasticity of money demand.

Since we have implicitly assumed that money demand is homogeneous of degree one in prices, equation (4) may be rewritten as

$$M = PY^{a_1}e/i^{a_2} \tag{5}$$

and setting money supply equal to money demand

$$a \cdot (R + D) = PY^{a_1}e/i^{a_2} \tag{6}$$

Since we are interested in percentage changes in the variables, a transformation is necessary. Defining

$$gx = (1/x)\,(dx/dt), \text{ where } x = a, R, D, Y, P, \text{ and } i$$

we obtain

$$ga + (R/(R + D))gR + (D/(R + D))gD = gp + a_1 gY - a_2 gi + e'. \tag{7}$$

Defining $(R/H)gR$ as the dependent variable,

$$(R/H)gR = a_1 gY - a_2 gi + gp - ga -(D/H)gD + e'. \tag{8}$$

As is evident from equation (8), the variation in the foreign reserve position depends upon the percentage change in income (gY), the percentage change in the price level (gp), the percentage change in the money multiplier (ga), and the percentage change in domestic credit (gD) multiplied by D/H. This follows from equation (3) and shows that changes in the money stock may be related to changes in the amount of reserves. Therefore, if changes in the money stock are a function of the postulated money demand relationship, movements in foreign reserves depend upon the same factors as do changes in money demand, all other things being equal.

As noted earlier, a positive a_1 is expected, since income is positively related to reserve flow via the money demand equation. Domestic credit is negatively related to reserve flows. Both of these conclusions are at variance with one or more Keynesian theories of the balance of payments.

Introducing World Price Determination

Following a strict monetary approach to price determination one may postulate an equation of exchange for the world. That is

$$M(w)V(w) \equiv P(w)Y(w) \tag{9}$$

where M = money supply; V = velocity; P = prices; Y = real income; and w = world.

The identity may be restated in terms of world prices

$$P(w) \equiv \frac{M(w)V(w)}{Y(w)}.$$

In growth terms the equation is

$$gP(w) \equiv gM(w) + gV(w) - gY(w). \tag{10}$$

The view of the world as a closed economy permits us to utilize a monetary approach to price determination. Substituting this identity in the reserve flow equation for country X

$$gR\frac{R}{H}(X) = a_1 gY(X) - a_2 gi(X) + gM(w) + gV(w) - gY(w) - ga(X)$$
$$- gD\frac{D}{H}(X) + z. \tag{11}$$

Assuming that both $gY(X)$ and $gY(w)$ have the same elasticity of money demand, equation (11) may be rewritten as

$$gR\frac{R}{H}(X) = a_1 [gY(X) - gY(w)] - a_2 gi(X) + gM(w) + gV(w) - ga(X)$$
$$- gD\frac{D}{H}(X) + z. \tag{12}$$

Equation (12) is important to the Third World economies because it highlights the impact of nondomestic influences on the level of reserves held by a country. In a sense, the equation shows how dependent the small country is on the rest of the world, but, more importantly, it highlights what variables are available to the authorities for conduct of policy. As before, the policy alternatives are straightforward; reserve management tools are the money multiplier and domestic credit. But even these tools must be used in conjunction with an accurate assessment of what is happening around the small country.

The Estimating Equations

The two equations relevant for empirical analysis are the equation for the standard reserve flow mechanism of the Zecher model, and the expanded alternative equation based on equation (12). The standard reserve flow equation for country X is

$$gR(\frac{R}{H})(X) = a_1 gY(X) - a_2 gi(X) + \beta_1 gp(X) - \beta_2 ga(X) - \beta_3 gD\frac{D}{H}(X) + z$$

where z = a stochastic disturbance.

The parameter β_1 is introduced to test the assumption of linear homogeneity in prices. The model explicitly assumes that money demand is homogeneous of degree one in prices. An estimated value of β_1 not significantly different from one would lend statistical support to the assumption.

The alternative reserve flow equation incorporating the world equation of exchange is

$$gR(\frac{R}{H})(X) = a_1 [gY(X) - gY(w)] - a_2 gi(X) + \xi_1 gM(w) + \xi_2 gV(w) - \beta_2 ga(X)$$
$$- \beta_3 gD\frac{D}{H}(X) + z$$

and is based upon equation (12).

A discussion of the results of these basic models found by various researchers is now preceded by a general discussion of why this model is important for Third World countries as well as development literature in general.

RELEVANCE OF THE APPROACH
TO THIRD WORLD ECONOMIES

While the role of demand and supply for money has been an implicit feature in most attempts to analyze balance of payments over the past five decades, more traditional tools of value theory—demand and supply schedules and their elasticities—occupied center stage during the 1920s and 1930s. With the collapse of international fixed exchange rates in the 1930s and mass unemployment, the Keynesian revolution viewed balance-of-payments adjustment not as an automatic process but as a policy problem for governments. Attention was concentrated on the "elasticity conditions" required for devaluation to have a favorable impact on the balance of payments.[8] Johnson argued that the "so-called 'elasticity approach' to devaluation proved to be demonstrably unsatisfactory for the immediate postwar period of full and over-full employment, owing to its implicit assumption of the existence of unemployed resources that could be mobilised."[9] Rudolf R. Rhomberg and Robert H. Heller note that "as public preoccupation with the insufficiency of aggregate demand and with unemployment gave way in the post-war period to concern about inflation the Keynesian analytical tools were ... replaced by ... instruments of monetary analysis. While there is still controversy about the role of monetarism in solving problems of inflation and unemployment, the monetary approach—all the proponents of which are not 'monetarists' in the narrower sense—has come to occupy a central place in the analysis of balance of payments problems."[10]*

It is clear that developing countries have experienced widely different inflation rates over time, whether they be on fixed or on flexible exchange rate systems. Those on stable fixed exchange rate structures have generally exhibited inflation rates not significantly different from the rest of the world, while others have had inflation rates commensurate with their devaluations—that is, purchasing-power parity appears to hold. Whether or not devaluation generates inflation or reverse causality exists, it is clear that domestic credit creation at some level, all other things being equal, requires fixed exchange rate adjustment through devaluation over time. The process has an impact upon the balance of payments. One can point to, for example, the Central American Common Market countries, which have maintained relatively stable fixed exchange rates over time and have, in general, observed inflation commensurate with that of the developed nations. Mexico, until recently, could also be included in this group of nations that have experienced increases in real output and balance of payments stability by control-ling the level of domestic credit creation.[11] Other Latin American nations—Brazil, Chile, Argentina, and Uruguay, for example—have experienced highly unstable exchange rates and dramatic inflation generated by huge government deficits, accompanied by devaluations over time. Bolivia has observed distinct periods of rapid inflation and devaluation (1952-58) with little growth, and impressive exchange rate stability (1958-70) and increases in real output. Both the inflation-prone and the relatively stable countries face similar structural bottlenecks, which have been elaborated in the monetarist-structuralist literature on Latin America.

The policy dictates of the monetary approach for Third World nations differ from the simple monetarist and structuralist conclusions espoused during the 1960s and, of course, from traditional Keynesian literature. Roberto Campos has noted that "the early controversy between monetarists and structuralists in Latin America has been exaggerated beyond all bounds"[12] and he observes that "we might jocosely define a monetarist as a structuralist in a hurry and a structur-alist as a monetarist without policy-making responsibility." The monetary approach as it relates to developing countries does not require the rigidly simplistic mone-

---

*At this juncture it is important to note that the so-called elasticities approaches isolated the trade or current accounts, while many times simply ignoring the capital account. One should be careful to differentiate among various definitions of the balance of payments for various discussions. See Donald S. Kemp (this book, Chapter 3).

tarist tenets of classical liberalism: strict reliance upon the quantity theory, rigorous free trade, nonintervention by government, and subordination of the structural problems of developing countries to stabilization policies. Indeed, the monetary approach argues that a balanced attack on these structural problems is hindered by misguided monetary and fiscal policies aimed at short-term improvement in the current account, policies that may lead to negative capital account movements and, therefore, obviate the policy goals. The monetary approach argues that resources for dealing with structural problems—including unemployment, supply rigidities, and trade dependence—may be generated through the capital account in an economy with a stable monetary policy and consequent capital inflow.* Specifically, the monetary approach hypothesizes that monetary expansion associated with government borrowing from the banking system is a key factor contributing to both balance of payment deficits and inflation.

The relevance of the monetary approach to balance of payments adjustment in the Third World is based on a number of factors. First, it is rooted in the simple premise that the balance of payments is essentially a monetary phenomenon. It therefore places principal responsibility for orderly growth with a developing country's central bank monetary planners, who cannot take a passive position on the matter of expenditure policy goals of government. Second, the monetary approach provides a less complicated empirical framework for policy evaluation. Rhomberg and Heller underscore the point, noting that "by focusing directly upon the relevant monetary aggregates, this approach eliminates the intractable problems associated with the estimation of numerous elasticities of international transactions and other parameters describing their interdependence, which are inherent in other approaches."[14] Third, the monetary approach aggregates the current and capital accounts, as opposed to the Keynesian preoccupation with current account implicit in the "elasticities" and "income-absorption" approaches. Through integrating the capital and current accounts and focusing on the demand and supply for money and their consequent influence on reserve positions, the monetary approach argues that a Third World country can maintain a negative current account balance yet promote balance of payments stability through attraction of capital inflows. This hypothesis has special relevance for developing countries in that it suggests that they can, through appropriate money management, create a stable climate to attract resources from abroad that may be utilized for development activities. In short, a stable monetary climate may permit the attraction of reserves through the capital account of reserves, which may be utilized to offset current account imports.

---

*Joshi concludes that economic theory cannot deal satisfactorily with structural obstacles. He notes that "they are either put into the ceteris paribus clause in which case they are considered 'given'; or they are not, in which case they represent an 'inefficiency' which can be corrected by the price system."[13]

If, as several monetary approach studies postulate, economic growth and foreign reserve flows are positively related, there follow implications for the savings and foreign exchange gap theories as postulated in the literature. The foreign exchange gap may certainly be reduced if growth accompanied by stable monetary policy permits inflow of foreign reserves to feed the current account import component. Development literature suggests that the internal swings and foreign exchange gaps constitute two separate constraints on the attainable rate of economic growth.[15] Even if savings are mobilized internally, growth may be frustrated by the inability of the system to utilize those resources to purchase requisite imports.* The monetary approach argues that growth with monetary stability contributes positively to the foreign exchange position. D. S. Wilford notes that Mexican international reserve flows for the 1954–74 period were

> as would be predicted by the monetary approach. . . . If money demand grows faster than Mexican authorities wish to expand the money supply via their own resources, then reserves flow inward. Another result is that reserves flow inward, not outward, in response to increases in real income. . . . Mexico experienced rapid growth during the period. Therefore, reserves generally flowed inward, despite a worsening balance of trade. . . . The financial policies of the Central Bank . . . led to a stable reserve position for most of the period.[16]

R. Zecher confirms a similar relationship among output, prices, and reserves for Australia. He notes that

> when demand for money grows faster than the supply of money would have grown due to domestic sources alone, international reserves tend to accumulate and to bring actual growth in the money stock closer to desired growth. As implied by the hypothesis, growth in output and the price level are associated with balance of payments surpluses, while growth in the domestically determined portion of the money stock tends to be associated with deficits and reserve outflows. . . .[17]

J. Marcus Fleming and Lorette Boissonneault noted in an empirical examination of 36 nations that

> to the extent that capital is attracted by credit scarcity and high interest rates, an autonomous policy to reduce the expansion of credit

---

*Joshi notes that the distinction between the savings and foreign exchange constraints is of very limited usefulness and that it may indeed be harmful, since such a distinction lends respectability to the view that developing countries are hampered in their development solely by external foreign exchange factors.

would tend to reduce the flow of net capital exports or increase that
of net capital imports, thus bringing about a swifter remedial effect on
the balance of payments. . . .[18]

In short, if the foreign exchange gap is the critical development bottleneck,
it would appear that appropriate management of domestic money stocks can, in a
growth economy, encourage foreign reserve inflows.

Fourth, supporters argue that policy prescriptions are more simple and
manageable for developing countries, where data on monetary variables from central banks are often more readily available and reliable than are the data from
numerous accounts recording transactions of various goods, services, and capital
items that are required in the "elasticities" approach. Indeed the International
Monetary Fund (IMF) cites as one major reason that it has used monetary approach
models for developing countries during the past 25 years the fact that monetary
statistics have usually been available, while more detailed national income accounting data for the "elasticities" and "income-absorption" approaches were less
available and/or reliable.

Fifth, it is contended that the developing countries typically have simpler
financial structures and there are, therefore, fewer alternatives to holding these
funds in monetary form or spending them on domestic or foreign goods and
services or on foreign financial instruments. Indeed, the IMF suggests that the
monetary approach permits a "meaningful approximate analysis of the relevant
aggregates with the help of models that are small enough to be calculated with
pencil and paper."[19]

Sixth, the monetary approach framework is especially appropriate for
developing countries in Latin America, where control over domestic credit is
utilized as a major instrument of money management and balance of payments
control. Further, the approach pinpoints ultimate administrative responsibility
for reserve flows in the small, open economy. J. J. Polak notes that

> it may be difficult, perhaps in some circumstances humanly impos-
> sible, for the system to withstand demands for credit from govern-
> ment or from other insistent borrowers; and in such circumstances,
> the desire to make public development expenditure, or to construct
> private factories, may be considered the cause of the expansion in the
> economy. But for purposes of monetary analysis and monetary pol-
> icy, there is a clear gain in clarity if the responsibility is pinpointed for
> credit expansion. The economic development could also have been
> financed by higher taxes or by a foreign loan. In these situations, the
> desire to spend for a particular purpose would not have led to a pay-
> ments problem. In a real sense, the credit expansion is the cause of the
> payments problem.[20]

Seventh, the monetary approach permits monetary authorities to measure more effectively the overall equilibrium adjustment of prices, output, and foreign reserve positions to discretionary policies aimed at influencing domestic credit. D. Lachman[21] reiterates the uniqueness of the monetary approach by noting that "in the closed economy ... the monetary ... base is regarded as a policy instrument," while in the relatively open economies that generally characterize the Third World, the "monetary base is no longer regarded as being determined solely by policy since it may be changed by balance of payments surpluses or deficit." D. S. Wilford and W. T. Wilford conclude, based on empirical evidence for Honduras and Mexico, that "monetary authorities can control the composition of money stock between foreign reserves and domestically created credit," but that they cannot influence the absolute level of monetary stocks without sacrificing the fixed exchange rate." Further, it can be noted that "restrictive monetary policy by the small economy is rendered ineffectual and central banks of such economies are, by and large, dependent upon movements of world monetary variables beyond their control."[22] Manuel Guitian notes that in "any economy the public determines the *real* quantity of money that it desires to hold ... the banking community and, in particular, the monetary authorities do not directly control the total money supply but only the part that is made available through domestic credit." Further, he notes that "the attainment of a quantity of money desired by the community is compatible with different movements in international reserves that may not be consistent with the balance of payments objectives of the authorities."[23] The monetary approach, therefore, highlights for the developing country the equilibrium adjustment impacts of domestic credit as the control variable for stabilization purposes.

In summary, given that most developing countries are small, open systems, the monetary approach may, therefore, permit planners in Third World countries to implement and evaluate development strategies by focusing upon relatively few monetary variables, which are generally more statistically reliable than the myriad of national accounts data required by other approaches. Further, the monetary approach requires less discretionary intervention in planning decisions, intervention that is often based on imperfect knowledge in the developing country and that, therefore, tends to obfuscate, rather than promote, development objectives.

SOME EMPIRICAL RESULTS
FOR THIRD WORLD NATIONS

In this section, some results of empirical studies of the monetary approach are reported. Although various models were used by different researchers, the basic formulations can find their roots in the model presented in this chapter's first section. The reader of this survey of results for Third World economies may find it useful to refer back to equations (8) and (12), at least, as well as to their counterpart estimating equations.

Michael Connolly and Dean Taylor: Eighteen Devaluations in Developing Countries

Michael Connolly and Dean Taylor[24] test the proposition that a devaluation will improve the balance of payments unless accompanied by an "approximately equiproportionate expansion in domestic credit."[25] The sample includes 18 independent devaluations in developing countries over the 1959–70 period. They conclude: devaluation in developing countries is successful in improving payments imbalances, "particularly in light of the fact that it serves the second objective of dismantling exchange controls;"[26] the price adjustment following devaluation involves primarily a substantial increase in the price of traded goods and secondarily a moderate increase in the overall rate of inflation; and, contrary to the findings of Richard Cooper, correlation exists between the change in domestic credit in the banking system in the year following devaluation and the improvement in the goods and service balance for the same year. Connolly and Taylor reconcile their findings with those of Cooper by noting that

> his [Cooper's] finding differs from ours primarily in that his is for only the merchandise account, while the monetary approach has to do with the overall balance of payments. The monetary argument is basically that one cannot expect devaluation to improve the overall balance of payments unless it leads to an increased demand for money unmatched by an increase in domestic credit.[27]

M. S. Khan: Venezuela

M. S. Khan applies the monetary model to the Venezuelan economy over the 1968–73 period. During this period Venezuela maintained a fixed exchange rate and operated with relatively few restrictions on trade and none on international movement of capital. Khan finds that his 11-equation model, which was estimated on a quarterly basis for Venezuela during 1968–73, gave encouraging results, in terms of both the estimates of the structural equations and the model's ability to track the behavior of key macroeconomic variables. He views the model as "sufficiently general to appear to be relevant to a number of countries."[28]

Maxwell Fry: Afghanistan

Maxwell Fry applies the monetary approach to Afghanistan, a country that has maintained a flexible exchange rate historically.[29] Using the model of John

Rutledge,[30] Fry finds that Afghanistan, with its highly undeveloped monetary sector, fits the reduced-form equation (derived from a conventional demand-for-money function and the purchasing power parity relationship) very well for the period 1955-72. He notes that the model showed quite remarkable explanatory power, with an R^2 = .99, D-W = 2.65, and F = 2705.78.*

D. S. Wilford and W. T. Wilford: Honduras

In this analysis an estimation is made of a form of the reserve flow equation as it follows from the assumption of linear homogeneity in prices.[31] The specification below constrains money demand to be free of money illusion and is, therefore, a strict monetarist case. The equation is

$$(\frac{R}{H})gR - gP = a_1 gy - a_2 gi - \beta_2 ga - \beta_3 (\frac{D}{H})gD + u. \tag{8}$$

Table 7.1 gives the empirical results for estimating equations utilizing annual data for 1950-74. The results conform closely to the expectations, as all coefficients are significantly different from zero; have the hypothesized signs; and are statistically close to their hypothesized values at the .05 risk level. The size of the interest elasticity coefficients is of interest in that it suggests that changes in interest rates do not significantly affect holding of money vis-a-vis less liquid assets. The results are consistent with those of other studies analyzing less developed countries.† In less developed financial markets, the costs of rearranging portfolios on the basis of interest rate movement are higher than they are in developed

---

*However, it must be noted that Fry's results are somewhat tenuous, as pointed out by B. Putnam and J. Van Belle in "A Monetary Approach to Afghanistan's Flexible Exchange Rate: A Comment," *Journal of Money, Credit and Banking* (February 1978): 117-18. Although some of Fry's results were found to be statistically unclear, Bluford H. Putnam and John J. Van Belle confirmed his eventual conclusions supporting the monetary approach.

†One almost universal result of Third World empirical balance of payments studies is the lack of significance of the interest variable in the money demand equations. The J. Villasuso, W. T. Wilford, and A. M. Agapos study found interest to be consistently insignificant in Costa Rica.[32] D. S. Wilford and J. R. Zecher find "the signs for the coefficient of the interest variable are consistent with the model though standard errors are high . . . [and] could be due to lack of a well developed capital market. . . ."[33] Their substitution of U.S. interest rates as proxies yielded insignificant differences. (On the assumption that Mexican reported rates were questionable in accuracy and not representative of market rates, they substituted U.S. interest rates. The results were not significantly improved, however.) D. Lachman notes for South Africa that "the variables included to measure the opportunity cost of holding money although in all cases of the expected sign are not always significantly different from zero."[34] Insignificance of interest rates is probably attributable to a number of factors, including inaccurate reporting of interest rate data for many developing countries, undeveloped financial markets, and interest rate structures established by nonmarket influences. The rate of inflation might be a better measure of the opportunity cost of capital.

TABLE 7.1

Foreign Reserve Flow Regressions for Honduras: 1950–74*
(annual data)

Regression Number	Dependent Variable a_1	Income Elasticity a_1	Interest Rate Elasticity a_2	Price Elasticity β_1	β_2	β_3	R^2	DW	F Level
1	$\frac{R}{H}gR$	1.11 (4.09)	-0.16 (-2.01)	1.12 (3.61)	-0.94 (-3.47)	-0.88 (-6.76)	.81	2.46	19.11
2	$\frac{R}{H}gR - gp$	1.07 (4.42)	-0.149 (-2.16)	— —	-0.968 (-3.85)	-0.88 (-6.99)	.79	2.41	25.24

*Data sources are Central Bank of Honduras and *International Financial Statistics* (IFS) (Washington, D.C.: International Monetary Fund). The U.S. long-term (as reported by IFS) interest rate is used as a proxy for the world interest rate and therefore the Honduran rate, since no reliable series on the Honduran market rate of interest are available. This U.S. proxy for the world rate follows from the assumption of unified capital markets.

Source: D. Sykes Wilford and Walton T. Wilford, "On the Monetary Approach to the Balance of Payments: The Small, Open Economy," *The Journal of Finance* 33 (March 1978): 322.

financial markets, since there are fewer asset alternatives. Thus the estimated $|a_2| < .2$ is entirely consistent with rational behavior in some less developed capital market economies. The reserve flow equation shows that a 1 percent increase in domestically created money, all other things being equal, will generate approximately a 1 percent loss in foreign reserves. All coefficients are close to predicted values, and the coefficient for gP in regression 3 supports the assumption of the absence of money illusion. The coefficients, as expected, remain stable between regressions 3 and 4, with the F-levels for both acceptable at the .01 risk level. The R^2's indicate that about 80 percent of the variation in the dependent variable is explained.

The most important coefficients for the policy maker, β_2 and β_3, are significantly different from zero and not significantly different from their hypothesized values. Perhaps most important from the policy standpoint is that the coefficients of (D/H)gD are very close to the predicted value of –1 in Table 7.1.

The data show that, as the monetary approach to balance of payments hypothesizes, the Central Bank of Honduras cannot control the level of its money stock in the long run. The composition of the stock, however, may be influenced, in that domestic monetary policy can meet the demands for money either through domestically created money stock or through foreign reserves. The implications for monetary policy are, therefore, clear. If the central bank desires a balance of payments position appropriate for maintenance of a fixed exchange rate, it should select a rate of growth in domestic credit and the money multiplier at a rate equal to, or slightly less than, the internal demand for money. Since a stable exchange rate has been one of the major goals of monetary policy in this Central American nation during the past 25 years, it would do well to consider the implications of the monetary approach to balance of payments in the implementation of its monetary policy.

B. B. Aghevli: Indonesia

B. B. Aghevli develops a model including four broad areas: demand for real money balances, supply of nominal money, government budget, and balance of payments, with real income considered exogenous; he tests the model for Indonesian quarterly data for 1968-73.[35] The period was characterized by relative price stability and rapid economic growth. He finds that demand for real balances for both the narrow and broad definitions of money, with a R^2 at the .99 level, and that long-run income elasticity for narrow and broad definitions of money demand are 2.18 and 2.29 respectively. The elasticities are "high but by no means unusual for a developing country in which in the absence of other financial assets, the public holds most of its savings in monetary form, and in which, moreover, the monetised sector of the economy is exanding rapidly."[36] Indonesian supply elasticity of exports with respect to income was close to unity (implying that the export sector grows in the same proportion as the rest of the economy), and the coefficient of the relative price term is also significant.

Aghevli estimates the long-run rate of growth of reserve, narrow, and broad money consistent with a 7 percent real growth rate for Indonesia and an 18 percent inflation rate to be a relatively high 30 percent, attributable largely to the high long-run income elasticity of demand for real balances.*

D. Sykes Wilford and J. Richard Zecher: Mexico

D. Sykes Wilford and J. Richard Zecher analyze the fixed exchange rate period 1955–75 for Mexico under monetary model assumptions. Mexico throughout the 20-year period experienced negative trade balances. However, in all but six years, there were net inflows of foreign reserves, and the capital account for the 20 years was consistently sufficient to maintain a positive balance of payments. Wilford and Zecher note that "contrary to many standard balance of payments theories, rapid economic growth (averaging 6–7 percent) has been coincidental with the strengthening of Mexico's foreign reserve position."[37] They contend that this was achieved by pursuing deficit financing policies not through excessive increases in domestic credit, but through transference of savings from the private to the public sector by use of financial intermediaries. They further contend that a number of international and internal factors operated together to diminish the ability of the central bank to control injections of domestic credit and that these influences contributed to the instability of the peso, culminating in devaluation.

Their standard monetary reserve flow equations for the period, equation (8), exhibited low standard errors and consistently high R^2's, ranging from .85 to .92, and respectable levels. Interest rates were insignificant in the money demand equations. The model was useful in explaining the data throughout the period until 1975. The authors note that "the experience in 1975 was far different from that predicted by the model. Instead of the implied outflow of reserves sufficient to reduce money growth by about 16 percent, there was an inflow sufficient to increase money growth by 14.5 percent. This whopping error largely reflects the desperate attempts of the Mexican authorities to hold the exchange rate by borrowing from abroad, particularly in the fourth quarter of 1975."[38] They conclude that Mexico can again achieve and maintain a fixed exchange with the United States and an approximate zero balance of payments, expanding domestic credit at a rate approximately equal to U.S. inflation plus the rate of growth in real output in Mexico.

---

*It is becoming increasingly clear that in developing countries where monetization of the barter sector is proceeding at a substantial pace, the demand for money-income elasticity coefficients are higher than those observed for industrialized nations. Further empirical and theoretical research remains to be undertaken in explaining the secular changes in the elasticities over time as nonmarket sectors are monetized.

N. C. Miller and S. S. Askin: Brazil and Chile

N. C. Miller and S. S. Askin examine the degree to which the balance of payments of

> two small, relatively open economies influences the ability of their monetary authorities to control the money supply . . . and . . . investigate to what extent variations in the domestic component of the monetary base are *offset* via international payments imbalances, and then to what extent the authorities sterilize the effects of payments imbalances on the monetary base.[39]

They test for the classical payments adjustment for Brazil and Chile, and conclude that monetary authorities "have essentially complete monetary autonomy in the long run as long as international reserves are large enough to finance a payments deficit [and] there is not evidence that the classical adjustment mechanism functions in either country."[40] Although they find that "even if their exchange rates had remained constant, Brazil and Chile would have had almost complete control over their money supplies," such control only extended *as long as they were able to finance a payments deficit.* One wonders, however, how long international reserves can remain large enough to finance payments deficits and, therefore, the extent to which their findings actually deny monetary predictions. In general, it is the reserve position (precipitated by excessive expansion of domestic credit) that has a direct impact on those reserves utilized to sterilize payments imbalances.

Summary

Most of the monetary studies for Third World nations appear to confirm the Johnson hypothesis that international reserve levels are positively related to the level of domestic income and the exchange rate, and negatively related to the domestic component of the monetary base.

Further, in economies that are highly dependent upon foreign trade, as are the developing countries, the money supply grows at a rate that, over the long run, maintains an equilibrium in the foreign balance. Finally, monetary authorities can influence short-term movements in the money supply, but they cannot indefinitely counteract long-term excess money stocks unless they are prepared to alter the foreign exchange rate from time to time.

NOTES

1. Harry G. Johnson, *Further Essays in Monetary Economics* (Cambridge, Mass.: Harvard University Press, 1973); and Robert A. Mundell, *International Economics* (New York: Macmillan, 1968).

2. See, for example, J. A. Frenkel, "A Monetary Approach to the Exchange Rate: Doctrinal Aspects and Empirical Evidence," *Scandinavian Journal of Economics* 78 (1976): 200–24; J. A. Frenkel and C. A. Rodriguez, "Portfolio Equilibrium and the Balance of Payments: A Monetary Approach," *American Economic Review* 65 (September 1975): 674–88; Harry G. Johnson, "Money and the Balance of Payments," *Banca Nazionale del Lavoro—Quarterly Review* no. 116 (March 1976): 3–18; Harry G. Johnson, "The Monetary Approach to the Balance of Payments Theory," in *International Trade and Money*, ed. M. B. Connolly and A. K. Swoboda (London: George Allen and Unwin, 1975); Harry G. Johnson, "The Monetary Approach to the Balance of Payments Theory: A Diagrammatic Analysis," *The Manchester School* (1975); Donald S. Kemp, "A Monetary View of Balance of Payments," *Federal Reserve Bank of St. Louis Review* 57, no. 4 (April 1975): 14–22; A. R. Nobay and Harry G. Johnson, "Monetarism: A Historic-Theoretic Perspective," *Journal of Economic Literature* 15 (June 1977): 470–85; and R. Ramanathan, "Monetary Expansion, Balance of Trade and Economic Growth " *Economic Record* 51 (March 1975): 31–39.

3. W. Michael Cox, "Some Empirical Evidence on an Incomplete Information Model of the Monetary Approach to the Balance of Payments: The Canadian Experience," this book, Chapter 6; W. Michael Cox and D. Sykes Wilford, "The Monetary Approach to the Balance of Payments and World Monetary Equilibrium," Mimeographed, 1977; Frenkel, op. cit.; Thomas Courchene, "The Price-Specie Flow Mechanism and the Gold Exchange Standard: Some Exploratory Empiricism Relating to the Endogeneity of Country Money Balances," in *The Economics of Common Currencies*, ed. H. G. Johnson and A. K. Swoboda (London: Allen and Unwin, 1973); and R. Zecher, "Monetary Equilibrium and International Reserve Flows in Australia," *Journal of Finance* 29 (December 1974): 1523–30.

4. See, among others, B. B. Aghevli, "Money, Prices and the Balance of Payments: Indonesia 1968–73," *Journal of Development Studies* 13 (January 1977): 37–57; Bijan B. Aghevli and Mohsin S. Khan, "The Monetary Approach to Balance of Payments Determination: An Empirical Test," in *The Monetary Approach to the Balance of Payments* (Washington, D.C.: International Monetary Fund, 1977), pp. 275–90; M. I. Blejer, "The Monetary Approach to Devaluation: A Graphical Presentation," *Weltwirtschaftliches Archiv* 113 (1977): 348–52; M. J. Fry, "A Monetary Approach to Afghanistan's Flexible Exchange Rate," *Journal of Money, Credit, and Banking* 8 (May 1976): 219–25; Manuel Guitian, "Credit Versus Money as an Instrument of Control," in *The Monetary Approach*, op. cit., pp. 227–42; M. S. Khan, "A Monetary Model of Balance of Payments: The Case of Venezuela," *Journal of Monetary Economics* 2 (July 1976): 311–32; Mohsin S. Khan, "The Determination of the Balance of Payments and Income in Developing Countries," in *The Monetary Approach*, op. cit., pp. 243–74; D. Lachman, "A Monetary Approach to the South African Balance of Payments," *South African Journal of Economics* 43 (September 1975): 271–83; N. C. Miller and S. S. Askin, "Monetary Policy and the Balance of Payments in Brazil and Chile," *Journal of Money, Credit, and Banking* 8 (May 1976): 227–38; I. Otani and Y. C. Park, "A Monetary Model of the Korean Economy," *International Monetary Fund Staff Paper* 23 (March 1976): 164–99; Rudolf R. Rhomberg, "Money, Income, and the Foreign Balance," in *The Monetary Approach*, op. cit., pp. 163–84; Rudolf R. Rhomberg and Robert H. Heller, "Introductory Survey " in *The Monetary Approach*, op. cit., pp. 1–14; and D. Sykes Wilford, *Monetary Policy and the Open Economy: Mexico's Experience* (New York: Praeger, 1977).

5. See D. Sykes Wilford and Walton T. Wilford, "Monetary Approach to Balance of Payments: On World Prices and the Reserve Flow Equation," *Weltwirtschaftliches Archiv* no. 1 (1977): 31–39, for empirical tests on Mexico and Honduras using the equations developed in this section.

6. See R. Zecher, "Monetary Equilibrium and International Reserve Flows in Australia," *Journal of Finance* 29 (December 1974): 1523–30; and Harry G. Johnson, *Further Essays*, op. cit

7. Stock of high-powered money includes coins, currency, commercial bank deposits at the central bank minus interbank deposits.

8. For short reviews of the evolution of theoretical thought on balance of payments theory, see Johnson "The Monetary Approach," op. cit.; Rhomberg and Heller, op. cit.; and Marina v. N. Whitman, "Global Monetarism and the Monetary Approach to the Balance of Payments," *Brookings Papers on Economic Activity* no. 3 (1975): 491–536. A dissenting view of the monetary approach presented in an historical context is found in D. A. Currie, "Some Criticisms of the Monetary Analysis of Balance of Payments Correction," *Economic Journal* 86 (September 1976): 508–22.

9. Johnson, "The Monetary Approach," op. cit., pp. 208–09.

10. Rhomberg and Heller, op. cit., p. 2.

11. For empirical studies of Central America and Mexico from the monetary approach perspective, see D. Sykes Wilford, op. cit.; D. Sykes Wilford, "Price Levels, Interest Rate, Open Economies, and a Fixed Exchange Rate: The Mexican Case, 1954–1974," *Review of Business and Economic Research* 12, no. 3 (Spring 1977); Wilford and Wilford, op. cit.; D. Sykes Wilford and Walton T. Wilford, "On the Monetary Approach to the Balance of Payments: The Small, Open Economy," *The Journal of Finance* 33 (March 1978): 319–23; D. Sykes Wilford and J. Richard Zecher, "Monetary Policy and the Balance of Payments in Mexico 1955–73," unpublished manuscript, 1978; and Walton T. Wilford and D. Sykes Wilford, "Efectos de la Creación de Crédito Sobre la Balanza de Pagos en El Salvador," Caribbean Studies, forthcoming.

12. Roberto de Oliviera Campos, "Economic Development and Inflation with Special Reference to Latin America," in Organization for Economic Cooperation and Development, *Development Plans and Programmes*, OECD Development Center, Paris (1964): 129–37.

13. See Vijah Joshi, "Saving and Foreign Exchange Constraints," in *Unfashionable Economics*, ed. P. P. Streeten (London: 1970).

14. Rhomberg and Heller, op. cit., p. 4.

15. H. B. Chenery and M. Bruno, "Development Alternatives in an Open Economy," *Economic Journal* (1962).

16. D. Sykes Wilford, *Monetary Policy*, op. cit., p. 50.

17. Zecher, op. cit., p. 1530.

18. J. Marcus Fleming and Lorette Boissonneault, "Money Supply and Imports," in *The Monetary Approach*, op. cit., p. 146.

19. Rhomberg and Heller, op. cit., pp. 6–7.

20. J. J. Polak, "Monetary Analysis of Income Formation and Payments Problems," in *The Monetary Approach*, op. cit., p. 27.

21. Lachman, op. cit., p. 272.

22. Wilford and Wilford, "Monetary Approach to Balance of Payments: On World Prices and the Reserve Flow Equation," op. cit., p. 38.

23. Guitian, op. cit., p. 235.

24. Michael Connolly and Dean Taylor, "Adjustment to Devaluation in a Small Country," *De Economist* 124 (1976): 319–27.

25. Ibid., p. 849.

26. Ibid.

27. Ibid., p. 858.

28. M. S. Khan, "A Monetary Model of Balance of Payments: The Case of Venezuela," *Journal of Monetary Economics* 2 (July 1976): 330.

29. M. J. Fry, "A Monetary Approach to Afghanistan's Flexible Exchange Rate," *Journal of Money, Credit, and Banking* 8 (May 1976): 219–25.

30. John Rutledge, *A Monetarist Model of Inflationary Expectations* (Lexington, Mass.: Lexington Books, 1974).

31. Wilford and Wilford, "On the Monetary Approach to the Balance of Payments: The Small, Open Economy," op. cit.

32. See J. Villasuso, W. T. Wilford, and A. M. Agapos, "The Demand for Money in an Emerging Nation: Costa Rica," *Philippine Economic Journal* 24 (Second Trimester 1974), no. 2: 130–34.

33. D. Sykes Wilford and J. Richard Zecher, "Monetary Policy and the Balance of Payments in Mexico 1955–73," *Journal of Money, Credit, and Banking* 11 (1979).

34. Lachman, op. cit., p. 280.

35. Aghevli, op. cit.

36. Ibid., p. 46.

37. Wilford and Zecher, op. cit.

38. Ibid.

39. Miller and Askin, op. cit., p. 227.

40. Ibid., p. 236.

M. A. Akhtar

8

SOME COMMON MISCONCEPTIONS ABOUT THE MONETARY APPROACH TO INTERNATIONAL ADJUSTMENT

The "monetary approach" to international adjustment is the subject of substantial controversy in international economics. A good deal of the dispute is due to misconceptions concerning the basic features of the approach. The matter has not been helped when in the heat of controversy the proponents of the approach have made unrealistic claims for the revealed truth. While the proponents have, upon occasion, claimed too much, the critics have generally seriously underestimated the contribution of the monetary approach and, in some cases, have failed to understand its widely useful implications for the international adjustment process. In this paper, the general framework of the monetary approach will be outlined, followed by a discussion of some of the common criticisms and misconceptions concerning the approach.

AN OVERVIEW OF THE MONETARY APPROACH

The basic framework of the monetary approach is built on the following relationships:[1]

$$M_s = f(R + D(\ )); f > 0 \tag{1}$$

$$M_d = g(\ )P^a \tag{2}$$

$$P = EwP_F(\ ) \tag{3}$$

The author is grateful to Bluford H. Putnam and D. Sykes Wilford for discussions and comments on various aspects of the arguments in this paper.

$$B = \frac{dR}{dt} \tag{4}$$

$$M_s = M_d \tag{5}$$

where M = nominal money balances (subscripts s and d denote supply and demand, respectively),

f( ) = supply of money function,

R = foreign exchange reserves,

D ( ) = domestic credit function,

g( ) = demand for money function,

P = domestic price level,

P_F( ) = foreign price level function assumed to be related to the foreign money demand function,

E = exchange rate (units of domestic currency per unit of foreign currency), and

B = the overall (official settlements basis) balance of payments.

Equation (1) specifies the money supply process; the supply of money is a stable and increasing function of foreign exchange reserves and the domestic credit; the latter may be exogenous or endogenous. Equation (2) represents the demand for money, which is a stable function of a few key variables; specifically, an income or wealth constraint, interest rates, and probably some other variables such as expectations, exchange risk, and so on. Note that the money demand function is not necessarily homogeneous of degree one in the price level. Equation (3) states the relationship between the domestic price level and the foreign or world price level with *w* as a factor that accounts for deviations from the purchasing power parity. Equation (4) defines the balance of payments, while equation (5) is the stock equilibrium condition. Inserting (3) into (2) and combining the result with (1) and (5) yields:

$$f(R + D( )) = g( )[EWP_F( )]^a \tag{6}$$

Under a fixed exchange rate system, E is fixed and R is endogenous. A rise in g( ), a rise in P_F( ), or a fall in D( ) will result in a rise in the overall balance of payments, that is, dR/dt rises. On the other hand, a fall in g( ), a fall in P_F( ), or a rise in D( ) leads to a fall in dR/dt. The process and speed of adjustment, as well as the impact of initial disturbance on the balance of payments, depend upon a number of considerations including institutional arrangements. However, the ultimate result is determined by the equilibrium condition between money supply and money demand. Under freely flexible exchange rates, R is fixed, that is, $(dR/dt) = 0$. Changes in g( ), P_F( ), and D( ) lead to changes in exchange rates, which in turn may affect the arguments of g( ), P_F( ), and probably of D( ). Eventually changes in the exchange rate will bring money demand into equilibrium with money supply. Finally, under a regime of controlled floating the monetary approach to international adjustment is a combination of the alternative theories under fixed and flexible exchange rates. The authorities choose a combination of R and E constrained by (6).

Equations (1) through (6) represent the *basic* structure of the monetary approach, but do not present a *complete* model. They are consistent with any number of formulations ranging from the limiting case where all or most of the determinants of g( ), P_F( ), and D( ) are exogenous, to the more general case where most of the determinants of these functions are endogenous. Moreover, there is no specification of the adjustment to equilibrium; again, any number of ways of specifying the speed and process of adjustment are consistent with the basic framework outlined here. Thus, as noted by M. Mussa, the monetary approach is not embodied in any single theoretical model; rather, it is represented by a large set of models that have certain features in common but differ in many important ways.

Four basic features emerge from the preceding summary view of the monetary approach.[2] First, the balance of payments defined on official settlements basis is an *essentially* monetary phenomenon and balance of payments problems are largely monetary problems that should be analyzed through explicit specification of monetary behavior, and its integration with "real" factors. This does not mean that real forces do not affect the balance of payments (or vice versa), rather that to do so they must affect the demand for and supply of money. This subject is pursued a bit further in the next section.

Second, the monetary approach explicitly recognizes that money is a stock and not a flow, and analyzes international adjustment problems through stock equilibrium conditions and stock adjustment processes. The analysis emphasizes that an adequate theory of the balance of payments must integrate stocks and flows.

Third, money stock is endogenous and can change through changes in domestic credit and/or through international reserve flows. The distinction between domestic origin and foreign origin components of the money stock is important for an analysis of balance of payments problems.

Fourth, the exchange rate is determined in the asset market, and as an approximation it may be taken as the relative price of different national monies, determined by the conditions for stock equilibrium for national monies. However, the exchange rate is not a purely monetary phenomenon; both "real" and monetary factors are important in determining its behavior. Changes in real factors that affect money demand and money supply also affect the exchange rate. In this respect, the monetary approach recognizes the simultaneity between the exchange rate, and the determinants of money demand and money supply.

COMMON MISCONCEPTIONS AND CRITICISMS

This section deals with some of the misconceptions and confusions concerning the monetary approach. The discussion below is a somewhat dispassionate look at the issues involved. It is not intended to be comprehensive in terms of its coverage of the criticisms and misconceptions. Instead, the emphasis is on those issues that have led to confusions about the general framework as presented in the preceding section.

An Essentially Monetary Phenomenon

As noted in the previous section, the monetary approach treats the balance of payments as a monetary phenomenon. The view is generally accepted but it is not without its critics. In his review of the theoretical papers in *The Monetary Approach to the Balance of Payments* edited by Frenkel and Johnson, F. H. Hahn has labelled it as a "false scent."[3] Specifically, referring to Mussa's statement that "the balance of payments is an essentially (but not exclusively) monetary phenomenon ... The official settlements balance is in surplus (deficit) when the monetary authorities of a country are purchasing (selling) foreign exchange assets in order to prevent their own money from appreciating (depreciating) relative to other monies,"[4] he argues that "on similar grounds the market for cheese is an essentially monetary phenomenon. Why? Because if some cheese is sold for stock rather than current production then cheese makers must be purchasing money stock from households, etc., etc."[5] While Mussa's rationale is somewhat ambiguous and weak, Hahn's reasoning fails to recognize the nature of exchange rates and misses the whole point. An outline of the rationale for the view that the balance of payments is an *essentially* monetary phenomenon is in order at this point.

Two interrelated points should be made regarding the rationale for the view in question. First, consider the consolidated balance sheet identity of the monetary sector in an open economy (for the sake of simplicity we ignore the money multiplier):

$$M = R + D$$

or

$$R = M - D$$

This identity differentiated with respect to time yields:

$$\frac{dR}{dt} = \frac{dM}{dt} - \frac{dD}{dt} \tag{7}$$

which indicates that the overall balance of payments is identically equal to the difference between the rate of change of money and the rate of change of domestic credit. Both monetary and "real" influences on the balance of payments are reflected in equation (7); however, real influences must appear through monetary factors. Thus, monetary factors have the *primary* role because they transmit the disturbances from the monetary side as well as from the real side. Indeed, it would be impossible to have a balance of payments surplus or deficit in a barter economy. Putting the matter in a somewhat different light, in an open economy excess demands and supplies of goods or bonds may be eliminated by exchanging them for money in the international market.

Second, since there is a direct relationship between the money stock and the overall balance of payments, the latter is approximately analyzed by *explicitly* specifying monetary behavior rather than treating it as a residual of "real relationships." To say that money is not a residual from the real side is to say much more than what Hahn appears to believe, that is, "money makes an appearance."[6] In the latter sense, money flows can appear as residuals of real flows determined by incomes and relative prices.

Domestic Credit

Domestic credit is usually, but not always, treated as an exogenous variable under the control of the monetary authorities. This has led to the view that the monetary approach ignores the determinants of the money supply and relies too heavily on the money supply identity. The view is most forcefully expressed by D. A. Currie and Max Corden.[7] The monetary approach theorists have, of course, long recognized that the fiscal policy and other "real" variables influence domestic credit creation, but most of them appear to believe that even so the monetary authorities have control over domestic credit. For many cases, the treatment of domestic credit as exogenous may be appropriate. If, however, domestic credit is responding passively to real forces, then the monetary approach should be (and can be) adapted to those forces.

In principle, domestic credit creation may be specified as a function of other variables that are believed to be the major influences or it may be related to the government budget constraint. The latter approach has been taken frequently in the monetary approach literature.[8] Specifically:

$$\Delta D = G - T - B \tag{8}$$

where ΔD = change in domestic credit, D

G = government expenditure

T = fiscal revenue, and

B = addition to borrowing from the private sector,
  both foreign and domestic

The introduction of the government budget constraint enables us to treat domestic credit creation as passively responding to the fiscal variables. Thus, fiscal influences on domestic credit can be (and have been) incorporated into the structure of the monetary approach without endangering the internal consistency of the general model.

General Misconceptions About the Money Demand Function

The question of exogenous versus endogenous determinants of the money demand function is taken up in the next section. However, before this is done it is important to mention three general misconceptions concerning the role of the money demand function in the monetary approach. First, there appears to be a view that the "specific" form of the money demand function is important for the monetary approach conclusions or results to hold. In a recent article, S. C. Tsiang, while appreciating the importance of the money demand function in the monetary approach, writes that

> there does not yet seem to be general agreement among the proponents of the monetary approach about its [money demand function] precise form . . . the actual decision to pick one or the other seems to depend mostly upon expediency in relation to the problem that the author is tackling.[9]

The *general* agreement for the precise form of the money demand function is not important for the monetary approach; what is important is that it should be a stable function of a few key variables over the period of analysis. What those variables are is an empirical question and is likely to differ according to the time period and circumstances.

Second, some authors have criticized the monetary approach by using an extremely restrictive Cambridge form of the money demand function, where money demand is assumed to be interest inelastic. This is the type of function Whitman attributes to the "global monetarists."[10] There are probably no "global monetarists" in Whitman's sense but, if there are any, they probably would include interest rate as an argument in their money demand function.*

---

*The "skeleton" model used by Whitman is a slightly modified version of Dornbusch's model in his article in the December 1973 issue of the *American Economic Review*. Apparently, Whitman is cognizant of the fact that Dornbusch is not a "global monetarist" and that

Third, sometimes, though not often, critics have ignored the importance of the money demand function in the monetary approach and have criticized it for focusing attention on "the accounting identity between reserves, domestic credit and money" and for confusing accounting identities with causal economic relationships.[11] This type of criticism has also appeared in reference to empirical analyses based on the monetary approach. On the theoretical side, in view of equations (1) through (6) this charge is clearly invalid. On the empirical side, this criticism, as shown in a subsequent section, is due to some confusion about the derivation of estimating equations.

Exogenous Versus Endogenous Variables

Some of the more forceful monetary approach literature makes the assumptions of full employment and "small country" (or alternatively the so-called law of one price in the multicountry context), so that the main arguments of the money demand function become exogenous. This has led to the rather popular impression that the monetary approach is relevant only for small countries or that the exogeneity of the determinants of the money demand function is a necessity for the monetary approach.[12] Neither of these views is correct.*

In principle, the proponents of the monetary approach visualize a general equilibrium model of the macroeconomic type with stock and flow variables. But in practice they attempt to reduce the general equilibrium model to manageable proportions by singling out money as the center of analysis. The treatment of the arguments of the money demand function as endogenous is in no way inconsistent with the monetary approach. In fact, some of the recent monetary approach models treat interest rates, prices, or income as endogenous.[14] However, much remains to be done to develop models that determine income and prices simultaneously with the exchange rate and/or the balance of payments within the context of the monetary approach. This is, by far, the weakest area in the monetary approach literature.

In general, two important considerations bear on the issue of exogeneity versus endogeneity of the determinants of the money demand function. The first

---

he chose a simple model to "emphasize the monetary aspects of the problem," and the Cambridge form of the money demand function so as "not to detract from the main line of argument."[13]

It may be useful to note one other source of confusion in Whitman's conception of "global monetarism." She treats global monetarism as the "full package" and the monetary approach as an extension of it. This is incorrect; global monetarism is a limiting or a polar case of the monetary approach.

*As is obvious from our discussion in the previous sections, on the money supply side R is endogenous except in the case of perfectly flexible exchange rates, and D can be specified as a function of fiscal and other "real" sector variables.

deals with the length of the time period involved. For very short periods such as days or a few weeks the levels of aggregate real income and prices may be assumed given. However, virtually nothing is known about the stability of the demand for money over such periods. For periods ranging from a quarter to one or two years, the demand for money is generally believed to be fairly stable. But over such periods the simultaneity between the money supply process and the determinants of the money demand may be substantial. In this case, the second consideration becomes important. In other words, whether or not the determinants of the demand for money are exogenous may depend upon the particular circumstances of the country, such as the degree of openness, integration of domestic financial markets with similar markets abroad, and the size of the economy. Thus if the law of one price describes the relevant "reality," interest rates and prices should be treated as exogenous. Obviously, these matters require empirical analysis, which is the subject matter of the next section.

Some Empirical Confusions

Most of the critics have rejected any conclusions based on reduced or quasi-reduced form tests of the monetary approach models. Probably the main reason for this is that they feel the assumptions required to produce reduced or quasi-reduced form models are unduly restrictive or altogether erroneous due to the simultaneous equation bias. This quarrel with reduced form models is not new and, of course, has a great deal of merit. However, as noted above, some of the issues involved are empirical, and cannot be resolved a priori.

The monetary approach can be tested through either direct tests of the models or tests of the models as well as their assumptions.[15] The direct test may be of structural models (which treat some, most, or all of the determinants of the money demand or money supply functions as endogenous) or of reduced and quasi-reduced form models. While the direct tests of structural models are rather rare thus far, though not altogether unknown, such tests for reduced or quasi-reduced form models are very common. However, the latter may appear to be more favorable to the monetary approach than the underlying structural models. This is what makes it necessary to test the key assumptions introduced in order to produce the reduced form version. Tests of the assumptions of reduced form models are fairly common in the empirical literature on the monetary approach.

The empirical tests of the small country assumption (or the law of one price in multicountry models), often made in the limiting case of the monetary approach, indicate that for many countries the assumption or some modified version of the assumption captures the relevant "reality." Similar results have been found for the nonsterilization assumption regarding the balance of payments surplus underlying the money supply process under a fixed exchange rate system. However, neither of the assumptions holds universally. The tests of the assumptions combined with the direct tests of the monetary approach suggest that the usefulness of the empirical studies can be determined only on a case-by-case basis, taking full account of the circumstances of the problem as well as the craftsmanship of the researcher. Judged in these terms, many of the empirical tests of the monetary approach can be said to have contributed a great deal to our knowledge.

Some critics have not only rejected empirical findings based on the reduced form models but have gone so far as to argue that "direct estimation of the balance of payments equation implied by the monetary approach involves the estimation of an accounting identity rather than a true behavioral relationship."[16] This appears to be the result of a confusion regarding the derivation of the estimating equation(s). Even in the limiting case of the monetary approach, a single reduced form equation for international reserve flows is obtained by combining the money supply identity with the money demand function under the assumption of monetary equilibrium. Thus, the estimating equation explicitly incorporates the influence of money supply factors as well as the influence of factors underlying the money demand function.[17]

Monetarism and the Monetary Approach

Despite the proponents' claim that the monetary approach is neither entailed by nor entails monetarism,[18] it is commonly believed that the monetary approach is a direct descendant of M. Friedman's restatement of the quantity theory. Presumably this view finds its main support in the fact that the monetary approach largely assumes "normal" full employment in the long run. In this section, some of the distinguishing features of the monetary approach vis-a-vis "monetarism" are noted. The conclusion reached—a rather obvious one—is that the monetary approach does not imply monetarism.

First, the monetary approach treats the money supply as an endogenous variable, whereas it is generally treated as an exogenous variable by the monetarists. As noted elsewhere in this study, R is endogenous under a fixed rate regime as well as under a controlled floating regime. Moreover, D may be exogenous or endogenous regardless of the exchange rate regime.

Second, unlike the monetarists, the proponents of the monetary approach do not consider fiscal policy as impotent, while placing "too much" emphasis on the use of monetary policy. Specifically:

> The monetary approach to the balance of payments asserts neither that monetary mismanagement is the only cause, nor that monetary policy change is the only possible cure, for balance of payments problems; it does suggest, however, that monetary process will bring about a cure of some kind—not necessarily very attractive—unless frustrated by deliberate monetary policy action, and that policies that neglect or aggravate the monetary implications of deficits and surpluses will not be successful in their declared objectives.[19]

As should be evident from the overview of the monetary approach in the first section, the exchange rate problems also have both monetary and nonmonetary causes as well as cures.

Third, the monetary approach, like the modern monetarists' theory, assumes that the aggregate money demand function is a stable function of a few aggregate economic variables. However, in this respect its assumptions are also similar to those of the Keynesian theory. At a more specific level, the monetary approach, unlike that of the monetarists, does not require the assumption that "the demand for money is homogeneous of degree one in all prices and nominal money assets (absence of money illusion)."[20]

Fourth, the monetary approach can be applied to a system in which prices and wages are rigid. In this case, monetary changes affect quantities—employment, output, and consumption—rather than prices and wages. This application has been investigated by, for example, Carlos A. Rodriguez in the context of a Keynesian model.[21]

Fifth, it is worth noting that the proponents of the monetary approach do not have a common stance on the issue of flexible versus fixed exchange rates. In fact, in contrast to the findings of the monetarists, the limiting case seems to favor a fixed exchange rate in that changes in the exchange rate are regarded as unnecessary as well as ineffective for achievement of payments equilibrium.

Finally, an important methodological difference between the monetary approach and the monetarists's theory is evident in the treatment of assumptions. Following Friedman, the monetarists regard the "realism" of their assumptions as unnecessary to the "correctness" of their models and instead emphasize the predictions the models yield.[22] By contrast, the proponents of the monetary approach attempt to test, as noted above, the assumptions as well as the predictions of their models. In a more general sense, the monetary approach emphasizes the need for general equilibrium methodology and, unlike the monetarists' theory, does not necessarily presume that the private sector is inherently more stable than the public sector or that the monetary impulses dominate in all cases. For example, Johnson warns against "the dangers of the politically popular belief that desirable real results can be achieved by manipulation of monetary magnitudes and maneuvers with the monetary mystique."[23]

NOTES

1.The most relevant contributions to the contemporary revival and development of the monetary approach were made by R. A. Mundell and Harry G. Johnson. See, in particular, R. A. Mundell, *International Economics* (New York: Macmillan, 1968) and *Monetary Theory* (Pacific Palisades: Goodyear, 1971); Harry G. Johnson, *Further Essays in Monetary Theory* (London: Allen and Unwin, 1972). Most of the recent contributions are listed in the bibliography of this book. The presentation of the basic framework of the monetary approach in this study is based primarily, but not exclusively, on R. Dornbusch, "The Theory of Flexible Exchange Rate Regimes and Macroeconomic Policy," *Scandinavian Journal of Economics* 78, no. 2 (1976): 255–75; M. Mussa, "Tariffs and the Balance of Payments: A Monetary Approach," in *The Monetary Approach to the Balance of Payments*, ed. J. A. Frenkel and Harry G. Johnson (Toronto: University of Toronto Press, 1976), pp. 187–221; M. Mussa, "The Exchange Rate, the Balance of Payments and Monetary and Fiscal Policy Under a Regime of Controlled Floating," *Scandinavian Journal of Economics* 78, no. 2 (1976): 229–48; J. A. Frenkel and Harry G. Johnson, "The Monetary Approach to the Balance of Payments: Essential Concepts and Historical Origins," in *The Monetary Approach*, op. cit., pp. 21–45; and A. K. Swoboda, "Monetary Approaches to Balance-of-Payments Theory," in *Recent Issues in Monetary Economics*, ed. E. Classen and P. Salin (New York: North-Holland, 1976), pp. 3–23.

2. The first three features are noted in Harry G. Johnson, "The Monetary Approach to Balance of Payments Theory and Policy: Explanation and Policy Implications," *Economica* 44 (August 1977): 217–29, and Harry G. Johnson, "The Monetary Approach to the Balance of Payments: A Nontechnical Guide," *Journal of International Economics* 7 (August 1977): 251–68. See also Mussa, "Tariffs," op. cit., and Swoboda, op. cit. The last feature emerges from adaptation of the theory to flexible or controlled floating exchange rate regimes. For an emphasis on this aspect see Dornbusch, op. cit.; Mussa, "The Exchange Rate," op. cit., and P. J. K. Kouri, "The Exchange Rate and the Balance of Payments in the Short Run and in the Long Run: A Monetary Approach," *Scandinavian Journal of Economics* 78, no. 2 (1976): 280–304.

3. F. H. Hahn, "The Monetary Approach to the Balance of Payments," *Journal of International Economics* 7 (August 1977): 241.

4. *The Monetary Approach*, op. cit., p. 189.

5. Hahn, op. cit., p. 241.

6. Ibid.

7. D. A. Currie, "Some Criticisms of the Monetary Analysis of Balance of Payments Correction," *Economic Journal* 86 (September 1976): 508–22; and Max Corden, "General Discussion: What Have We Learned? Where are the Fundamental Conflicts of Opinion?" proceedings of a conference on *Flexible Exchange Rates and Stabilization Policy*, published in *The Scandinavian Journal of Economics* 78, no. 2 (1976): 387, 403–05.

8. See, for example, G. H. Borts and J. A. Hanson, "The Monetary Approach to the Balance of Payments," Mimeographed, 1975; P. D. Jonson, "Money and Economic Activity in the Open Economy: The United Kingdom, 1880–1970," *Journal of Political Economy* (October 1976): 979–1012; Johan Myhrman, "Balance-of-Payments Adjustments and Portfolio Theory: A Survey," in *Recent Issues*, op. cit., 203–37; D. Sykes Wilford, *Monetary Policy and the Open Economy: Mexico's Experience* (New York: Praeger, 1977), pp. 21–26; and M. A. Akhtar, Bluford H. Putnam and D. Sykes Wilford, "Fiscal Constraints, Domestic Credit and International Reserve Flows," *Journal of Money, Credit, and Banking* 11 (1979).

9. S. C. Tsiang, "The Monetary Theoretic Foundation of the Modern Monetary Approach to the Balance of Payments," *Oxford Economic Papers* 29 (November 1977): 321.

10. See Marina v. N. Whitman, "Global Monetarism and the Monetary Approach to the Balance of Payments," *Brookings Papers on Economic Activity*, no. 3 (1975): 491–536.

11. Currie, op. cit., pp. 514 and 516.

12. See, in particular, Joanne Salop, "A Note on the Monetary Approach to the Balance of Payments," in *The Effects of Exchange Rate Adjustment*, ed. P. Clark, D. Logue, and R. Sweeney (Washington, D.C.: U.S. Department of the Treasury, 1976), pp. 23–31; and Whitman, op. cit.

13. R. Dornbusch, "Devaluation, Money, and Non-traded Goods," *American Economic Review* 63 (December 1973): 871.

14. See, for example, Dornbusch, op. cit., and Jonson, op. cit.

15. Some of the recent empirical studies are discussed by S. P. Magee, "The Empirical Evidence on the Monetary Approach to the Balance of Payments and Exchange Rates,"

American Economic Review 66 (May 1976): 163-70. Many others, published and unpublished, are listed in the bibliography of this volume.

16. Whitman, op. cit., p. 525. See also Currie, op. cit.

17. For a detailed discussion of this issue see Bluford H. Putnam and D. Sykes Wilford, "Monetary Equilibrium and International Reserve Flows: An Empirical Treatment of the Money Supply Identity Issue," unpublished paper, 1977. See also Magee, op. cit.

18. See Frenkel and Johnson, op. cit., pp. 24-25. Elsewhere Johnson complained that "there has been a noticeable tendency to dismiss the new [monetary] approach as merely an international economic application of an eccentric and intellectually ludicrous point of view of a contemporary lunatic fringe referred to as 'monetarism.'" Harry G. Johnson, "The Monetary Approach to Balance-of-Payments Theory: A Diagrammatic Analysis," *The Manchester School* 44 (September 1975): 221.

19. Frenkel and Johnson, op. cit., p. 24.

20. Ibid.

21. Carlos A Rodriguez, "Money and Wealth in an Open Economy Income-Expenditure Model," in *The Monetary Approach*, op. cit., pp. 222-36.

22. See M. Friedman, "The Methodology of Positive Economics," in his *Essays in Positive Economics* (Chicago: University of Chicago Press, 1953), pp. 3-43.

23. Harry G. Johnson, "Money, Balance-of-Payments Theory, and the International Monetary Problem," *Essays in International Finance*, no. 124 (Princeton, N.J.: Princeton University Press, November 1977).

FLEXIBLE EXCHANGE RATES

PART II

INTRODUCTION
Bluford H. Putnam
D. Sykes Wilford

In the first part of this volume, the monetary approach to international adjustment under the assumption of fixed exchange rates was addressed. Thus the interest was in the balance of payments adjustment or in the quantity adjustments necessary in the money market (through a country's holdings of international reserves) to maintain equilibrium in goods and assets markets. In the second part of this volume, international adjustment is analyzed in the context of flexible exchange rates. Price adjustments will bear the burden of maintaining equilibrium in goods and assets markets. But, basically, the pressures at work in the fixed rate system still operate and the transition to flexible rate models is quite smooth.

Since the breakup of the Bretton Woods system, the international macro economist has been challenged by new and ever-changing economic data. Although the flexible period is still an infant at the time of this writing, the system has already managed to generate a plethora of offical, business, and academic debate. Part of this debate has been stimulated by the flexible rate system's failure to behave as expected. In particular, flexible exchange rates have not guarnteed the independence of national monetary policies, and exchange rates have not shifted to equilibrate fully current account balances. Various adaptations of the monetary approach have much to say about these issues. This collection of studies starts with the basic monetary approach to flexible exchange rates and then moves quickly to some rather interesting and complex extensions.

Also worth noting is the fact that students of the monetary approach do not tend to fall into easily predictable camps when the question of fixed versus flexible exchange rates is raised. The monetary approach is providing ammunition for both sides of the debate. New concepts from the monetary approach will surely be at the forefront of future discussions on proper policy as more and more is learned about how the international monetary system, under flexible exchange rates, functions.

The ease with which the basic monetary approach model to fixed exchange rates can be converted to a model of exchange rate determination under flexible rates is demonstrated by the initial chapter in Part 2, "Factors Determining Exchange Rates: A Simple Model and Empirical Tests," by Thomas Humphrey and Thomas A. Lawler. Besides providing the theoretical transition from fixed to flexible rate models, this study also includes some interesting empirical estimates underscoring the relevance of the approach.

With the basic theory in hand, the next study, "The Monetary Approach to Exchange Rates: Its Historical Evolution and Role in Policy Debates," by Thomas Humphrey, takes a close look at three exchange rate controversies in which the monetary approach was forcefully argued. In this study, it is possible to trace the growing sophistication of the approach, as each successive debate produced new thoughts and ideas.

The first monetary approach models of exchange rate determination all assumed that the monetary authorities conducted monetary policy by controlling the money supply. Bluford H. Putnam, in "Monetary Policy, Interest Rate Targets, and Foreign Exchange Markets," assumes that the monetary authorities set interest rates, and derives conclusions concerning movements in the domestic money supply and the spot exchange rate that are worth the attention of policymakers.

The next three studies focus on an important extension of the approach that is critical in understanding the interdependence of monetary policies under flexible exchange rates. This is the issue of currency mobility or currency substitution. Essentially, these models assume that residents can hold assets denominated in more than one currency in their portfolios. This allows international adjustment to occur either through price changes (exchange rate movements) or demand-side quantity adjustments (portfolio shifts at existing exchange rates). Demand substitutability among currencies may be considered the counterpart of the perfect supply substitutability imposed by the assumption of fixed exchange rates. Marc A. Miles's "Currency Substitution: Perspective, Implications, and Empirical Evidence," provides a basic model adaptable for empirical testing. His results and his summary of other relevant empirical results are quite supportive of this new development in the monetary approach. "Currency Mobility and Balance of Payments Adjustment," by Russell S. Boyer, ranks as the first modern theoretical statement of the currency mobility concepts. First drafted while he was still a student at the University of Chicago, this study has been widely circulated and has had a major role in stimulating interest in this topic. The final chapter in this group, "A Currency Portfolio Approach to Exchange Rate Determination," by David T. King, Bluford H. Putnam, and D. Sykes Wilford, returns to the basic model presented in the Humphrey-Lawler article and redefines the demand for money function to encompass the concept of currency substitution.

Working this extension through the model points out with the interdependence of monetary policy under flexible exchange rates.

The contribution of Lance Girton and Don Roper, "The Evolution of Exchange Rate Policy," argues that significant changes in exchange rate policies will occur as national monetary authorities evaluate such policies in the context of domestic stabilization policies. In deriving their conclusions, a rather interesting alternative statement of purchasing power parity is presented and related to intervention policies.

Monetary approach models tend to focus on long-run trends, because of their dependence on the purchasing power parity assumption. Charles D. Cathcart, in "A Monetary Approach to the Exchange Rate in the Short Run," does not assume purchasing power parity, but does retain the basic features of a monetary approach model. His essay is especially provocative and provides an interesting interpretation of "overshooting" phenomena. David T. King, in "Expectations and Exchange Rate Dynamics," presents an alternative view of the overshooting problem by incorporating an analysis of risk into the general monetary exchange rate determination model.

The final chapter, "Money Illusion and Its Influence on International Adjustment," by John J. Van Belle, could have been placed in either the fixed or the flexible exchange rate sections of this volume, since its conclusions are easily applied to either system. In this study, money illusion distorts perceptions of real balances and thus can impede or promote adjustment to equilibrium depending on the type (or cause) of the money illusion.

Thomas M. Humphrey
Thomas A. Lawler

9

FACTORS DETERMINING
EXCHANGE RATES:
A SIMPLE MODEL AND
EMPIRICAL TESTS

This article constructs and tests a simple static equilibrium model of exchange rate determination.[1] The model assumes a regime of freely floating currencies and posits that the exchange rate, by definition the relative price of two national moneys, is determined by the basic factors underlying the demands for and supplies of those national money stocks. Besides the money supply itself, these factors include real income and interest rates—the latter reflecting expectational influences that enter into exchange rate determination.

The article proceeds as follows. First, it discusses the logic and economic content of the individual equations that constitute the major building blocks of the model. Second, it condenses the model to one reduced-form equation that expresses a functional relationship between the exchange rate and its ultimate determinants. Third, it fits the foregoing equation to the statistical data on several foreign exchange rates, assesses the accuracy of the fit, and discusses some problems involved in testing the model.

THE MODEL AND ITS ELEMENTS

The model itself consists of two hypothetical national economies represented by a set of equations containing the following variables. Let M be the nominal money stock (assumed to be exogenously determined by the central bank) and m the demand-adjusted rate of growth of that stock, that is, the differ-

This article, in a slightly different form, appeared in the *Economic Review* of the Federal Reserve Bank of Richmond.

ence between the respective growth rates of the nominal money supply and real money demand, this difference by definition being equal to the rate of price inflation. Furthermore, let D be the real demand for money, that is, the stock of real (price-deflated) cash balances that the public desires to hold, Y the exogenously-determined level of real income, and i and r the nominal and real rates of interest, respectively. Also let X be the exchange rate (defined as the domestic currency price of a unit of foreign currency), P be the price level, and E be the expected future rate of price inflation. Omicrons are used to distinguish foreign-country variables from home-country variables, and the subscript w denotes the entire world economy. The foregoing elements are linked together via the relationships described below.

Monetary Equilibrium Equations

The first part of the model consists of monetary equilibrium equations, one for each country

$$P = M/D \quad \text{and} \quad P^O = M^O/D^O \tag{1}$$

These equations, which can also be written in the form $M/P = D$, state that the price level in each country adjusts to bring the real (price-deflated) value of the nominal money stock into equality with the real demand for it, thereby clearing the market for real cash balances. This market-clearing price-adjustment process relies chiefly on equilibrating changes in aggregate expenditure induced by discrepancies between actual and desired real balances. For example, if actual balances exceed desired, cashholders will attempt to get rid of the excess via spending for goods. Given the exogenously-determined level of real output, however, the increased spending will exert upward pressure on prices, thereby reducing the real (price-deflated) value of the nominal money stock. Prices will continue to rise until actual real balances are brought down to the desired level. Conversely, a shortfall between actual and desired real balances will induce a cut in expenditure leading to a fall in prices and a corresponding rise in the real value of the money stock. This process will continue until actual real balances are brought into equality with desired balances. To summarize, disequilibrium between actual and desired real balances generates the changes in spending that cause prices to alter sufficiently to eliminate the disequilibrium.

Note that the equations also imply that, given the real demand for money, the price level is determined by and varies equiproportionally with the nominal money supply. This latter result, of course, is the essence of the quantity theory of money. For that reason, the equations could also be called quantity theory equations.

Real Cash Balance Equations

National demand for money functions constitute the second part of the model. Written as follows

$$D = KYi^{-a} \quad \text{and} \quad D^o = K^o Y^o_i o^{-a} \tag{2}$$

these equations express the public's demand for real cash balances as the product of a constant K and two variables, namely real income and the nominal interest rate. The income variable is a proxy for the volume of real transactions effected with the aid of money and thus represents the transaction demand for money. By contrast, the interest rate variable measures the opportunity cost of holding money instead of earning assets. The parameter $-a$, which appears as the exponent of the interest rate variable, is the interest eleasticity of demand for money. It measures the sensitivity or responsiveness of money demand to changes in the interest rate and is assumed to be a negative number indicating that the quantity of real balances demanded varies inversely with the cost of holding them. For simplicity the numerical magnitude of the interest elasticity parameter is assumed to be the same for both countries. For the same reason the income elasticity of demand for money, as represented by the exponential power to which the income variable is raised, is assumed to possess a numerical value of unity.

The Purchasing Power Parity Equation

The third equation of the model is the purchasing power parity relationship

$$P = XP^o \tag{3}$$

showing how national price levels are linked together via the exchange rate. As indicated by the equation, prices in both countries are identical when converted into a common currency unit at the equilibrium rate of exchange. This means that the exchange rate equalizes such common-currency price levels and, by implication, the buying power of both moneys expressed in terms of a common unit. In other words, exchange-rate adjustment insures that a unit of a given currency commands the same quantity of goods and services abroad when converted into the other currency as it commands at home. This condition of equalized purchasing power is of course necessary if the two national money stocks are to be willingly held and monetary equilibrium is to prevail in both countries. For if the purchasing powers were unequal, people would demand more of the high- and less of the low-purchasing power currency on the market for foreign exchange. The resulting excess demand for the former and the corresponding excess supply of the latter would cause the exchange rate between the two currencies to adjust until purchasing power was equalized and both money stocks were willingly held. Note also that the purchasing power parity equation can be rearranged to read $X = P/P^0$, thus corresponding to the economic interpretation of the exchange rate as the relative price of the two currencies, that is, as the ratio of the foreign currency's internal value in terms of goods to the domestic currency's internal value in terms of goods. Since the internal value of a unit of currency in terms of a composite market basket of commodities is the inverse of the general price level $1/P$, it follows that the relative price of the two moneys is simply the ratio of the national price levels as indicated by the equation.

Nominal Interest Rate Equations

The fourth group of relationships in the model are the nominal interest rate equations, one for each country. Written as follows

$$i = r + E \text{ and } i^0 = r^0 + E^0 \tag{4}$$

they define the nominal interest rate as the sum of the real rate of interest and the expected future rate of inflation, the latter variable being the premium added to real yields to prevent their erosion by inflation.

Real Interest Rate Parity Condition

The fifth equation expresses the interest-parity condition

$$r = r^0 = r_w \tag{5}$$

according to which the real rate of return on capital assets tends to be everywhere the same and independent of the currency denomination of the asset. This equation reflects the model's assumption of a highly-integrated efficient world capital market. In such a world capital is mobile internationally, that is, foreigners can purchase domestic securities and domestic citizens can purchase foreign securities. Given these conditions it follows that real yield equalization is necessary if all asset stocks are to be willingly held. Accordingly, the equation states that real interest rates in both countries are the same and are equal to a given constant world rate r_w. Note that equations (4) and (5) taken together imply that international nominal interest rate differentials reflect differences in expected future national rates of inflation. For example, if the market expects the future rate of inflation to be 12 percent in the United Kingdom and 5 percent in the United States, then the U. K. nominal interest rate will be 7 percentage points above the corresponding U.S. interest rate.

Price Expectations Equations

Completing the model are price expectations equations that describe how the public forms its anticipations of the future rate of inflation. These inflationary expectations constitute the anticipated future rates of depreciation of money holdings. As such, they enter the foreign and domestic demand for money functions via the nominal interest rate variables and thereby play an important role in exchange rate determination. Written as follows

$$E = m \text{ and } E^O = m^O \tag{6}$$

the price expectations equations state that the expected rate of inflation E is equal to the demand-adjusted rate of monetary expansion m, that is, the difference between the respective growth rates of the nominal money supply and real money demand.

As written, these equations embody the so-called *rational expectations hypothesis* according to which the public correctly bases its price forecasts on the variable that the model contends actually determines the rate of inflation. This feature ensures that the model is internally consistent, that is, that the equations describing the formation of inflationary expectations are consistent with equations describing how inflation is actually generated. Such consistency is characteristic of the forecasting behavior of rational agents who use knowledge about the actual inflation-generating process in forming expectations of future inflation. Since the model asserts that the actual rate of price inflation is determined by the demand-adjusted growth rate of money (see equation 1), it follows that the expected rate of inflation is determined by that same variable as shown in equation (6).

LINKAGES AND CAUSATION

Taken together, the foregoing relationships constitute a simple six-equation model of exchange rate determination. For convenience the model is summarized below.

$$P = M/D \text{ and } P^O = M^O/D^O. \tag{1}$$

$$D = KYi^{-a} \text{ and } D^O = K^O Y^O_i{}^{O-a}. \tag{2}$$

$$P = XP^O. \tag{3}$$

$$i = r + E \text{ and } i^O = r^O + E^O. \tag{4}$$

$$r = r^0 = r_w \,.$$
(5)

$$E = m \text{ and } E^0 = m^0$$
(6)

The foregoing equations imply two unidirectional channels of influence—one direct, the other indirect—running from money and income (both exogenous variables) to prices to the exchange rate. Regarding the former channel, the model implies that both exogenous variables affect prices and the exchange rate directly through the monetary equilibrium and purchasing power parity equations. As for the indirect channel, the model implies that the rates of growth of the exogenous variables influence prices and the exchange rate indirectly via the price expectations component of the nominal interest rate variable that enters the demand for money function. More specifically, the model postulates the following causal chain:

1. The demand-adjusted money-stock growth rate determines the expected rate of inflation.
2. Given the real rate of interest, the expected rate of inflation determines the nominal rate of interest.
3. The latter variable, together with the given level of real income, determines the demand for money.
4. Given the demand for money, the nominal money stock determines the price level.
5. Finally, the two price levels, foreign and domestic, together determine the exchange rate.

In brief, when the demand-adjusted money growth rate rises, price expectations also rise and so too does the nominal interest rate (the cost of holding money). This reduces the quantity of real cash balances that people desire to hold, that is, cashholders will want to get out of money and into goods. The resulting increased spending for goods puts upward pressure on the price level and, via the purchasing power parity nexus, also on the exchange rate. Clearly the linkages run from money stocks and real incomes to prices to the exchange rate.* Moreover, all variables affecting the exchange rate do so through monetary channels, that is, through the demand for and supply of money. In this sense, money demand and supply may be said to constitute the *proximate* determinants of the exchange rate. The *ultimate* determinants, however, are the variables that underlie and determine the monetary factors themselves.

---

*Note that reverse causality is effectively ruled out by the assumed exogeneity of the money stock and income variables. Therefore, while these variables can affect the exchange rate the exchange rate cannot influence them—at least not within the context of the model.

DETERMINANTS OF THE EXCHANGE RATE

To show the relationship between the exchange rate and its ultimate determinants, simply substitute equations 1 - 2 and 4 - 6 into equation 3 and solve for the exchange rate. The resulting "reduced form" expression is

$$X = [K^O/K] \ [M/M^O] \ [Y^O/Y] \ [i/i^O]^a \tag{7}$$

or, since the nominal interest rate i is the sum of the real interest rate r and the expected rate of inflation E—the latter variable itself being equal to the growth rate of money per unit of money demand m—the equation can be alternatively expressed as

$$X = [\frac{K^O}{K}] \ [\frac{M}{M^O}] \ [\frac{Y^O}{Y}] \ [\frac{r+m}{r^O+m^O}]^a \ . \tag{7'}$$

Disregarding the fixed constants (the K's), equation 7 (or 7') collects the determinants of the exchange rate into three groups, namely relative money supplies, relative real incomes, and relative nominal interest rates comprised of a fixed real rate component and a variable price expectations component. Of these three groups, the first captures purely monetary influences on the exchange rate while the second and third capture real and expectational influences, respectively.

Regarding monetary and real influences, the equation predicts that a country's exchange rate will depreciate (that is, rise) if its demand-adjusted money stock is growing faster than in the other country. Conversely, a nation will find its currency appreciating on the foreign exchanges when its money stock grows slower and its real income faster than in the other country. Note that the model's conclusion that rapid real growth results in currency appreciation contradicts the conventional balance of payments view of exchange rate determination. According to this latter approach, income growth tends to depreciate a country's currency by inducing a rise in imports and a consequent trade balance deficit. By contrast, the present model depicts real growth as stimulating not imports but rather the demand for money. Given the nominal money stock, this increased real money demand necessitates a fall in the price level to clear the market for money balances. With foreign prices given, the fall in domestic prices requires an equivalent appreciation of the exchange rate to maintain purchasing power parity. In short, the model predicts that growth-induced rises in the real demand for money will raise the internal and therefore also the external value of a currency.

As for expectational influences, the equation predicts that a rise in the expected rate of inflation in one country (as reflected in its interest rate) relative to the other will cause the former's currency to depreciate on the foreign exchanges. The reason, of course, is that when interest rates rise, desired real cash balances fall. Cashholders attempt to get rid of unwanted balances via expenditure for goods thereby putting upward pressure on prices. According to the model, the rise in prices will be relatively greater in the country experiencing the larger rise in interest rates. In this way increasing relative interest rates cause corresponding increases in relative national price levels that must be offset by exchange rate depreciation to preserve purchasing power parity. Note again that the model's prediction of a direct relation between interest rate movements and exchange rate movements runs counter to the conventional balance of payments view. According to this latter approach, a rising interest rate should lower the exchange rate either by attracting capital from abroad (thereby improving the capital account of the balance of payments) or by reducing domestic expenditure for imports and potential exports (thereby improving the trade balance). This cannot happen in the present model where, instead of strengthening the balance of payments, a rising interest rate induces a shift from cash to goods resulting in domestic inflation and exchange rate depreciation. In short, equation (7) predicts that a country will experience currency depreciation when its relative money stock rises, its relative real income falls, and its relative inflationary expectations rise.

EMPIRICAL APPLICATION

This article has constructed a simple economic model that states that the bilateral exchange rate between any two national currencies is determined by relative money stocks, relative real incomes, and relative nominal interest rates— the last variable reflecting relative expectations regarding national inflationary prospects. All that remains is to illustrate how the model can be applied to empirical studies of exchange rate determination. With this objective in mind, an attempt is made below to estimate the model's reduced-form exchange rate equation (equation 7) and to use it to explain the behavior of the United States/ United Kingdom and United States/Italy exchange rates, respectively, over the post-1972 period of generalized floating. To do this, it is necessary to transform equation (7) into linear form by expressing the variables as logarithms. This step is required because equation (7) is nonlinear, and nonlinear equations are difficult to estimate directly. The resulting log-linear version of equation (7) is written as

$$\ln X = a_0 + a_1 (\ln M - \ln M^O) + a_2 (\ln Y^O - \ln Y) + a_3 (\ln i - \ln i^O) \qquad (8)$$

where ln stands for the logarithm of the attached variable and the a's are coefficients to be estimated from the statistical data. Note that according to equation (7) the a priori expected values of the coefficients attached to the money and income variables are unity whereas the coefficient attached to the interest rate variables should lie between zero and unity, consistent with previous empirical estimates of the interest elasticity of demand for money.

Equation (8) was estimated for quarterly United States/United Kingdom and United States/Italy data for the period 1973 I to 1977 II. The money supply variable used for each country was M_1. The income variables used were real gross national product for the United States and real gross domestic product for the United Kingdom and Italy, respectively. As for the interest rate variables, the treasury bill rate was used for each country in the United States/United Kingdom equation and the rate on medium-term government bonds was used for each country in the United States/Italy equation.

The results are shown in Table 9.1.

In general the empirical results are consistent with the theoretical model. According to the estimated equations, fully 94 percent of the variation of both the dollar/pound and dollar/lira exchange rates are explained by variations in the money stock, real income, and interest rate variables. In both cases the coefficients on the explanatory variables have the expected positive signs. All coefficients are statistically significant at the .01 level except for those on the United States/Italy income and interest rate variables. Moreover, the coefficient on United States/Italy money stock variable is close to its expected (theoretical) value of unity, as is the coefficient on the United States/United Kingdom income variable. The interest rate coefficients in both equations are also consistent with previous empirical estimates of the interest elasticity of demand for money.[2] These results are perhaps better than one might expect considering the extreme simplicity of the model, the degree to which floating rates are managed instead of free, the limited number of observations, and the fact that short-run data are used to test a long-run equilibrium model.

In sum, the equations reported above provide at least modest empirical support for the theoretical model developed earlier in the article. One should not make too much of these results, however. Just as one swallow does not make a summer, two regression equations do not prove a theory. In particular, equation (8) may not fit the data well for other countries and other time periods. In fact, an attempt was made to test the equation against recent data for Canada, Japan, and Germany, as well as for data pertaining to the United Kingdom during the early 1920s when that country was off the gold standard. For the first three countries, the equation performed poorly. For the United Kingdom from 1920 to 1924, however, it was at least partially successful. As shown in Table 9.2, the equation performed adequately except for the coefficient on the income variable, which bears the wrong sign. This of course may be due to the unreliability of United Kingdom income data for that period rather than to shortcomings inherent in the model.* Nevertheless, the fact that the equation does

---

*Since quarterly national income figures are not available for this period, the Federal Reserve's Index of Industrial Production was used as a proxy for U.S. real income. No such official index is available for the United Kingdom. Therefore a quarterly industrial production index constructed in 1927 by Rowe[3] was used as a proxy for U.K. real income. However, the reliability of this index is open to question.

TABLE 9.1

Regression Results for US/UK and US/Italy Exchange Rates (Quarterly Data: 1973 I to 1977 II)

Dollar/pound exchange rate

$$\ln X = 3.47 + .55(\ln M_{US} - \ln M_{IT}) + 1.39(\ln Y_{UK} - \ln Y_{US}) + .22(\ln i_{US} - \ln i_{UK})$$
$$(3.84)^o \qquad\qquad (4.00)^o \qquad\qquad\qquad (3.47)^o$$

$$R^2 = .94 \quad DW = 1.63^a$$

Dollar/lira exchange rate

$$\ln X = -4.05 + .89(\ln M_{US} - \ln M_{IT}) + .58(\ln Y_{IT} - \ln Y_{US}) + .13(\ln i_{US} - \ln i_{UK})$$
$$(4.98)^o \qquad\qquad (1.56) \qquad\qquad\qquad (1.85)$$

$$R^2 = .95 \quad DW = 1.03^a$$

aThe reported Durbin-Watson statistics are in the inconclusive region in testing for serial correlation. Correcting for first-order serial correlation using the Cochrane-Orcutt method did not significantly alter the results.

Note: Omicron indicates statistical significance at the 1 percent level of confidence. t-statistics are given in parentheses beneath the estimated coefficients.

Source: Compiled by the author with data from *International Financial Statistics* (Washington, D.C.: International Monetary Fund).

TABLE 9.2

Regression Results for US/UK Exchange Rates
(Quarterly Data: 1920 I - 1924 IV)

Dollar/pound exchange rate

$$\ln X = -.17 + .55(\ln M_{US} - \ln M_{UK}) - .16(\ln Y_{UK} - \ln Y_{US})$$
$$(4.48)^o \qquad\qquad\qquad (-1.55)$$

$$+ .10(\ln i_{US} - \ln i_{UK})$$
$$(2.77)^o$$

$$R^2 = .76 \quad DW = 1.31$$

Note: Omicron indicates statistical significance at the 5 percent level of confidence. t-statistics are given in parentheses beneath the estimated coefficients.
Source: Compiled by the author with data from *International Financial Statistics* (Washington, D.C.: International Monetary Fund).

not work well for all countries is reason to interpret the results reported here with caution.

PROBLEMS IN TESTING THE MODEL

In closing this article, it may be appropriate to consider why the data did not exactly fit the model like a glove. Regarding this question, at least three likely explanations come to mind. First, the model assumes that exchange rates are permitted to float freely while in fact governments still intervene in foreign exchange markets from time to time in order to achieved a managed float. This suggests that there may be some reverse causality running from exchange rates to money, at least in the short run. In brief, the model may not be a completely accurate description of existing exchange rate regimes.

Second, quarterly data may not be suitable for testing what is essentially a model of long-run equilibrium. Quarterly data are short-run data. As such they may be dominated by transitory dynamic adjustment phenomena that are absent in long-run static equilibrium. Annual (or longer) data are more appropriate for testing an equation that is based on assumptions of purchasing power parity, interest rate parity, monetary equilibrium, real income exogeneity, and undirectional causality between money and exchange rates—all propositions about long-run equilibrium. Unfortunately, the post-Bretton Woods era of floating rates is only five years old, and the number of annual observations is insufficient to test these propositions. Even the number of quarterly observations is distressingly low.

An alternative solution would be to augment the model with additional equations and variables to represent dynamic adjustment processes. While this might permit the specification of short-run influences affecting the exchange rate, it would unduly complicate the model, contrary to the objective of keeping it simple. Note, however, that this latter feature may constitute a third reason for the model's failure to conform exactly to the data, that is, the model may be far too simple to capture all the influences on the exchange rate. This does not necessarily mean that the model is conceptually unsound. The underlying theory may be correct even though its empirical form is inadequate to fit the facts. Thus the model can be faulted on the grounds that its empirical money demand equations are too simple, that it lacks dynamic adjustment mechanisms, and that it arbitrarily constrains the elasticity coefficients to be the same for each country. These considerations should be kept in mind when interpreting the results of the regression analysis.

SUMMARY

This article has developed and estimated a simple model of exchange rate determination. The model states that exchange rate movements are determined by shifts in relative money stocks, relative real incomes, and relative inflationary expectations as manifested in relative interest rate movements. Although the model receives some empirical support from post-1972 data for the dollar/pound and dollar/lira exchange rates, it does not perform well when applied to data for other countries and other time periods. One is therefore advised to take an agnostic attitude regarding the validity of the model until all returns are in. In short, additional experience with floating exchange rates, together with the application of empirical techniques of greater sophistication than those employed here, will be necessary to establish conclusively the validity or invalidity of the model.

NOTES

1. Variants of the model have been employed by a number of analysts to explain recent exchange rate movements. See in particular John F. O. Bilson, "The Monetary Approach to the Exchange Rate: Some Empirical Evidence," Mimeographed, 1976; John F. O. Bilson, "Rational Expectations and the Exchange Rate," Mimeographed, 1976. See also Jacob Frenkel, "A Monetary Approach to the Exchange Rate: Doctrinal Aspects and Empirical Evidence," *Scandinavian Journal of Economics* 78, no. 2 (1976): 200-24; and Bluford H. Putnam and John R. Woodbury, "Exchange Rate Stability and Monetary Policy: A Case Study," Federal Reserve Bank of New York, Mimeographed, 1976. For a survey of much of the relevant work see Peter Isard, "The Process of Exchange Rate Determination: A Survey of Important Models and Major Issues," Federal Reserve Board, International Finance Division Discussion Paper No. 101 (January 1977): 56–60; and Stephen P. Magee "The Empirical Evidence on the Monetary Approach to the Balance of Payments and Exchange Rates," *American Economic Review Papers and Proceedings* 66 (May 1976): 163-70.

2. See John T. Boorman, "The Evidence on the Demand for Money: Theoretical Formulations and Empirical Results," in *Current Issues in Monetary Theory and Policy*, ed. Thomas M. Havrilesky and John T. Boorman (Arlington Heights, Ill.: AHM, 1976). Boorman reports that recent empirical studies of the demand for money suggest an interest elasticity of about -0.2 for short-term rates, quite close to the estimates appearing in Table 9.1.

3. J. W. F. Rowe, "An Index of Industrial Production," *Economic Journal* 37 (June 1927): 186.

Thomas M. Humphrey

10

THE MONETARY APPROACH TO EXCHANGE RATES: ITS HISTORICAL EVOLUTION AND ROLE IN POLICY DEBATES

One of the oldest debates in economics is that between the monetary and balance of payments approaches to the determination of exchange rates in a flexible exchange rate regime. The monetary approach attributes exchange rate movements largely to actual and anticipated changes in relative money stocks. It stresses a channel of causation running from money to domestic prices to the exchange rate. By contrast, the balance of payments approach holds that autonomous nonmonetary factors affecting individual items in the balance of payments are to blame.* It stresses a causal channel running from real factors through the balance of payments to the exchange rate and thence to domestic prices and sometimes further to the money supply. Both views underlie current discussions of the weakness of the dollar—the monetary approach holding excessive U. S. money growth to blame while the balance of payments view sees excessive oil imports and the sluggish foreign demand for U. S. exports as the culprits. Although the difference between these two rival approaches is fairly well understood, what is not so fully appreciated is that the current debate between them is largely a repetition of earlier disputes going back more than 200 years.

The purpose of this study is to trace the emergence and development of the monetary approach in three of these early controversies, namely the Swedish bullionist controversy of the 1750s, the English bullionist controversy of the

---

*The balance of payments approach is not to be confused with the so-called monetary approach to the balance of payments (MABOP), which is the monetary approach applied to a regime of fixed or pegged exchange rates.

early nineteenth century, and the German inflation controversy during and immediately following World War I.[1] These debates are crucial to the evolution of the monetary approach in two respects. First, they establish the analytical foundations of the monetary approach. These foundations consist of a quantity theory relationship linking money to prices, a purchasing power parity relationship linking prices to the exchange rate, and an expectations theory specifying how anticipations of future money stocks are formed and how they influence the exchange rate. Second, the earlier debates are the origin of current monetarist policy prescriptions for strengthening the dollar. These prescriptions call for the gradual deceleration of the growth rate of the money supply to eliminate the excess supply of dollars alleged to be the basic cause of the fall of the internal and external value of the dollar.

THE SWEDISH BULLIONIST CONTROVERSY (1755-65)

One of the earliest debates in which the monetary approach played a leading role was the Swedish bullionist controversy of the mid-1700s.[2] The events precipitating the debate were as follows. In 1745, Sweden shifted from a metallic monetary system with fixed exchange rates to an inconvertible paper system with flexible exchange rates. The suspension of convertibility was followed by a steady rise in the prices of commodities and foreign exchange. A debate then arose between the two main political parties of the time—known as the Hats and Caps—over the cause of these price increases.

The Hat Political Party

The Hats advanced the balance of payments theory, blaming both the external and the internal depreciation of the Swedish mark on Sweden's adverse trade balance. Specifically, they held that the adverse trade balance had produced a depreciating exchange, that exchange depreciation had rendered imported goods more expensive, and that the rise in import prices had spread to the rest of the economy, thereby raising the general level of prices. Here is an early example of the tendency of balance of payments theorists to attribute both domestic inflation and exchange rate depreciation to external nonmonetary shocks and to assert a chain of causation running from the exchange rate to prices, rather than vice versa as in the monetary approach. Consistent with their balance of payments view, the Hats prescribed export promotion and import restriction schemes as remedies for inflation and exchange rate depreciation. Nothing was said about money.

The Cap Party

The opposition Cap party emphatically rejected the Hat's balance of payments theory and instead pointed to the importance of the monetary factor. They blamed both domestic inflation and the external depreciation of the Swedish mark on the Riksbank's overissue of banknotes following the suspension of convertibility. They favored a policy of monetary contraction to roll back prices and the exchange rate to preinflation levels.

The Caps also adhered to an evil-speculator theory of exchange rate movements. This conspiracy theory is no part of the monetary approach. For that reason the Caps cannot be considered as fullfledged advocates of the monetary approach.

Pehr Niclas Christiernin

One participant who did articulate the monetary view was Pehr Niclas Christiernin, an academic economist at the University of Uppsala, who advanced a quantity theory explanation of the transmission mechanism linking money with the exchange rate. In his *Lectures on the High Price of Foreign Exchange in Sweden* (1761),[3] Christiernin maintained that the chief cause of currency depreciation was an over issue of banknotes by the Riksbank and that causation flowed from money to spending to all prices including the prices of commodities and foreign exchange. He saw monetary expansion as stimulating demand. Part of the demand pressure falls on domestic commodity markets raising prices there. The rest spills over into the current account of the balance of payments in the form of increased demand for imports. The resulting import deficit then puts upward pressure on the exchange rate, which consequently rises to restore equilibrium in the current account. Clearly, money-induced changes in total spending constitute the driving force in Christiernin's version of the transmission mechanism, running from money to the exchange rate. This component has been a hallmark of the monetary approach ever since.

As for policy recommendations, Christiernin was opposed to the Caps' plan to restore the exchange rate to its original preinflation level via contraction of the note issue. His opposition stemmed from his belief that prices adjusted sluggishly in response to deflationary pressure, so that the monetary contraction required to restore the exchanges to parity would bring painful declines in output and employment rather than the desired price decreases. For this reason he recommended stabilizing the exchange rate at a level established during the inflation level. Unfortunately, his advice was ignored and the Caps enacted a deflationary policy that resulted in the very drop in output and employment that he had predicted.

THE ENGLISH BULLIONIST CONTROVERSY (1797–1819)

The monetary and balance of payments theories clashed again in the famous controversy over the cause of the fall of the British pound following the Bank of England's suspension of the convertibility of banknotes into gold during the Napoleonic wars.[4] As in the earlier Swedish controversy, one side blamed currency depreciation on the central bank's overissue of notes while the other side blamed it on an adverse balance of payments. This time, however, the proponents of the monetary and the balance of payments views were known as the bullionists and the antibullionists, respectively.

The bullionists did more than any group before or since to develop and clarify the monetary view. The so-called strict bullionists crystallized the theory in rigorous form and the moderate bullionists refined and extended it. The strict bullionists included William Boyd, David Ricardo, and John Wheatley, while the moderate bullionists included William Blake, Francis Horner, William Huskisson, and, above all, Henry Thornton.

The Strict Bullionists: Ricardo and Wheatley

The strict bullionists made several major contributions to the monetary approach. They were the first to specify both the quantity theory and purchasing power parity links in the transmission mechanism connecting money and the exchange rate. In addition, they stated the monetary approach in its most rigid and uncompromising form, asserting that, under conditions of inconvertibility, where money cannot drain out into foreign trade, the exchange rate varies in exact proportion with changes in the money supply. They arrived at this latter conclusion via the following route.

First they assumed that under inconvertibility domestic prices (P) vary in strict proportion with the quantity of money in circulation (M). This of course is the rigid version of the quantity theory, which may be expressed as

$$P = kM \tag{1}$$

where k is a constant equal to the ratio of the circulation velocity of money to real output, both treated as constants by the strict bullionists.

Second, they maintained that under inconvertibility the exchange rate (E) moves in proportion to the ratio of domestic to foreign prices (P/P^0). First enunciated by Wheatley in 1803, this proposition is the famous purchasing power parity doctrine, so christened by Gustav Cassel, who rediscovered it more than 100 years later in 1918. The Wheatley-Ricardo-Cassel purchasing power parity condition may be written as

$$E = P/P^0 \tag{2}$$

implying that external currency valuations derive from their real internal values and that the general price level or the purchasing power of money is everywhere the same when converted into a common unit at the equilibrium rate of exchange.

Third, they assumed that the foreign price component (P^O) of the purchasing power parity ratio was a constant equal to the given world bullion price of commodities, so that exchange rate movements reflected corresponding movements in domestic paper money prices only. Given this assumption, the exchange rate is a good proxy for domestic prices and may be expressed as

$$E = P \tag{2$'$}$$

assuming the constant foreign price level is "normalized" and set equal to unity.*

Finally, they substituted the exchange rate proxy for the price variable in the quantity theory relationship, obtaining the result

$$E = kM \tag{3}$$

which states that the exchange rate varies in exact proportion with the money supply. On this basis they were able to conclude that a rise in the exchange rate above its gold parity constituted both proof and measure of overissue of inconvertible currency. In other words, if the exchange rate stood 5 percent above its gold parity, then this was prima facie evidence that the note issue was 5 percent above what it would have been under convertibility. This was most clearly stated by Ricardo:

> If a country used paper money not exchangeable for specie, and, therefore, not regulated by any fixed standard, the exchanges in that country might deviate from par *in the same proportion* as its money might be multiplied beyond that quantity which would have been allotted to it by general commerce, if . . . the precious metals had been used.[5]

Wheatley extended the analysis to the case where both countries are on an inconvertible paper standard. He simply substituted quantity theory relationships for both the domestic and foreign price variables in equation (2). This gave him the result that the exchange rate varies in proportion with relative money supplies, that is

$$E = kM/k^O M^O = K(M/M^O) \tag{4}$$

---

*Due to the unavailability of reliable general price indexes, the classical economists also used the paper money price of bullion as an empirical proxy for the commodity price level. Accordingly, they interpreted a rise in the market price of gold above its mint price as both a sign and a measure of the fall of the internal purchasing power of money.

where K is the ratio of the constants k and k^0. Wheatley stated this result when he declared that "the course of exchange is the exclusive criterion [of] how far the currency of one [country] is increased beyond the currency of another."[6]

Another contribution of the strict bullionists was their assertion that exchange rate movements are purely a monetary phenomenon. They rejected the antibullionist argument that real disturbances to the balance of payments—such as harvest failures, wartime disruption of trade, and military expenditures abroad—were responsible for the fall of the paper pound during the Napoleonic wars. Regarding supply shocks and foreign remittances, they denied that such factors could influence exchange rates even in the short run. Their position was that the slightest real pressure on the exchange rate would, by making British goods cheaper to foreigners, result in an instantaneous expansion of exports sufficient to eliminate the pressure. In their view, an adverse exchange was solely and completely the result of an excess issue of currency. Ricardo even went so far as to argue that even if foreign transfers and domestic crop failures *did* affect the exchanges by reducing real income and hence the demand for money, the cause of exchange depreciation is still an excess stock of money, albeit one arising from a reduction of money demand rather than an expansion of money supply. Ricardo's point was simply that real factors could affect the exchange rate only through shifts in money demand not offset by corresponding shifts in money supply. In such cases the latter was to blame for exchange rate movements. The notion that all factors affecting the exchange rate must do so through monetary channels, that is, through the demand for or supply of money, is of course central to the modern monetary approach.

Finally, the strict bullionists prescribed monetary restraint as the *only* cure for a depreciating currency. They held that a rise in the price of foreign exchange constituted an infallible sign that the currency was in excess and must be contracted. Ricardo even defined an excess issue in terms of exchange depreciation, thus implying a single unique correct money stock, namely one associated with the exchange being at its former gold standard parity.[7]

The Moderate Bullionists: Blake and Thornton

The moderate bullionists modified the strict bullionists' analysis in three respects. First, they pointed out that it applies to long-run equilibrium situations but not necessarily to the short run. Second, while acknowledging that long-run (persistent) exchange depreciation stemmed solely from note overissue, they were willing to admit that real shocks could affect the exchanges in the short run. Their position is best exemplified by William Blake's distinction between the Real and the Nominal exchange.[8] According to Blake, the real exchange or real barter terms of trade R are determined by nonmonetary factors—crop failures, unilateral transfers, structural changes in trade, and the like—that affect the balance of payments. The nominal exchange N, however, reflects the relative purchasing powers of different currencies as determined by their relative supplies (M/M^o). Blake's analysis can be summarized by the equation

$$E = RN \tag{5}$$

which expresses the actual exchange rate as the product of its real and nominal components, both of which contribute to exchange rate movements in the short run. Blake maintained, however, that in the long run the real exchange (R) is self-correcting (that is, returns to its original level) and that only the nominal exchange (N) can remain permanently depressed. Therefore, persistent exchange depreciation is a sure sign of an excess issue of currency.

The third modification was made by Henry Thornton, whose analysis of the money-price-exchange rate nexus was much more subtle and sophisticated than that of the strict bullionists. In particular, he argued that interest rates and the velocity of money enter the nexus, that velocity is extremely variable in the short run owing to shifts in business confidence, and that this variability invalidates the rigid money-price-exchange rate linkage postulated by the extreme bullionists.[9] In terms of equation (3) he argued that k is a variable determined by the interest rate (i) and the state of business confidence (c). That is,

$$k = k(i, c) \tag{6}$$

Since k varies in the short run, the exchange rate and money do not exhibit exactly equiproportional movements. A given change in the money stock affects k as well as the exchange rate. In the long run, however, k is a constant and the equiproportionality proposition holds.

The Antibullionists

Except for an expectations mechanism, the bullionists had assembled and integrated all the elements of the monetary theory of exchange rate determination. Compared to this accomplishment, the contributions of the antibullionists appear quite meager indeed. They attributed exchange depreciation and domestic inflation solely to real factors—crop failures, overseas military expenditures, and the like—operating through the balance of payments. They correctly asserted that the exchange rate is determined by the supply and demand for foreign exchange arising from external transactions. But they fail to see that an important factor influencing supply and demand might be relative price levels, as determined by relative money stocks. In fact, they rejected all monetary explanations, claiming that banknote expansion could not affect the exchanges in the slightest. They thought the price of foreign exchange could rise indefinitely without indicating the existence of an excess note issue. As for policy recommendations, they urged curtailment of imports and overseas expenditures to improve the balance of payments and to strengthen the pound. They doubted that any conceivable reduction in the banknote issue could restore the exchanges to parity.

Their main analytical tool was the real bills doctrine, which they employed in an unsuccessful attempt to refute the charge that the Bank of England had overissued the currency. The real bills doctrine states that money can never be issued to excess as long as it is tied to bills of exchange arising from real transactions in goods and services. Henry Thornton, however, exposed the fallacy of this doctrine when he pointed out that rising prices would require an ever-growing volume of bills to finance the same level of real transactions. In this manner inflation would justify the monetary expansion necessary to sustain it and the real bills criterion would not effectively limit the quantity of money in existence. Thornton's demonstration of the invalidity of the real bills doctrine constituted a victory for the bullionists and for the monetary approach to the exchange rate. The victory, however, was not definitive. For when the debate erupted again in World War I, the balance of payments approach was the dominant view.

THE GERMAN INFLATION CONTROVERSY (1918-23)

The debate reopened in 1918 when Gustav Cassel used his purchasing power parity doctrine, together with the quantity theory to attack the official balance of payments explanation of the wartime fall of the German mark. Whereas the policymakers blamed the currency depreciation on real disturbances to the balance of payments—for example, obstructions to German shipping, wartime disruption of trade, and the like—Cassel blamed it on excessive monetary expansion in Germany as compared to that of her trading partners.

Cassel's Critique of the Balance of Payments Approach

Cassel's criticism of the balance of payments theory was virtually the same as that of his strict bullionist counterparts, Wheatley and Ricardo. Like them, he argued that the exchange rate is automatically self-correcting in response to real shocks to the balance of payments. Therefore the theory is incapable of accounting for persistent exchange rate depreciation.

Regarding the operation of the self-correcting mechanism, he noted that when balance of payments disturbances push the external value of a currency below its internal value, the currency becomes undervalued on the foreign exchanges, that is, its domestic purchasing power is greater than that indicated by the exchange rate. Such undervaluation, he held, will immediately invoke forces returning the exchange rate to equilbrium. For as soon as a country's currency becomes undervalued relative to its purchasing power parity, foreigners will find it profitable to purchase the currency for use in procuring goods from that country. The resulting increased demand for the currency will bid its price back to the level of purchasing power parity. In short, deviations of the exchange rate from purchasing power parity generate corrective alterations in the trade balance that eliminate the deviations. Both the balance of payments and the exchange rate return swiftly to equilibrium. Thus, contrary to the balance of payments view, external nonmonetary shocks have no lasting impact on the exchange rate.[10] It follows that any persistent depreciation must be due to excessive monetary growth that raises domestic prices and thereby alters the purchasing power parity or equilibrium exchange rate itself. In this connection he repeated Ricardo's dictum that an excess supply of money, whether stemming from a rise in money supply or stemming from a fall in money demand, is always and everywhere the cause of exchange rate movements.

Cassel also criticized the proposition that exchange depreciation causes domestic inflation rather than vice versa. He acknowledged that currency depreciations relative to purchasing power parity produce import price increases. But he denied that these import price increases could be transmitted to general prices provided the money stock and hence total spending were held in check. He maintained that, given monetary stability, the rise in the particular prices of imported commodities would be offset by compensating reductions in other prices, leaving the general price level unchanged. In short, he denied that, as proponents of the balance of payments approach contended, causation ran from the exchange rate to domestic prices.[11]

Hyperinflation and the Reverse Causality Argument

Despite Cassel's forceful and vigorous attack, the debate did not go into high gear until the postwar hyperinflation episode of the early 1920s.[12] During this episode the price of foreign exchange rose to fantastic multiples of its prewar level and everybody wanted to know why. Advocates of the monetary approach, including Cassel and his followers, pointed to the explosive growth of the money supply as the obvious answer. But proponents of balance of payments approach dismissed the monetary factor and instead attributed exchange depreciation to the adverse balance of payments caused by the burden of reparations payments combined with Germany's alleged "fixed need for imports" and "absolute inability to export." In their view money had nothing to do with the fall of the mark. On the contrary, they claimed that causation ran from the exchange rate to money rather than vice versa. They specified the following causal order of events: depreciating exchanges, rising import prices, rising domestic prices, consequent budget deficits, and increased demand for money requiring an accommodative increase in the money supply.

Regarding the increase in the money supply, they contended that the exchange-induced rise in prices created a need for money on the part of business and government, that it was the Reichsbank's duty to meet this need, and that it could do so without affecting prices.* Far from seeing currency expansion as the source of inflation, they argued that it was the solution to the acute shortage of money caused by skyrocketing prices. Here is the familiar argument that the central bank must accommodate supply-shock inflation in order to prevent a disastrous contraction of the real (price-deflated) money stock. German proponents of the balance of payments view, however, pushed this argument to ridiculous extremes. In 1923, when the Reichsbank was already issuing currency in denominations as high as 100 trillion marks, Havenstein, the president of the Reichsbank, expressed hope that the installation of new high speed currency printing presses would help overcome the money shortage. Citing the real bills doctrine, he refused to believe that the Reichsbank had overissued the currency. He also flatly denied that the Reichsbank's discount rate of 90 percent was too low although the market rate on short term loans was an astronomical 7,300 percent per year.[13]

Characteristics of the Balance of Payments School

It is instructive at this point to identify the chief characteristics of the German balance of payments school if only because some of these characteristics survive in vestigial form in popular discussions of the fall of the dollar. First, members of the school tended to adhere to superficial supply-and-demand explanations of the exchange rate. Some merely asserted that the exchange rate is determined by supply and demand without saying what influences supply and demand. Others specified certain autonomous real factors affecting the balance of payments as the underlying determinants of foreign exchange supply and demand. None recognized that relative price levels and/or relative money stocks might also play a role. These variables were effectively excluded from the balance of payments school's list of exchange rate determinants.

The school's second characteristic was its tendency to identify exchange depreciation with one or two items in the balance of payments. In particular, members singled out raw material imports as the culprit, just as some analysts currently blame petroleum imports. Third, they tended to treat the items in the

---

*Balance of payments theorists placed the blame for government deficits financed by new money issues squarely on inflation rather than on the actions of the policy authorities. Inflation, they said, caused government expenditures, which were largely fixed in real terms and thus rose in step with prices, to rise faster than revenues, which were fixed in nominal terms in the short run and thus adjusted sluggishly to inflation. The result was an inflation-induced deficit that had to be financed by money growth. The authorities had nothing to do with the deficit. The monetary school rejected this argument on the grounds that the government possessed the power to reduce its real expenditures and, moreover, that the authorities had deliberately engaged in deficit spending for several years before the hyperinflation, thus establishing the monetary preconditions essential to that episode.

balance of payments as predetermined and independent, when in fact they are interdependent variables determined by prices and the exchange rate. For example, they asserted that Germany's import requirements were irreducible regardless of price and that her exports were likewise fixed. They then extended this reasoning to the other accounts of the balance of payments . Fourth, they denied the operation of a balance of payments adjustment mechanism. This denial followed from their assumption that both the balance of payments and the exchange rate are exogenously determined by factors that are independent of money, prices, and the exchange rate itself. This assumption permitted no equilibrating feedback effects from the exchange rate to the balance of payments. M. J. Bonn, a prominent balance of payments theorist, expressed the point as follows.[14] Suppose, he said, that import contraction is impossible given Germany's dependence on imported raw materials and foodstuffs. Likewise export expansion is impossible because of tariff barriers and economic depression abroad. Now assume a disturbance that produces a deficit in Germany's trade balance, thereby causing an exchange rate depreciation of the mark relative to its purchasing power parity equilibrium. According to Cassel and his school, the depreciation, by lowering the foreign currency price of German goods and raising the mark price of foreign goods, should spur exports and check imports, thereby restoring equilibrium in the trade balance. But these price-induced readjustments in trade are impossible when imports and exports are independent of exchange rate changes. In such a case, an adverse trade balance may persist in the face of an undervalued currency, contrary to the conclusion of the monetary school. Finally, the fifth characteristic of the German balance of payments school was its categorical rejection of the proposition that money influences prices and the exchange rate. As previously mentioned, this antimonetarist view was implicit in the school's reverse causation, money shortage, and real bills doctrines.

The Monetary School's Critique

Members of the monetary school had little trouble exposing the fallacies in these views. They noted that supply and demand constitute only the *proximate* determinants of the exchange rate, that the *ultimate* determinants are the factors underlying supply and demand themselves, and that these factors include the relative levels determined by relative money stocks. They pointed out that the components of the balance of payments are variables, not constants, that they are determined simultaneously by prices and the exchange rate, and that exchange rate movements reflect primarily monetary pressure on the entire balance of payments, rather than nonmonetary disturbances to particular accounts. Regarding the reparations account, they noted that the depreciation of the mark was not caused by these payments themselves but rather by the inflationary way they were financed, that is, by fresh issues of paper money. As for

Germany's alleged need for a fixed physical quantity of imports regardless of prices, they argued that needs are not imcompressible and that even the import demand for absolute necessities possesses some price elasticity. Moreover, they pointed out that exports too are responsive to changes in relative prices and that the exchange rate mechanism would therefore tend to equilibrate exports and imports were it not continually frustrated by inflation. They maintained that had domestic prices stopped rising, a further depreciation of the mark, by making German goods cheaper to foreigners and foreign goods dearer to Germans, would have stimulated exports and restrained imports until new equilibrium was reached. In their view, it was only the rise in domestic prices consequent upon the increase in the money supply that prevented the expansion of exports and the contraction of imports. Otherwise current account equilibrium would have been restored by the exchange-induce shift in relative prices of exports and imports.

Most important, advocates of the monetary approach argued convincingly that exchange depreciation originated in excessive money growth and that the monetary authorities could have stopped the depreciation had they been willing to exercise control over the money stock. In short, they showed that the price of foreign exchange could not have risen indefinitely unless sustained by inflationary money growth. Had the latter ceased, the exchange rate would have stabilized.

The Expectations Element

The German inflation controversy contributed the last of the three major elements to the monetary approach. The English bullionist writers had already established the quantity theory and purchasing power parity elements. All that remained was the statement and development of the expectations channel, linking anticipations of future money supplies with the current exchange rate. This step was taken during the hyperinflation debate when the monetary school sought to explain why the dollar/mark exchange rate actually rose faster than the German money supply. According to the strict quantity theory and purchasing power parity hypotheses, the two variables should rise at roughly the same rate. Their failure to do so was taken by the balance of payments school as constituting evidence of the invalidity of the monetary approach. Advocates of the monetary approach, however, rescued it from this criticism by explaining the exchange rate/money growth disparity in terms of market expectations. In a nutshell, they contended that in disequilibrium, the exchange rate is influenced by the expected future exchange rate (that is *anticipated* purchasing power parity), which depends on prospective price levels, governed by expected money stocks. Howard Ellis, in his *German Monetary Theory 1905-1933* (1934),[15] cites several economists, notably Gustav Cassel, Walter Eucken, Fritz Machlup, Ludwig von Mises, Melchior Palyi, A. C. Pigou, and Dennis Robertson, who claimed that exchange rate movements reflected anticipated increases in the money stock, and argued that the external value of the mark varied in proportion to the expected future quantity of money rather than to the actual current quantity. In sum, observers watching the money supply accelerate month after month came to expect future money growth to exceed present money growth; these expectations caused the exchange rate to outpace the money supply.

Similar explanations were advanced to account for disparities between the rate of domestic price inflation and the rate of currency depreciation in Germany. Eucken, Machlup, and von Mises argued that the exchange rate embodies inflationary expectations and that exchange rate movements parallel movements in expected future prices, not actual current prices. For this reason, they claimed, the exchange rate may deviate from the purchasing power parity computed from current price levels. Cassel perhaps put the matter most clearly when he wrote:

> A depreciation of currency is often merely an expression for discounting an expected fall in the currency's internal purchasing power. The world sees that the process of inflation is constantly going on, and that the condition of State finances, for instance, is rendering a continuance of the depreciation of money probable. The internal valuation of the currency will, then, generally show a tendency to anticipate events, so to speak, and becomes more an expression of the internal value the currency is expected to possess in a few months, or perhaps in a year's time.[16]

As this passage suggests, members of the monetary school explained not only how expectations affect the exchange rate, but also how expectations themselves are determined. In essence, they said that people base their exchange rate expectations on observations of the behavior of the policy authorities, especially the latter's monetary and fiscal response to large budgetary commitments like reparations payments. These observations yield information about the authorities' policy strategy, and people use this information in predicting future policy actions affecting the exchange rate. As Dennis Robertson put it in his famous textbook *Money* (1922), "the actual rate of exchange is largely governed by the *expected* behavior of the country's monetary authority. . . . "[17] In the case of Germany, the authorities were already demonstrating a pronounced tendency to finance reparations payments with budget deficits and excessive monetary growth. People expected this policy to continue and these expectations were embodied in the exchange rate.*

---

*Expectations were not the only factor cited by the monetary school as causing the exchange rate to lead prices and money. Another was currency substitution, that is, the substitution of stable dollars for unstable marks in German residents' transactions and asset money balances.

CONCLUSION

This study has surveyed the development of the monetary approach to the exchange rate in three historical controversies with the rival balance of payments approach. The study offers some support for Sir J. R. Hicks's argument that monetary theory, unlike other branches of economic theory, tends to be influenced by historical events and episodes, notably severe monetary disturbances and institutional change that alter the character of the monetary system.[18] In the case of the monetary theory of the exchange rate, at least, Hick's argument seems validated. For, as discussed above, the main elements of the monetary approach emerged from controversies triggered by currency, price, and exchange rate upheavals following the suspension of metallic parities. Specifically, the study argues that the monetary approach originated in the Swedish bullionist controversy of the 1750s, that its quantity theory and purchasing power parity components were thoroughly established during the English bullionist controversy of the early 1800s, and that the expectations component was added during the German inflation debate of the early 1920s. Thus all the elements of the modern monetary approach were firmly in place by the mid-1920s.

NOTES

1. For another treatment of the role of the monetary and the balance of payments approaches in these debates see John Myhrman, "Experiences of Flexible Exchange Rates in Earlier Periods:Theories, Evidence, and a New View," *Scandinavian Journal of Economics* 78, no. 2 (1976): 169–96.

2. On what follows, see Robert V. Eagly, *The Swedish Bullionist Controversy* (Philadelphia: American Philosophical Society, 1971).

3. Pehr Niclas Christiernin, *Lectures on the High Price of Foreign Exchange in Sweden, 1761.*

4. On the English bullionist controversy see Denis P. O'Brien, *The Classical Economists* (London: Oxford University Press, 1975), pp. 147–53; and Jacob Viner, *Studies in the Theory of International Trade* (New York: Augustus Kelley, 1965), pp.119–70.

5. David Ricardo, *The Principles of Political Economy and Taxation* (London: J. M. Dent and Sons, 1917), p.151, quoted in James W. Angell, *The Theory of International Prices* (New York: Augustus Kelley, 1965), p. 69, n. 3.

6. John Wheatley, *Remarks on Currency and Commerce* (London: Burton, 1803), p. 207, quoted in Angell, op. cit., p. 52.

7. Regarding the policy implications of the Ricardian definition of excess, see O'Brien, op. cit., p. 148.

8. On Blake, see O'Brien, op. cit., pp. 150–51.

9. Thornton's contribution is discussed in O'Brien, op. cit., pp. 149–50.

10. Gustav Cassel, *Money and Foreign Exchange After 1914* (New York: Macmillan, 1922), pp. 149, 164–65.

11. Ibid., pp. 145, 167–168.

12. What follows relies heavily on Ellis's classic survey of the German inflation controversy. See Howard S. Ellis, *German Monetary Theory, 1905-1933* (Cambridge: Harvard University Press, 1934), Chapters 12–16.

13. Leland Yeager, *International Monetary Relations: Theory, History, and Policy,* 2nd ed. (New York: Harper and Row, 1976), p.314.

14. Bonn's views are discussed in Paul Einzig, *The History of Foreign Exchange* (London: Macmillian, 1962), pp. 271–72, and Ellis, op. cit., pp. 248–52.

15. Ellis, op. cit.

16. Cassel, op. cit., pp. 149–50.

17. Dennis Robertson, *Money* (London: Cambridge University Press, 1922), p. 133.

18. Sir John Hicks, *Critical Essays in Monetary Theory* (London: Oxford University Press, 1967), pp. 156–58.

Bluford H. Putnam

11

MONETARY POLICY, INTEREST RATE TARGETS, AND FOREIGN EXCHANGE MARKETS

The interaction between domestic monetary policy and foreign exchange markets has been analyzed only from the perspective of an exogenous change in the money supply causing a change in the exchange rate of the domestic currency vis-a-vis the currency of a specific trading partner. Studies such as those by Jacob Frenkel or by Thomas Humphrey and Thomas Lawler always assume that monetary policy is conducted through changes in the money supply, and conclude, all other things being equal, that increases in the domestic money supply *cause* a depreciation of the domestic currency in terms of foreign currency.[1] Monetary policy, however, is not always conducted through the money supply, particularly in the very short run. For instance, U.S. monetary authorities set targets for the growth of monetary aggregates, but day-to-day and week-to-week policy actions follow federal funds interest rate targets. Furthermore, the central bank discount rate is a very active policy tool for many foreign countries.

If central banks conduct monetary policy in the short run with respect to interest rate targets, then variations in the money supply may be caused by events in the foreign exchange markets, particularly changes in expectations of future exchange rates. The argument is developed in the following manner. Should some exogenous event result in reformulation by exchange market participants of their expectations of future exchange rates, the market forward exchange rate would not reflect the change in expectations, because central banks in adhering to an interest rate target are implicitly fixing the interest rate differential between assets denominated in different currencies. International arbitrage will ensure that the market forward exchange premium (or discount) will correspond quite closely to this interest rate differential. Since the forward exchange rate does not shift when exchange rate expectations do, market participants have an incentive to increase their liabilities in the depreciating currency and increase their assets in the appreciating currency. This change in the demand for certain monies will be validated by the central banks if they maintain constant interest rates. Substantial shifts in exchange market expectations, then, result in swings in the money supply, and, as will be apparent later, changes in the spot exchange rate, too.

The study is organized as follows. First, a behavioral relationship is postulated between the demand for domestic liabilities and differences between forward exchange rates and expected future spot rate. Second, the supply of domestic liabilities is specified by assuming that central banks set interest rate targets and meet them. Third, with the supply and demand for domestic liabilities already specified, an examination of the foreign exchange markets completes the model, determining the equilibrium spot and forward exchange rates and the domestic money stock. In the final section, the conclusions of the model are reviewed with particular attention to their policy implications.

DEMAND FOR DOMESTIC LIABILITIES

In well-integrated international capital markets the mechanism known as international arbitrage serves to guarantee that the interest rate differential between comparable assets denominated in different currencies will be nearly equal to the forward exchange premium or discount. This arbitrage assumption can be expressed as follows:

$$(F - S)/S = rd - rf \tag{1}$$

where F = the forward exchange rate (in terms of foreign currency units per unit of domestic currency)

S = the spot exchange rate

rf = the interest rate on foreign assets

rd = the interest rate on domestic assets, and

F, rf, and rd are all quoted with respect to the same time dimension (maturity date)

If international markets function efficiently they will reflect some aggregate forecast of the future spot exchange rate and provide an expected return to the bearer of the foreign exchange risk.[2] In equation form,

$$F = F^e + v \tag{2}$$

where F^e = market forecast of the future spot exchange rate, and

v = expected return due to foreign exchange risk

For the purposes of this analysis, the expected return due to foreign exchange risk, v, will be set equal to zero. While this need not be the actual case, recognition of a risk return is unnecessary in the context of this study.

Equation (2) is essentially an equilibrium condition. For if market expectations of the future spot exchange rate do not equal the forward rate ($F \neq F^e$), then some market participants have an incentive to borrow in one currency and lend in another. Such portfolio optimizing actions would cause movements in the spot exchange rate, the domestic interest rate, and the foreign interest rate until equilibrium values were reached.

Expanding on the adjustment process noted in the preceding paragraph, one can focus initially on the demand for liabilities denominated in the currency that is expected to depreciate in excess of that predicted by the forward exchange rate.* In equation form,

$$\Delta DL^d = f(\Delta K, (F - F^e)/S) \tag{3}$$

where DL^d = the demand for liabilities denominated in the domestic currency
 K = all other demand factors, which are held constant in this analysis, and
$$\partial((F - F^e)/S)/\partial DL^d > 0$$

Whenever actual market expectations differ from the market forward exchange rate, there will be a demand for liabilities in the currency that is expected to depreciate in excess of the forward rate. This demand for liabilities in the currency expected to depreciate is matched by a demand for assets denominated in the currency whose expected appreciation is greater than that indicated by the forward rate.

Without being specific concerning the type of liabilities being discussed here, a reasonable assumption is that a stable set of these liabilities will be included in standard definitions of the money supply for any particular country. Thus, money supply changes should be in the same direction and of similar relative magnitude as changes in domestic liabilities. Explicitly,

$$\Delta M^d = h(\Delta DL^d) \tag{4}$$

where M^d = the domestic money supply demanded.

---

*The text assumes that the domestic currency is also the currency expected to depreciate with respect to some particular foreign currency. To analyze the reverse case, in which the domestic currency is expected to appreciate, one need only substitute "domestic" for "foreign" and vice versa.

CENTRAL BANK POLICY

Turning now to the supply of domestic liabilities, the key factors are the private banking system and the monetary authorities or central bank. The private banking system is assumed to supply credit (liabilities) to demanders for some market-determined spread over the interest rate at which the banking system can acquire the funds to lend. The interest rate on the "wholesale" funds market is determined by the central bank. That is, the central bank conducts monetary policy by fixing some interest rate, and in this case, the interest rate fixed by the authorities is the interest rate on the interbank market for loanable funds.*

The assumption that the central bank fixes the interest rate is expressed as follows:

$$rd = \overline{rd} \tag{5}$$

The banking system is essentially passive and loans funds at some spread over the wholesale interest rate. This spread is set equal to zero for simplicity, and it can be noted that the supply of domestic liabilities will expand to meet demand. That is,

$$\Delta DL^s = \Delta DL^d \tag{6}$$

And, correspondingly, the money supply will also accommodate the quantity of money demanded:

$$\Delta M^s = \Delta M^d \tag{7}$$

By assuming that the banking system is passive, that is, that banks do not change their net position, the analysis focuses directly on the monetary policy of the central bank. And, instead of assuming that the money supply is the control variable, the analysis assumes that the interest rate is the control variable. While this assumption is certainly anything but new to large segments of the economic literature, it provides a different focus in the context of recent developments in international monetary theory, such as the monetary approach to the balance of payments literature. In any case, the assumption has two implications. First, the supply of money will accommodate changes in the demand for money, as the

---

*For the United States, this compares to the federal funds markets.

Editor's Note: This study was written originally in 1972, and was the product of research done while the author was a graduate student at the University of Chicago. Minor revisions were made in the process of editing this manuscript to make it suitable for publication in this volume.

central bank acts to fix prices in the bond market. Secondly, in terms of practical applications, the model is essentially short-run in nature, for two reasons. First, many central banks use interest rate targets only for short-run policy and adjust these targets over the course of a year to control certain monetary aggregates, and second, to preserve the simplicity of the argument this model does not allow for feedback effects of central bank policy into any real variables affecting money demand (see equation (3), the constant K).

On the foreign side, the foreign central bank acts to fix the interest rate on foreign assets, hence,

$$\text{rf} = \overline{\text{rf}} \tag{8}$$

Coupling these two central bank policy assumptions, equations (5) and (8), with the international arbitrage assumption, equation (1), the market forward exchange premium or discount is determined. This implies that the demand for domestic liabilities is also determined, equation (3), given the spot exchange rate and expectations of its change.

FOREIGN EXCHANGE PRESSURES

At this stage, the process generating an expansion in domestic liabilities is clear, but the model contains no mechanism for reaching any kind of equilibrium. Looking at the demand for domestic liabilities, equation (3), one can identify three areas for further attention. First, nothing has yet been said about the determination of the expectations of the future spot rate (F^e). Second, the spot exchange rate is also undetermined. And third, the counterpart of the demand for domestic liabilities, that is, the demand for foreign assets, has yet to be discussed.

With respect to the formation of expectations concerning the future spot exchange rate, only the briefest of specifications is required here. Thus,

$$F^e = \overline{F^e} \tag{9}$$

which is to say that expectations of the future spot rate are determined outside the scope of this model.*

The determination of the spot exchange rate and the discussion of the demand for foreign assets are intertwined. In this analysis, the change in demand

---

*A more sophisticated specification might include feedback effects from changes in the money supply to changes in expectations of the future spot exchange rate. While such a specification would affect the dynamic path of this model, it would not alter the basic conclusion concerning the direction of change in the money supply and spot exchange rates that are derived later in this section.

for domestic liabilities is desired specifically for use in acquiring foreign assets. That is, when the forward exchange rate does not equal the markets' expectations of the future spot rate ($F \neq F^e$), there is a demand for domestic liabilities to finance the purchase of foreign assets. The price of foreign assets is fixed in foreign currency terms by the foreign central bank's policy of fixing the interest rate (equation 8). But the price of a foreign asset is not fixed in terms of the domestic currency price. In other words, the exchange rate can change in response to pressures in the foreign exchange market, and changes in the spot exchange rate effectively change the domestic value of any foreign assets bought or sold. With respect to the foreign exchange market, the demand for foreign currency is, thus, established as directly related to the change in demand for domestic liabilities. Or simply,

$$FC^d = g(K, 1/S, \Delta DL) \tag{10}$$

where FC = foreign currency, and

$$\partial \Delta DL / \partial FC^d > 0$$

K = other relevant factors (held constant here), and

$$\partial (1/S)/\partial FC^d < 0$$

The supply function is held constant with respect to changes in the demand for domestic liabilities since there is no incentive to borrow funds denominated in the appreciating currency. So,

$$FC^s = h(K, 1/S) \tag{11}$$

where $\partial 1/S/\partial FC^s > 0$

and for equilibrium,

$$FC^s = FC^d \tag{12}$$

Equations (10), (11), and (12) describing foreign exchange market pressures indicate that the domestic currency will depreciate whenever there is a demand for domestic liabilities due to differences between the forward exchange rate and the market's expectations of the future spot rate.

The spot rate can be solved from equations (10), (11), and (12), plus the interest arbitrage assumption, (1), and the central bank policy assumptions, (5) and (8), given the expected future spot rate, (9). That is, the spot exchange rate will adjust to equilibrate the actual forward exchange rate and the expected future spot rate.* Substituting the interest rates from (5) and (8) into the arbitrage equation (1) yields the actual market forward discount, $(F - S)/S$. When equilibrium conditions (2), (7), and (12) hold, $F = F^e$, and $(F - S)/S = (F^e - S)/S$. This uniquely determines the spot exchange rate.

A numerical example is useful. Initially, the domestic and foreign central banks set interest rates such that the forward exchange discount is 5 percent on the domestic currency. Also, the spot exchange rate is 100 units of foreign currency per unit of domestic currency. Starting from equilibrium in which $F = F^e$, the forward exchange rate can be calculated from equation (1) and equals 95 units of foreign currency per unit of domestic currency. Now, some exogenous event causes market expectations of the future spot rate to change such that now $F^e = 92$. Since $(F - F^e)/S$ is now a positive value, the demand for domestic liabilities and foreign assets increases. This results in the spot foreign exchange markets in a depreciation of the domestic currency until $F = F^e$. With no change in the forward discount of 5 percent, since central banks have not altered interest rates, the spot exchange rate must fall to 96.84 foreign currency units per unit of domestic currency. At this rate, $F = F^e = 92$. The actual increase in domestic liabilities and the money supply is determined by the elasticity of the demand for foreign assets in terms of the domestic currency price, but the direction is clear. Furthermore, the greater the difference between the forward exchange rate and the expected future spot rate, the greater the equilibrating increase in the money supply.

CONCLUSION

Essentially, the model indicates that the decision by central banks to fix interest rates (stabilize local bond prices) implies a willingness to accept deviations in both the money supply and the spot exchange rate when exogenous events occur that shift foreign exchange expectations. Central banks often fail to admit this and on occasion can be observed intervening in exchange markets to resist downward spot exchange rate changes and intervening in the domestic bond markets to resist upward interest rate movements. One of these operations is doomed to failure.

NOTES

1. See Jacob Frenkel, "A Monetary Approach to the Exchange Rate: Doctrinal Aspects and Empirical Evidence," in *Flexible Exchange Rates and Stabilization Policy*, ed. Jan Herin, Assar Linbeck, and Johan Myhrma (Boulder, Colo.: Westview Press, 1977),

---

*This was alluded to earlier in the discussion of equation (2).

pp. 68–92; Thomas M. Humphrey and Thomas A. Lawler, "Factors Determining Exchange Rates: A Simple Model and Empirical Tests," Federal Reserve Bank of Richmond *Economic Review* (May-June 1977): 10–15 also reprinted in this volume (Chapter 9).

2. While this risk premium is not critical to this study, it is worth noting that it does exist. For related papers, see B. Cornell, "Spot Rates, Forward Rates and Exchange Market Efficiency," *Journal of Financial Economics* 5 (1977): 55–65; F. Modigliani and R. Sutch, "Innovations in Interest Rate Policy," *American Economic Review* 56 (May 1966): 178–97; and J. R. Hicks. *Value and Capital* (Oxford: Clarendon Press, 1946), p. 138 in particular.

Marc A. Miles

12

CURRENCY SUBSTITUTION:
PERSPECTIVE, IMPLICATIONS,
AND EMPIRICAL EVIDENCE

One possible way of differentiating between the neo-"Keynesian" and "monetarist" approaches to macroeconomic theory is by the degree of substitution that is assumed to exist among the various commodities in the models. For example, in the neo-Keynesian model, while the financial commodities money and bonds are assumed to be close subsitutes, neither is assumed to be a close substitute for goods. Thus changes in the demand or supply for money or bonds is not believed to have a direct effect on the demand for goods. Instead, changes in, for example, the net supply of money will have direct effect on the net demand for its only close substitute, bonds, causing an adjustment in the interest rate. It is only through the indirect avenue of "interest rate mechanics" that moentary policy can affect the net demand for goods. Because the nonsubstitutability between goods and money or bonds insulates the goods market from the direct effects of the other two markets, neo-Keynesians often feel justified in analyzing the behavior ot the goods market in isolation.

Monetarists, however, extend the degree of substitution among the three commodities. More specifically, within the Walrasian framework money and bonds are assumed to be direct substitutes not only for each other, but for goods as well. The direct substitution implies that changes in the net supply of money can be translated into changes in the net demand for goods and bonds. The monetarist model of national income therefore requires the simultaneous consideration of the money, goods, and bond markets.

But while the monetarist model does extend the range of substitutable commodities, it still imposes its own strict limitations on substitution within the model. In particular it strictly limits the range of assets that can be considered substitutes for money. The motivation for limiting the range of substitutable money assets is quite obvious. Since money is assumed a direct substitute for goods and therefore capable of influencing the level of aggregate demand, if "money" consists of a limited range of money assets, then by controlling the quantity of these assets the central bank can directly influence aggregate demand. The traditional monetarist position has therefore been that the relevant definition of "money" is something approximating the M1 or M2 definition of money, that any other money asset is a poor substitute.

This narrow concept of money has not gone unchallenged. During the 1960s, an empirical debate ensued over the degree to which other money assets, such as deposits at mutual savings banks or savings and loan associations, are close substitutes for demand and time deposits.[1] The debate set the stage for the challenge of some basic assumptions of the monetarist model. If the proper range of money assets is much broader than that hypothesized by the monetarists, and if the central bank has only limited control over the quantity of some of the additional assets, then even if the quantity of money does influence the level of aggregate demand, the central bank's ability to influence aggregate demand is diminished.

Yet the debate over the proper definition of money concentrated only on possible domestic assets that serve the functions of money. A basic assumption was maintained that individuals and businesses demand only money assets denominated in the domestic currency. However, with the resurgence of the monetary approach to the balance of payments, monetarists realized that it is possible for foreign money assets to serve as substitutes for domestic money assets. In particular, under fixed exchange rates, where the central bank fixes the value of domestic currency in terms of foreign currency, an individual can increase his quantity of money balances by demanding either foreign or domestic currency. For example, if the money demand of a Frenchman rises, he has two alternative sources of satisfying that increased demand. First, the central bank of France may increase the French money supply. The Frenchman may then obtain some of the increased money supply from the government by exchanging a bond (an open market operation) or by expanding a good or service (work for the government). Alternatively, the Frenchman can increase his money holdings by exchanging the same bond or the same good or service with a foreigner. In return he will receive currency. But since under the fixed rate system the central bank of France is fixing the value of francs in terms of foreign currency, the Frenchman can convert the foreign currency directly into francs. He presents the foreign currency at the central bank, which in turn is obliged to give him francs.

Thus, under a fixed rate system, foreign money assets are direct substitutes for domestic money assets. Increased ownership of either allows the individual to increase the quantity of domestic money he holds.

The source of the substitution in this fixed exchange rate case can be traced to the role of the central bank. Under the fixed rate system the central bank assures that domestic and foreign money assets are perfect substitutes on the supply side. By fixing the exchange rate, the central bank assures that domestic money will always exchange at a fixed ratio with foreign money. An individual is therefore indifferent to whether he is in domestic or in foreign money, because when he holds foreign money he knows he holds an equivalent amount of domestic money. This substitution on the supply side in turn invalidates one of the basic monetarist assumptions. There is no longer a limited range of money assets clearly under the control of the central bank. Domestic residents can alter the domestic money supply by exchanging money and goods and bonds with foreigners. Since the domestic central bank cannot control the quantity of money in foreign countries, the central bank cannot control the quantity of money available to domestic residents. Even if changes in the quantity of money influence aggregate demand, the central bank is unable to exploit this influence because it is unable to control changes in the quantity of money. Should the central bank of France increase the money supply once and for all, the domestic money supply would initially exceed domestic money demand. But Frenchmen can alleviate the excess supply of money by purchasing goods and bonds from abroad. Money would therefore immediately flow out through the balance of payments, offsetting the central bank's actions. Furthermore, the domestic balance of payments deficit must be matched by a balance of payments surplus abroad. Thus money supplies abroad simultaneously increase. The substitutability of international monies therefore makes the money supply of countries interdependent, and a common rate of inflation is observed among countries.

THE MONETARIST ARGUMENT
FOR FLEXIBLE EXCHANGE RATES

Because the fixed rate system creates substitutability among money assets and produces policy-offsetting flows of money and common rates of inflation among countries, the fixed rate system is undesirable from a closed economy monetarist perspective. The money supply instead should be used to help achieve internal stability. Therefore, the monetarists argue that a preferable system is one that stops these money flows and again limits "money" to a narrow range of assets. In other words, the substitution of money on the supply side must be eliminated.

The proposed solution for the interdependence of money supplies is perfectly flexible exchange rates. Under a perfectly flexible exchange rate system, the central bank does not intervene in the foreign exchange market to guarantee the value of domestic money. This lack of intervention has two assumed benefits. First, because the central bank no longer guarantees the value of the domestic money, foreign money is no longer a perfect substitute for domestic money on the supply side. Holding a given quantity of foreign currency no longer means holding a specific quantity of domestic currency. There is no central bank willing to convert domestic and foreign currency at some constant rate. Second, because the central banks no longer intervene in the foreign exchange market, the net movements of money among countries is assumed to be zero. There are no longer leakages in the money supply, and all the effects of domestic monetary policy are felt within the domestic country. Milton Friedman writes:

> In effect, flexible exchange rates are a means of combining interdependence among countries through trade with a maximum of internal monetary independence; they are a means of permitting each country to seek for monetary stability according to its own lights, without either imposing its mistakes on its neighbors or having their mistakes imposed on it.[2]

Flexible rates, then, are assumed to provide countries with the monetary independence that permits the implementation of the monetary policies proposed by the closed economy monetarists.

THE IMPLICATION OF CURRENCY SUBSTITUTION FOR FLEXIBLE RATES

The monetarist argument for flexible rates is logically consistent as far as it goes. However, the argument concentrates exclusively on the nonsubstitution of monies on the supply side. The issue of substitution on the demand side is not explicitly addressed. Instead, the argument implicitly assumes that monies denominated in different currencies are also nonsubstitutes in demand, that is, that Frenchmen hold only francs and Germans only Deutsche marks. It is assumed that no foreign money is held by domestic transactors for either transactions or speculative or precautionary purposes. In other words, by eliminating substitution of monies on the supply side and assuming away substitution in demand, the relevant definition of money is reduced to a range of assets that can be influenced by the central bank to produce the domestic monetary effects that are a necessary condition for monetarist theories to be relevant.

However, in the context of the existing international economic environment, the assumption of zero demand substitution is quite dubious. For example, multinational corporations have strong incentives to diversify the currency composition of their cash balances in order. to facilitate their endeavors in various countries. Even individuals and businesses that are clearly domiciled in a particular country often have transactions or precautionary or even speculative motives for diversifying the currency composition of their money holdings. Anyone who consistently makes purchases from foreign countries has at least the same transactions motives for demanding domestic currency balances. Importers and exporters, businessmen who travel abroad, tourists, and residents of border areas all have incentives to diversify their money balances. By holding foreign money, the transactions costs of their foreign purchases are reduced.

With a significant subset of a country's citizens and businesses maintaining diversified currency portfolios, the conclusion that monies are nonsubstitutes on the demand side is no longer valid. Now changes in the relative costs of holding monies of different denominations will cause changes in the relative amounts of these monies held within individual portfolios. The portfolio readjustments in turn produce net flows of money among countries even under perfectly flexible exchange rates. Such net flows are impossible under the monetarist argument because Frenchmen hold only francs. Hence, there cannot be a net flow of dollars or Deutsche marks into France unless the French central bank is willing to convert these foreign monies into francs. Under flexible rates the French central bank is no longer willing to perform such a conversion, so all the dollars must be returned to the United States where they are used, and all the Deutsche marks must be returned to Germany. There is no way for dollars to escape the United States, since no one in another country will hold them.

However, with substitution among currencies on the demand side, when dollars or Deutsche marks flow into France Frenchmen who are diversifying their currency portfolios may now demand them. Dollars can flow into France and remain there without any intervention by the French central bank. When the Federal Reserve increases the dollar money supply, the entire increase does not remain within the United States, with the price level in the United States adjusting to eliminate the excess supply of money balances; rather, some dollars can be redistributed through private markets to France. With currency substitution in demand, therefore, the effects of the Federal Reserve's monetary policy are again not internalized within the United States. The increased supply of dollars is dispersed throughout the world, raising money supplies abroad. The increased money supplies imply that price levels abroad will rise as well. Thus inflation is transmitted among countries without having to assume any government intervention in the foreign exchange market. Yet transmission of inflation is precisely the type of phenomenon against which flexible rates are assumed to insulate a country.

The degree to which inflation will be transmitted between two countries will of course be proportional to the degree of substitution between the corresponding monies. The limiting case is where two monies are perfect substitutes in demand. In that case there is the equivalent of one currency, just as when central banks make currencies perfect substitutes on the supply side by fixing exchange rates. In that case no distinction can be drawn between the two currencies. An increase in the nominal money supply in either country will increase the money balances used in both countries and cause the price level in each country to rise by precisely the same amount.

The issue of currency substitution therefore has important implications for the issue of the proper world monetary system. Should the world system emphasize independent country monetary control for internal stability? Alternatively, should the system emphasize cooperation and coordination at the expense of monetary independence? Currency substitution provides a good criterion for resolving this issue. For example, if the currencies of two countries are close substitutes in demand, then the monetary policies of these two countries cannot be independent. A world monetary system that emphasizes independent policies is therefore less than optimal in this situation. Instead, the two countries should be encouraged to coordinate their monetary policies as a bloc, rather than moving in separate directions. The greater the number of currencies that are close substitutes, the larger should be the bloc. The limiting case, of course, is the one in which all currencies are close substitutes. In that case the bloc becomes the whole world, and the countries should return to a fixed exchange rate system that encourages synchronization of monetary policies. The degree of substitution in demand between currencies therefore becomes an important empirical question.

EMPIRICAL MODELS OF CURRENCY SUBSTITUTION

There are at least two different methods for testing the presence of currency substitution. One method is to measure directly the degree of currency substitution. This method involves postulating a theoretical model of why some individuals in a country hold more than just domestic currency and how the relative quantities of the currencies held respond to changes in economic variables. A testable functional relationship is then derived from the theoretical model.

A second, less direct method is to compare the empirical relevance of a model that assumes currency substitution to one that does not. Both types of empirical models have appeared recently in the economic literature, and a summary of each is now presented.

A Direct Measurement of the Degree of Substitution

Individuals hold foreign currency money balances for the same reason that they hold domestic currency money balances: the money balances provide the individuals with monetary services or other types of benefits. These benefits of course are not costless. There is a specific interest rate or opportunity cost attached to holding money balances in each currency. Thus, given the relative efficiencies of domestic and foreign currency balances in producing the benefits, and the relative opportunity costs of obtaining the benefits, the individual will choose the relative amounts of foreign and domestic balances that maximize the amount of services he can obtain from a money portfolio of a given size. Equilibrium conditions require that the amount of benefits received for the last dollar's worth of domestic balances held be equal to the benefits received for an equivalent amount of foreign currency balances. A dollar's worth of balances is defined here as the sum of the additional balances held plus the cost of holding the balances. Thus, if the cost of holding a currency is 6 percent, a dollar's worth of balances involves purchasing only about 94 cents of additional balances. The remaining 6 cents is the cost of holding the additional balances.

With the relative quantities of money balances at equilibrium in this way, as long as the relative costs of holding the different balances or the desired size of the money portfolio do not change, the individual will not want to change the quantity held in either domestic or foreign balances. However, should the relative costs of holding the balances change, the desired ratio of balances will also change. Specifically, the individual will want to hold relatively less of the balances whose opportunity cost has risen and more of the balances whose opportunity cost has fallen. With a higher opportunity cost, the last dollar's worth of balances is now composed of fewer balances and more holding costs. Fewer services are therefore provided per dollar. Conversely, if opportunity costs fall there are more balances per dollar and thus more services per dollar. In order to return the money portfolio to equilibrium, one denomination of money will now be substituted for another.

The substitution process among currencies of different denominations can be described in terms of either cross-interest elasticities or the elasticity of substitution.[3] The cross-interest elasticities approach concentrates on the demand for money balances of a specific currency and how the demand varies as the opportunity cost of these balances or alternative balances changes.[4] A drawback of this approach is that it employs partial equilibrium analysis. An underlying assumption of an equation concentrating on the demand for only one type of money balance is that the quantity of other balances is constant or that there is no prevailing constraint on the total quantity of money balances held.

In contrast, the elasticity of substitution approach concentrates on the relative quantities of different money balances held within a limited overall quantity of balances.[5] The elasticity of substitution is defined as the percentage change in the relative holdings of different money balances with a one percent change in the relative opportunity costs. This approach recognizes that a rise in the relative quantity held of a particular denomination of money balances can be accomplished by either a rise in the absolute quantity of that denomination of balances or a fall in the absolute quantity of the other denominations of balances. Given a constant overall quantity of balances to be held, the substitution process should involve both quantity changes. The elasticity of substitution approach is therefore a general equilibrium approach because all quantities are permitted to change simultaneously within the overall constraint.

To date the only published estimate of the degree of substitution has been an estimate by Marc A. Miles[6] of the elasticity of substitution between Canadian and U.S. dollars in Canada. Real balances, denominated in terms of both U.S. and Canadian dollars from an individual's cash balance portfolio, are assumed to be combined in a constant elasticity of substitution (CES) production function for money services. Given the relative efficiencies of U.S. and Canadian dollars in producing money services (defined by the production function) and the relative opportunity costs of holding the two currencies (reflected in the asset constraint), the individual tries to maximize the production of money services. Maximizing the production function relative to the asset constraint yields the following functional form for the estimation:

$$\log(\frac{C\$}{US\$}) = a + \sigma \log(\frac{1 + i_{US}}{1 + i_{CAN}})$$

(1)

where   C\$ = Canadian dollars held

US\$ = U.S. dollars held

σ = elasticity of substitution between Canadian and U.S. dollars

i_{US}, i_{CAN} = opportunity costs of holding U.S. and Canadian dollars respectively.

The results of estimating the equation (1) over the period Q4/60-Q4/75 are

$$\log(C\$/US\$) = 2.56 + 5.43 \log(\frac{1 + i_{US}}{1 + i_{CAN}})$$
$$(18.0) \quad (2.59)$$

(2)

$\bar{R}^2 = 0.78$ $F(1,58) = 215.6$ RHO = 0.88   D.W. = 1.44

The estimated value of the elasticity of substitution is large at 5.4. It is significantly different from zero at the 99 percent level (two-tailed test), permitting the rejection of the hypothesis that foreign and domestic currencies are nonsubstitutes.

This equation is also estimated for three subperiods. For the purposes of this analysis it is fortunate that Canada has experienced periods of both fixed and floating rates. The values of the elasticities of substitution under the different exchange rate regimes can therefore be estimated. Two possible hypotheses concerning these values arise. One hypothesis states that the only reason the elasticity of substitution is large, as found for the period as a whole, is that for a significant subperiod the exchange rate of Canada was fixed. The Bank of Canada was willing during this subperiod to exchange Canadian dollars for U.S. dollars, and all that the elasticity of substitution measures is the substitution on the supply side during this subperiod. This hypothesis would be consistent with high values of elasticities of substitution during fixed rate periods and low values during floating rate periods.

The second hypothesis has just the opposite conclusion. It states that during periods of fixed rates the public does not have to substitute between currencies in private markets since the government is already making currencies perfect substitutes on the supply side. Alternatively, during floating rate periods the public will have to resort to performing all of its substitution through private markets. This hypothesis would be consistent with low or insignificant estimates of the elasticity of substitution during fixed rate periods, when the substitution mechanism is not needed, but large estimates during the floating rate periods.

Canada was on floating rates until May 2, 1962 and returned to floating rates on June 1, 1970. The subperiods examined are therefore Q4/60–Q2/62 (floating), Q3/62–Q2/70 (fixed), Q3/70–Q4/75 (floating). The results are presented in Table 12.1. The most striking difference among the subperiods is that in subperiods where the exchange rate was fixed, the estimated coefficient is smaller and insignificantly different from zero. In contrast, in both subperiods where the exchange rate was floating, the estimated values of σ are large and significantly different from zero at the 95 percent level (one-tailed test).

The results from analyzing the subperiods are therefore consistent with the second hypothesis and not the first. The large, significant elasticity of substitution for the period as a whole seems to be the result of substitution not during the fixed rate subperiod, but rather during the floating rate subperiods. The concept of substitution between U.S. and Canadian dollars by private Canadians appears to be statistically valid when the Canadian government is not performing that service for them. The results are even more impressive when one considers that the above data have not even included holdings of U.S. dollar-denominated Eurodollars, whose elasticity of substitution with respect to Canadian dollars could quite possibly be even higher.

Preliminary estimates for the elasticity of substitution in the United States between U.S. dollars and all foreign currency are very similar to the results for Canada.[7] The elasticity for the United States is in the range 3.0–5.0, depending on the definition of the U.S. money supply used in the analysis. Furthermore, the same pattern of values appears in the fixed versus flexible exchange rate periods. Under the Bretton Woods system, the estimated value of the elasticity of substitution is again insignificantly different from zero. However, as in the Canadian case, when the system of fixed rates is abandoned, the elasticity in the private market is estimated in the range of 3.0–5.0.

The preliminary results for the United States have three important implications. First, the similarity to the Canadian results indicates that the initial results for Canada are not a special case. Second, that there appears to be a significant degree of currency substitution in a major country like the United States indicates that the concept of currency substitution is important for explaining the behavior of international money markets. Third, given the apparent significant degree of substitution among major currencies, the current system of floating exchange rates, which emphasizes independent monetary policies among nations, is probably not the optimal international monetary system.

TABLE 12.1

Estimates of the Elasticity of Substitution During Subperiods of Fixed and Floating Exchange Rates

Subperiod	Exchange Rate Regime	Type of Equation	Constant Term	Elasticity of Substitution	$\bar{R}^2$	D.W.	F	Rho
Q4/60–Q2/62	Floating	OLSQ	2.78 (50.8)	12.8 (2.54)	0.48	1.66	6.47	
Q3/62–Q2/70	Fixed	CORC	2.31 (12.7)	2.66 (0.79)	0.78	1.41	107.4	0.9
Q3/70–Q4/75	Floating	CORC	2.79 (16.1)	5.78 (1.83)	0.79	1.27	74.0	0.8

Source: Compiled by the author with data from *International Financial Statistics* (Washington, D.C.: International Monetary Fund).

An Alternative Test for the Presence of Currency Substitution

A less direct but still plausible test of currency substitution is to measure whether the more aggregate empirical data are consistent with the hypothesis. Such a test has been performed by Paul Evans and Arthur Laffer.[8] Evans and Laffer focus their tests on the relationship among the excess demand for money in the domestic country, the excess demand for money in the foreign country, and the exchange rate. If currencies are perfect nonsubstitutes, then during periods where the exchange rate is not fixed, adjustments must occur through price rather than quantity changes. Changes in the exchange rate will be determined by changes in the excess demand for money in one country relative to that in another. If France increases its money supply, all other things being equal, then the supply of money will increase relative to demand in France, creating excess supply, a rise in the French price level, and a depreciation of the French franc. However, if currencies are perfect substitutes in demand, such price adjustments are unnecessary. If France increases its money supply, the excess supply can now be alleviated by francs flowing to, for example, Germany, and by an increase by the same percentage of the price level in both countries. The exchange rate will be unaffected.

The test used by Evans and Laffer is to differentiate between these two cases by observing whether the exchange rate responds to changes in relative excess supplies of money. The model tested is derived from three equations:
- the purchasing power parity relationship

$$ER_{i/j} = P_i/P_j \qquad (3)$$

where $ER_{i/j}$ is the number of units of Country i's currenty per unit of Country j's currency and P_i, P_j are the price levels in the two countries;
- a quantity theory equation for Country i

$$M_i V_i = P_i y_i \qquad (4)$$

where V_i is the income velocity of money and y_i is real income;
- a quantity theory equation for Country j

$$M_j V_j = P_j y_j . \qquad (5)$$

Solving equations (4) and (5) for the price levels and substituting into (3) yields

$$ER_{i/j} = \frac{V_i}{V_j} \cdot \frac{M_i}{M_j} \cdot \frac{y_j}{y_i} . \qquad (6)$$

Taking the logarithm of (6) and computing the period-to-period change yields the percentage change form

$$\%\Delta ER_{i/j} = b_0 \%\Delta(V_i/V_j) + b_1 \%\Delta M_i - b_2 \%\Delta M_j - b_3 \%\Delta y_i + b_4 \%\Delta y_j.$$
$$(7)$$

Equation (7) becomes the testable model. If currencies are perfect nonsubstitutes, then the exchange rate should be proportionately affected by a change in any of the right-hand variables. In other words, the estimated coefficients of b_0 to b_4 on each of the right-hand variables should be one in value. Conversely, if currencies are perfect substitutes, there should be no systematic relationship between the exchange rate and the right-hand variables. In other words, the estimated coefficients b_0 to b_4 should all be zero in value. So estimated values close to one are consistent with nonsubstitutability, and estimated values near zero are consistent with currency diversification.

Equation (7) is tested on monthly data from the period January 1968 through December 1975 for France, Germany, Italy, the United Kingdom, Canada, and Japan. The results are summarized in Table 12.2. Notice that the largest of the coefficients is only 0.38, which is far below one in value. All other coefficients are below 0.19 in value, some are even negative, and most are not significantly different from zero. The empirical results are again clearly more consistent with a world with a significant degree of currency substitution than a world where currencies are nonsubstitutes. So whether a direct or an indirect test is used, currency substitution appears to be a significant phenomenon for explaining the behavior of the international money markets.

SUMMARY AND CONCLUSIONS

This study has described how the concept of currency substitution is a logical extension of traditional monetary and financial theory. Rather than unrealistically constraining individuals and corporations to hold only the currency of the country in which they reside, the concept of currency substitution recognizes that economic units can potentially demand any currency in the world. The precise currencies and the relative quantities demanded will depend on both the relative efficiencies of different currencies in providing money services and their relative costs.

Empirical evidence of the existence of currency substitution is quite strong. For both Canada and the United States the estimated elasticity of substitution among currencies is quite high. Furthermore, the remarkable similarity of results in the two countries indicates that these results are probably not special cases.

In addition, the more aggregative tests on several additional countries indicate that the behavior of the exchange rate is more consistent with a world where currencies are close substitutes than with a world where currencies are nonsubstitutes.

These empirical results have profound theoretical implications. First of all, if major currencies are close substitutes, then traditional monetary theories that

TABLE 12.2

Testing the Exchange Rate Market for the Presence of Currency Substitution

Country	b_0	b_1	b_2	b_3	b_4	R^2	F	D.W.
Canada	.001 (.89)	-.002 (-.04)	.117 (.59)	-.000 (-.01)	.011 (.27)	.01	.1	1.61
France	.001 (.46)	.132 (1.10)	.149 (1.22)	.020 (1.38)	.082 (.82)	.04	1.0	1.78
Germany	.005 (1.75)	.149 (1.27)	.059 (.56)	.076 (1.55)	.032 (.25)	.04	1.0	1.56
Italy	-.001 (-.21)	.120 (1.73)	.190 (2.67)	-.008 (-.87)	-.074 (-1.14)	.09	2.2	1.97
Japan	.001 (.58)	-.027 (-.42)	-.001 (-.02)	-.002 (-.08)	.158 (2.23)	.06	1.4	1.86
United Kingdom	-.001 (-.26)	.383 (2.12)	.107 (.96)	.007 (.15)	.135 (1.19)	.11	1.3	1.56

Note: The "t" statistic for each coefficient appears below it in parentheses.
Source: Compiled by the author with data from *International Financial Statistics* (Washington, D.C.: International Monetary Fund).

assume all currencies to be nonsubstitutes do not realistically reflect the behavior of national or world money markets. The relevant money supply in the United States is not simply the number of U.S. dollars held. Instead, analysis of money demand and supply must incorporate foreign currencies held by Americans and dollars held by foreigners. Second, even perfectly flexible exchange rates no longer can guarantee monetary independence. While under perfectly flexible rates central banks do not permit net flows of money between countries, private markets now do. Third, the optimal system of international exchange rates is not one that emphasizes independent monetary policies. Instead, the various governments in the world should begin the process of developing an international system that promotes cooperation and coordination of monetary policies.

NOTES

1. For a good summary of this debate see Edgar L. Feige and Douglas K. Pearce, "The Substitutability of Money and Near-Monies: A Survey of the Time-Series Evidence," *Journal of Economic Literature* 15, 2 (June 1977): 439–69.

2. Milton Friedman, "The Case for Flexible Exchange Rates," in Milton Friedman, *Essays in Positive Economics* (Chicago: University of Chicago Press, 1953), p. 200.

3. The choice between the cross-elasticities approach and the elasticity of substitution approach for measuring the degree of substitution among currencies parallels the debate over the proper method of measuring the degree of substitution among domestic money assets. See Feige and Pearce, op. cit.

4. For a cross-interest elasticities approach to currency substitution, see, for example, Lance Girton and Don Roper, "Theory and Implications of Currency Substitution," Board of Governors of the Federal Reserve, *International Finance Discussion Papers*, No. 86, August 1976. For other studies of currency substitutions see Russell S. Boyer, "Currency Mobility and Balance of Payments Adjustment," this book, Chapter 13; and David T. King, Bluford H. Putnam, and D. Sykes Wilford, "A Currency Portfolio Approach to Exchange Rate Determination: Exchange Rate Stability and the Independence of Monetary Policy," this book, Chapter 14.

5. For an elasticity of substitution approach to currency substitution, see, for example, Marc A. Miles, "Currency Substitution, Flexible Exchange Rates, and Monetary Independence," *American Economic Review* 68 (June 1978): 428–36.

6. Ibid.

7. Marc A Miles, "Currency Substitution—The Case of the United States," Rutgers University, 1978.

8. Paul Evans and Arthur Laffer, "Demand Substitutability Across Currencies," University of Southern California, Mimeographed, 1977.

Russel S. Boyer

13

CURRENCY MOBILITY AND BALANCE OF PAYMENTS ADJUSTMENT

Most of the literature on balance of payments theory assumes that national currencies are held only by domestic residents.[1] The usual postulate is that citizens place any foreign exchange they accumulate through exports on the foreign exchange market in order to obtain domestic currency. This is in sharp contrast with the extensive analysis of financial capital mobility, in which foreigners can acquire interest-bearing assets from abroad, so that foreign assets are substitutable for domestic ones.[2] It is also at variance with the analysis of pure trade theory, in which foreign and domestic goods are often assumed to be perfect substitutes. This study attempts to ascertain some of the consequences of the relaxation of this restrictive assumption on currency mobility within the framework of the monetary approach to exchange rate determination.

Currency mobility, or trading in money, seems to be an important phenomenon in recent international financial dealings, as the extraordinary growth of the Eurodollar market in Canada, Europe and Japan demonstrates. In addition, one can surmise from Canadian data that foreign-currency holding was impor-

Editors Note: This study was written originally in 1972, and was the product of research done while the author was a graduate student at the University of Chicago. Minor revisions were made in the process of editing this manuscript to make it suitable for publication in this volume.

Earlier versions of this study were presented in workshops at the University of Western Ontario, at Purdue University, at the Federal Reserve System, Board of Governors, and in a session of the University of Western Ontario's conference on *International Monetary Problems*, April 1972. The author would like to thank R. A. Mundell, J. R. Melvin, and J. C. Leith for comments on a previous draft. They are, of course, not responsible for the views contained herein.

tant even before resident banks offered such deposits. This substitutability arises from asset demands and therefore does not depend on a particular exchange rate regime (as can be gathered from the continued growth of U.S. dollar holdings by residents of Canada since the decision to float).

This analysis is important because economists should attempt to fortify or dismiss the distinction central bankers have drawn between currency and capital markets: between currency mobility and capital mobility. The possibility of destabilizing speculation which has received substantial attention in the discussion of flexible exchange rate regimes, has not been discussed as seriously applicable to domestic bond or equity markets.[3] This study shows that, while capital mobility tends to stabilize international relations with fixed exchange rates, currency mobility causes instability in a world of flexible exchange rates, thus adding theoretical weight to the central bankers' distinction.

THE ADJUSTMENT PROCESS
WITHOUT CURRENCY MOBILITY

This section of the study develops a simple diagrammatic model of the balance of payments in order to describe the determination of the exchange rate in the monetary approach and to demonstrate the usual conclusions of international financial theory.[4] Throughout this section it is assumed that currencies are immobile (not substitutable), so that money of a particular denomination is held only by residents of the corresponding geographical currency area. The basic framework divides the world into two regions, A and B, of equal size and with different currencies. The totality of economic goods in the world is aggregated, for convenience, into these two currencies and all other things (AOT).* Currency is taken to be a financial asset without value in alternative uses, which provides some nonpecuniary service.

Equilibrium is attained in the world economy when excess demand in each market is equal to zero. By Walras' Law, when two of these markets clear, the third does as well. Therefore the analysis can concentrate upon only two market-clearing conditions; for simplicity, this study investigates the equilibrium conditions only in the two money markets. The model consists merely of the two demand functions for money equated to the supply of real balances:

$$\frac{M_i}{P_i} = \ell_i(y_i, \frac{M_i}{P_i}) \qquad\qquad \begin{array}{l} 0 < \ell_{i1} \\[2mm] 0 < \ell_{i2} < 1 \end{array} \qquad (1)$$

---

*This aggregation can be justified formally through the use of Hicks' composite good theorem.

where M_i, P_i, ℓ_i, and y_i are the nominal money supply, the money price of non-monetary items (AOT), the demand for real balances, and the level of real income, respectively, in each region, with i = A, B. Conspicuous for its absence from these functions is the rate of interest, measuring the opportunity cost of holding money. The reason is that this discussion deals only with problems for which this cost can be viewed as constant. Real balances are taken as arguments in these demand functions to represent the short-run wealth effects that such holdings have.[5] In order to ensure stability of the model, it is assumed that a unit increase in actual real balances increases the demand for them by less than a unit. This is shown in the constraints on ℓ_{i2}.

This model is represented diagrammatically in Figure 13.1. The values of real balances are measured along the axes, and excess demands for these monies are shown within the graph. In particular, along the E_i locus the excess demand for currency i is equal to zero. The extreme slopes of these loci, vertical and horizontal, indicate that the two currencies are not substitutable for each other, in the sense that the demand for either does not depend upon the supply of the other. To the right of E_A, there is excess supply of money A; to the left, there is excess demand. Similarly, above E_B, there is excess supply for that currency; below there is excess demand.

When there is excess supply of one currency, but an equal excess demand for the other, the third market is in equilibrium. The locus of points for which this is true is shown in Figure 13.1 as E_{AOT}. It must pass through point Q, since here two of the three markets clear; as a consequence, the third must clear as well. Furthermore, its negative slope is dictated by the fact that only in the southeast and northwest quadrants is there an excess demand for one currency and an excess supply of the other.

Prices in the two regions must be consistent with the exchange rate so that no arbitrage profits can be made by transacting in those goods that face no important trade barriers or transportation costs. Even in the case where non-traded goods exist, in the steady state prices satisfy relative purchasing power parity for the monetary experiments considered here. Thus, the exchange rate defined in the conventional way from the point of view of the A region (as the number of units of A currency required to purchase a unit of B currency) is equal to

$$\epsilon = \frac{P_A}{P_B} \qquad\qquad (2)$$

Figure 13.1 shows the determination of the real quantity of money held in the two currencies, under the assumption of zero substitutability between them. The method by which these real quantities are attained depends upon the exchange rate regime.

If the exchange regime is one of fixed exchange rates, then the authorities must supply whatever quantity of money is needed to keep the exchange rate at its par value. Thus, an excess demand for a particular currency is satisfied auto-

FIGURE 13.1

Currency Immobility

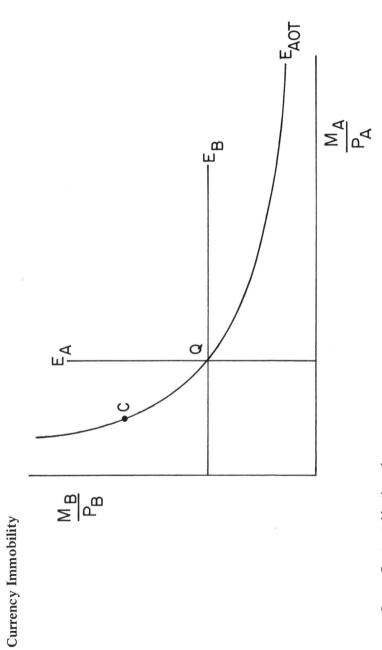

Source: Constructed by the author.

matically by an increase in its quantity as a consequence of the authorities' pegging operation. In this way the desired level of real balances is achieved through the appropriate adjustment of the quantity of nominal balances.

In contrast, if the authorities pursue a regime of flexible exchange rates, the quantities of the two monies are exogenous, since movements in prices and exchange rates do not alter the stance of financial policies. Under these circumstances, changes in the supplies of or demands for various monies cause alterations in this prices relative to other goods so as to re-equilibrate their markets. Desired real balances are attained under this exchange rate regime through the adjustment of these prices, rather than through the adjustment in quantities.

This figure has an interpretation also in terms of balance of payments analysis using a monetary approach. According to this view, the regions of excess demand for a particular money are the regions also of balance of payments surplus in an ex ante sense. The excess demand for money is satisfied through a surplus in the external sector. Similarly, deficits in the balance of payments, ex ante, exist for those points where there is an excess supply of money.

Whether these ex ante surpluses and deficits appear as imbalances in the balance of payments depends upon the exchange rate regime. Under flexible exchange rates, that there is no trade in money implies that the balance of payments ex post is zero. Instead prices and the exchange rate adjust to assure balance of payments equilibrium. In contrast, under fixed exchange rates, the surpluses and deficits ex ante are not eliminated by price movements, so that the balance of payments for each region can differ from zero.

To establish the mechanism behind this diagram, consider a situation in which the supply of money A is decreased by 10 percent; at the same time the supply of money B is increased by 10 percent. At unchanged prices, this shock puts the world economy at a point like C, where the market for all other things remains in equilibrium. The reason is that this experiment creates an excess demand for one currency and an equal excess supply of the other, leaving the state of excess demand for currency in total unchanged. However, there are distribution effects between the two regions.

The movement back to steady state, point Q, requires a decrease in real balances in economy B and an increase in real balances in economy A. In the case of fixed exchange rates, this is accomplished in the following way: The two economies trade money with each other, with the central banks acting as intermediaries altering the supplies of these currencies in the process of pegging the exchange rate. The balance of payments surplus of economy A is just equal to the deficit for B, so that the plans of agents in both countries are fulfilled. In this way, the economies move from point C to point Q over time, traversing along the E_{AOT} loci. For flexible rates, if prices can move rapidly, the readjustment is not a time-consuming process. The insufficient supply of A balances is eliminated through a fall in P_A; the excessive B balances cause inflation in B, which restores real balances to their desired levels. In this way, point Q is rapidly reattained.

THE WORLD ECONOMY WITH CURRENCY MOBILITY

Currency Mobility

The discussion so far has assumed that the world can be divided into two regions distinguished by their demands for different currencies. This was done to analyze the behavior of the balance of payments of regions, from both an ex ante and an ex post perspective. The purpose of this section is to eliminate these distribution effects, to permit citizens of any country to hold either currency; thus the concept of currency mobility can be modeled. In the absence of distribution effects, the important consideration for the determination of equilibrium is the excess supplies and demands for various assets in the world as a whole.

The analysis of the previous section is valid for such a model as long as the assumption that currencies have no substitutability is maintained. Under these circumstances, the fact that a particular currency is held worldwide does not alter the model except that now the concept of balance of payments must be applied to those agents holding a particular currency rather than to a grouping made according to geographical or political considerations. Now the polar slopes of E_A and E_B give evidence that the holdings of either currency do not affect the demand for the other, because of the assumption on demands for these currencies.

On an intuitive level, the meaning of substitutability between two currencies is quite clear. As financial assets, the relevant variable that, in the first instance, is crucial to determining the amount of each held is the rate of return on that asset as compared with other substitutable assets. For assets without pecuniary yield, their relative rate of return is just the rate of appreciation of one in terms of the other.

In this view, to say that the Canadian and U. S. dollars are perfect substitutes, or that either is a good substitute for pound sterling, means that none of these currencies is expected to change in value relative to any of the others. If this expectation were not held, then agents would accumulate the asset that was appreciating in value, while going short in market instruments denominated in the depreciating currency.

This analysis can be made more specific by widening it to include interest-bearing assets, with the assumption that capital mobility is perfect. In such a world, all expected real rates on interest-bearing assets are equated in accordance with the interest rate parity theorem. Therefore, differences in nominal rates of return must be associated with differences in inflation rates, and expected changes in exchange rates must be consistent with these. The population of currency substitutability forces changes in exchange rates to be zero, so that expected inflation rates must be equal. This implies that nominal rates of interest are the same when high capital mobility is combined with substantial currency mobility.

The argument so far has failed to mention the level of the exchange rates themselves, but, instead, considers the first derivative of exchange rates with respect to time. The reason for this is clear: Exchange rates themselves are irrelevant to the problem of currency substitution. Thus, the fact that U.S. and Canadian dollars are good substitutes implies nothing about which is more valuable. If individuals wish to hold a given quantity of real balances and are indifferent to whether they hold these real balances in Canadian or in U.S. dollars, for given expectations this indifference should be just as valid at an exchange rate of (C$/US$)1.08 as it is at (C$/US$).92. Clearly the fact that in one case the Canadian dollar is "cheaper" is not a valid reason for holding that currency. When a currency is less valuable relative to other currencies, it is less valuable relative to goods as well by purchasing power parity. Thus, more of it is needed to provide the same real balances.

Although it is true that exchange rates are not directly relevant to the question of currency substitution at a micro level, this analysis should model their role at a macro level. The reason for this is that the central concern here is to establish how currency substitution alters the process of exchange rate determination. In particular, this study is concerned with the nature of the equilibrium that exists for a world characterized by such substitution.

To focus attention on the determination of equilibrium exchange rates, it is postulated that expected changes in them are equal to zero. Thus, agents willingly hold nonzero quantities of currencies with different denominations, even when currencies are close substitutes.

When currencies are substitutes for each other, an increase in the real quantity held of one, all other things being equal, reduces the desired holdings of other currencies. There is a full offset only if the two currencies are perfect substitutes, since then agents are completely indifferent as to their holdings in real terms. With imperfect substitution, the offset is somewhat less. Thus a unit increase in real balances of a particular denomination causes less than a unit increase in desired real balances held in another denomination.*

This mechanism can be represented by modifying the equations in (1). Those equations now have the form:

$$\frac{M_A}{P_A} = \ell_A \left(y_A, \frac{M_A}{P_A}, \frac{M_B}{P_B} \right)$$

---

*Throughout this analysis it is assumed that demand for real balances has a wealth elasticity less than one with respect to both monies. In the case of perfect substitutes, the other-currency elasticity is equal to one minus the own-currency elasticity, so that an increase in money holdings of one form reduces demand for the other money by an equal amount.

and (3)

$$\frac{M_B}{P_B} = \ell_B (y_B, \frac{M_B}{P_B}, \frac{M_A}{P_A}).$$

where $0 \leqslant \ell_{i3} \leqslant 1 - \ell_{i2}$. Equations (1) are the special case of these specifications for which $\ell_{i3} = 0$. Under those circumstances, increases in real balances denominated in B have no influence on the demand for real A balances, and vice versa. However, in the present context $\ell_{i3} > 0$, and the higher the degree of substitutability the larger the value of this partial derivative.

The modification of Figure 13.1 caused by this substitution is shown in Figure 13.2. The vertical locus of points for which the market currency A clears was based on the assumption of zero substitutability, so that the demand for that currency was independent of holdings of other currencies. With nonzero substitution, desired holdings of this currency are negatively related to those of other currencies, since the two serve the same purpose. In this way, the E_A locus rotates about the steady-state equilibrium in a counterclockwise direction. A similar argument for currency B shows that it rotates clockwise. Thus both E_A and E_B rotate towards the E_{AOT} locus. That locus does not shift with the exogenous increase in substitution. The reason is that it is the degree of substitution between currencies only that is being investigated here rather than the degree of substitution between money and all other things.*

A Comparison with Mundell's Definition of Currency Mobility

Robert A. Mundell has considered the problem of currency mobility in a number of papers written during the late 1960s.[6] Indeed, Figures 13.1 and 13.2 are based largely upon the diagrammatic tools that he developed. These tools figure prominently in his later research but were presented earlier, when the concept of currency substitution was first mentioned.

The reader of that analysis will note the similarity between Mundell's diagrams and those presented here. Nonetheless, there is one striking difference between his framework and the present one. He finds that the loci E_A and E_B are positively rather than negatively sloped. This is disconcerting, since his model is trying to represent currency substitution in the same way as is this analysis. Mundell argues that E_A and E_B "have positive slopes ... if all currencies are gross substitutes. ..." For the case of two specific currencies, the reasoning is

---

*In order for E_{AOT} not to rotate, one must assume, in particular, that the influence of actual B-balances on desired A-balances equals the influence of actual A-balances on desired B-balances. In a linear model, E_{AOT} has a slope of -1 with this assumption.

FIGURE 13.2

Currency Mobility

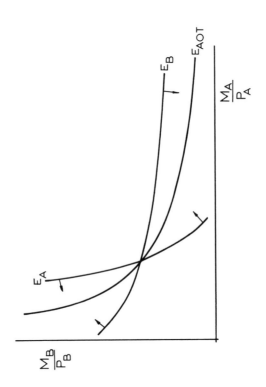

Source: Constructed by the author.

that "appreciation of the franc must be associated with appreciation of the pound to maintain equilibrium"[7] in each country's balance of payments.

It is clear that the Mundell definition of "gross substitutes" does not refer to a definition of the relationship between currencies so much as it refers to the substitutability in demand of the outputs of various economies. The reasoning is that if the domestic-currency price of exports is fixed, then the domestic-currency price of imports varies with the exchange rate. In this way the terms of trade for each country are tied to the value of the exchange rate.

Thus, Mundell's model must be seen as one describing substitutability among goods; this is inconsistent with the stated intention of modeling substitution among currencies. Furthermore, the Mundell analysis requires a good deal more structure to ensure that it is immune to the criticism that it is based on money illusion in the form of disregarding the effects of movements of the exchange rate on the levels of the real values of wages and profits. As the model stands, workers are apparently willing to take cuts in real incomes when they come in the form of devaluations, but may not be willing to take them when they occur through changes in domestic-currency wages.

It is of interest to note that Mundell's diagrammatic tools are applicable to the discussion of substitutability among interest-bearing assets when they are denominated in the same currency. This topic is considered next.

Substitutability of Bonds

It is important to distinguish between substitutability of assets denominated in the same currency and substitutability of those denominated in different currencies. In order to do this, consider two bonds that promise to pay one unit of currency per period indefinitely. Thus the price of these bonds is just equal to the inverse of their rate of return.

Assume initially that these two bonds, denoted again by A and B, are not substitutable for each other. Then a diagrammatic framework similar to that used in the previous section represents equilibrium in the economic system. Define the units of A and B bonds so that each has a fixed supply of one. Then the real quantity of each bond, equal to the unit supply multiplied by the price of the bond in terms of money, and divided by the exogenous unit price of goods in terms of money, is equal to the inverse of the rate of return on each bond. These real quantities are measured along the axes in Figure 13.3.

The E_{AOT} locus in Figure 13.3 has the same position and slope as it did in previous figures and serves a similar function here. Curves E_A and E_B, the loci of points for which there is zero excess demand for bonds A and B respectively, have their polar positions for the same reason as in sections above: the two financial assets are viewed as not substitutable for each other. Thus, for example, the E_A curve is completely vertical because the demand for A bonds depends positively upon its own rate of return, but is independent of the return on B bonds. This stringent assumption, of zero substitutability, must now be modified.

In relaxing this assumption, we employ the usual definition of substitutability among financial assets: a rise in the rate of return on either causes an excess supply of the other.[8] Thus, the demand functions for these assets are:

$$K_A^d = K_A^d \left(r_A , r_b \right)$$

$$K_B^d = K_B^d \left(r_B , r_A \right) \tag{4}$$

$$K_{i2}^d \leqslant 0 \leqslant K_{i1}^d , i = A, B.$$

As they become substitutes, K_{i2}^d becomes negative, becoming larger in absolute value without limit as substitutability increases.

The process of becoming substitutes of higher and higher degree can be represented as in Figure 13.3. Take A bonds to establish the diagrammatic consequences of this process. Zero excess demand for A bonds can be maintained (with a given nominal supply) if any rise in their rate of return is matched by a larger increase in the return on B bonds. Thus, E_A must have a positive slope, following the direction of rotation shown by the arrows in that figure. A similar argument shows that E_B rotates in a counterclockwise direction. That an increase in either rate of return must be more than matched by the increase in the other asset's return in order to keep each asset market cleared can be verified by the following argument: an equal increase in the two rates of return does not alter their relative rates, and therefore should not change portfolio balance decisions between the two bonds; rather it should create an excess demand for them both, and an excess supply for all other goods. This shows that E_A has a slope greater than one, while E_B has a slope less than one.

As these assets become closer substitutes for each other, the curves E_A and E_B rotate towards one another and away from E_{AOT}. Once again E_{AOT} does not need to rotate, because we are considering changes in substitutability between the two bonds, rather than between each of them and all other things.

In the limit when these bonds are identical in agents' utility functions, there are only two curves describing economic behavior in the economy:

1. E_{AOT}. This curve shows that the excess demand for the aggregate asset, A and B bonds together, varies directly with the average rate of return on these assets.

2. ZZ, the 45° line. This line shows that there cannot be any substantial deviation in the rates of return of two assets that are perfect substitutes for each other.

The reader will note that the diagram derived for substitutability between bonds is quite different from that representing a similar relationship between currencies. Furthermore, these differences become more important as the degree of substitutability becomes higher.

FIGURE 13.3

Bond Substitability

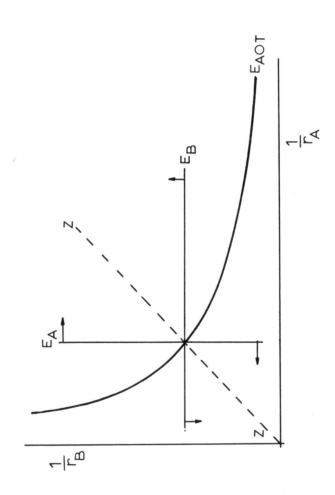

Source: Constructed by the author.

Perfect Substitution and Destabilizing Speculation

The discussion so far has shown that the analysis of substitution between financial assets denominated in different currencies is in marked contrast to that between assets of similar denomination. In particular, substitution between bonds leads to a diagrammatic analysis consistent with the tools used for goods that are gross substitutes; substitution between currencies yields a quite different diagram (Figure 13.2). This section continues the analysis of currency mobility, focusing on the limiting perfect mobility case.

Increasing substitution causes E_A and E_B in Figure 13.2 to rotate toward E_{AOT}. Indeed, in the limit of perfect substitutability, all these loci coincide. Thus, in the case where a unit increase in real A balances matched by a unit decrease in real B balances leaves both money markets in equilibrium, clearing of all markets occurs along the locus E_{AOT}. This shows that the static analysis of currency mobility leads to the conclusion that perfect substitutability yields a neutral equilibrium.

This conclusion is quite obvious in the case of fixed exchange rates. If Chicago dollars and New York dollars are perfect substitutes, then the total stock of either is indeterminate since agents at whim move their monies between these locations. A similar argument can be applied to Toronto dollars (that is, Canadian dollars) and Chicago dollars during a period of fixed exchange rates only.

It is during a period of flexible exchange rates that the theory of currency mobility yields interesting conclusions. The argument above shows that the supplies of Toronto dollars and Chicago dollars are indeterminate with perfect currency mobility (even though their real sum is constant). Under flexible exchange rates, the way in which agents in aggregate alter the supplies of real balances held is through the exchange rate and the price levels in different currencies, with these variables always satisfying purchasing power parity. Thus, this argument shows that the price levels in Canadian and U.S. dollars and the exchange rate are indeterminate. This conclusion is based on the argument that as currencies become substitutable, the expected opportunity cost of holding them is the dominant variable, more important than the exchange rate. Unless this expected opportunity cost is tied to it, the equilibrium exchange rate may become indeterminate.

Thus far the argument has been entirely static. However, this indeterminacy of equilibrium exchange rates assumes more importance when dynamic considerations are included in the discussion. For example, it is well known that adaptive expectation models of asset markets yield unstable solutions when the elasticity of demand and the coefficient of expectations become large.[9] The indeterminacy demonstrated here would modify this rule to make the stability condition even more stringent. Furthermore, the elasticity of demand with respect to opportunity cost becomes very large for such assets. Thus, there are no forces arising from static analysis to propel the exchange rate toward equilibrium, whereas dynamic considerations appear to force the model to be unstable.

The position of perfect currency mobility is a polar case toward which the world economic system appears to have moved recently. There do seem to be certain financial institutions and other multinational corporations for which monies of different denomination are very close substitutes. If these groups represent even a minor proportion of the total money supply of a particular denomination, their behavior can be destabilizing for the country as a whole. Furthermore, the analysis suggests that potential instabilities arise when less than perfect substitutability is combined with dynamic considerations.

CONCLUSIONS

The growth of Eurodollar markets has been so rapid that it has come upon international financial experts unawares. This study suggests that these markets do not represent a minor new phenomenon that is to be explained within the confines of existing theoretic structures. Instead, it finds that currency mobility must be analyzed using new techniques, since substitutability of financial assets denominated in different currencies has substantially different effects from substitutability of financial assets of the same denomination. In particular, exchange rates between currencies become indeterminate as the currencies become close substitutes; similar bonds, however, must have the same price if they have the same denomination.

Both the growth of currency mobility and the diminution of money illusion argue for a substantial degree of exchange rate fixity in the world economy. If this policy is carried out according to the rules of the gold standard, gearing monetary policy to external balance, then the system is completely viable. A serious commitment to such a regime would effectively create large unified currency areas in which speculative capital movements caused by expectations of parity changes would be eliminated. The resulting international financial system would be much more stable than are the present arrangements.

NOTES

1. See, for instance, the analyses of the foreign exchange market by Joan Robinson, "The Foreign Exchanges," in her *Essays in the Theory of Employment*, 2d ed. (Oxford: Blackwell, 1947), part 3, Chapter 1; F. Machlup, "The Theory of Foreign Exchanges," *Economica* 6 (November 1939): 75-97; and G. Harberler, "The Market of Foreign Exchange and the Stability of the Balance of Payments: A Theoretical Analysis," *Kyklos* 3 (fasc. 3, 1949); 193-218.

2. A detailed analysis of international capital mobility is contained in R. A. Mundell, *International Economics* (New York: Macmillan, 1968). See also L. Metzler, "The Process of International Adjustment Under Conditions of Full Employment: A Keynesian View," in *American Economic Association Readings in International Economics*, ed. R. Caves and H. Johnson (Homewood, Ill.: Irwin, 1968), pp. 465-86.

3. Modern discussion of this subject originated with Milton Friedman in his "The Case for Flexible Exchange Rates," in his *Essays in Positive Economics* (Chicago: University of Chicago Press, 1966). For examples that counter Friedman's contentions, see W. J. Baumol, "Speculation, Profitability and Stability," *Review of Economics and Statistics* 39 (August 1957): 263–71; and G. Telser, "A Theory of Speculation Relating Profitability and Stability," *Review of Economics and Statistics* 41 (August 1959): 295–301.

4. An extensive treatment of the theory supporting this approach is contained in Harry G. Johnson, "The Monetary Approach to the Balance of Payments Theory," *Journal of Financial and Quantitative Analysis* 7 (March 1972): 1555–72.

5. Such a specification for money demand is employed by D. Patinkin, in his *Money, Interest and Prices* (New York: Harper and Row, 1965).

6. Mundell, op. cit.; and *Monetary Theory: Inflation, Interest and Growth in the World Economy* (Pacific Palisades, Calif.: Goodyear, 1971).

7. Mundell, *International Economics*, op. cit., p. 52. Also, an early discussion of competing monies may be found in F. von Hayek, *Monetary Nationalism and International Stability* (London: Longmans, Green, 1939).

8. Such a definition is used in S. Royama and K. Mahada, "Substitution and Complementarity in the Choice of Risky Assets," in D. Hester and J. Tobin, eds., *Risk Aversion and Portfolio Choice* (New York: Wiley, 1967).

9. The stability condition is derived in P. Cagan, "The Monetary Dynamics of Hyperinflation," in *Studies in the Quantity Theory of Money*, ed. M. Friedman (Chicago: University of Chicago Press, 1956).

David T. King
Bluford H. Putnam
D. Sykes Wilford

14

A CURRENCY PORTFOLIO APPROACH TO EXCHANGE RATE DETERMINATION: EXCHANGE RATE STABILITY AND THE INDEPENDENCE OF MONETARY POLICY

The strongest argument traditionally made in favor of flexible exchange rates has been that they allow countries, not committed to buying and selling currencies at fixed prices, to pursue independent monetary policies according to their own welfare criteria. Actual experience with floating rates, however, has called into question the meaningfulness of monetary autonomy even under these conditions. Moreover, recent developments in the literature, specifically those adopting monetary approaches to international finance theory, have suggested that monetary independence may be illusory even in a positive sense. From R. Dornbusch,[1] it can be concluded (among other things) that independent monetary policies ultimately affect only nominal variables, simply altering (equivalently) inflation and exchange rate paths. J. Frenkel,[2] in underlining the money-expectations-exchange rate linkage, suggests that monetary independence in any real sense may be largely chimerical, even in the short run.

The Frenkel study is based on a generalization to a flexible exchange rate system of the "monetary" or "assets" view of balance of payments adjustment under fixed exchange rates.[3] The substitutability of currencies in the *supply* of credit that explains international reserves flows and connects monetary policies under fixed exchange rates in turn determines exchange rate fluctuations under flexible rates. As he observes,

> Being a relative price of two assets (moneys), the equilibrium exchange rate is attained when the existing *stocks* of the two moneys

This study benefited from comments by Richard Zecher, Richard Levich, William Gasser, Marc Miles, Alden Toevs, Ed Frydl, and M. A. Akhtar.

are willingly held. It is reasonable, therefore, that a theory of the determination of the relative price of two moneys could be stated conveniently in terms of the supply of and demand for these moneys.[4]

In this model, then, exchange rates are equilibrium solutions at which the existing stocks of the set of highly liquid financial assets—the world's currencies—are contentedly held.

The assets approach, through emphasis on the role of supply substitutability among the various monies, shows that the same fundamental force that induces monetary integration under fixed rates—optimizing international reallocation of credit demand in response to changing relative credit supply conditions—still creates pressures tending to frustrate monetary independence under flexible rates. The potential short-run benefits of divergent monetary policies quickly evaporate as the process of arbitrage among internationally substitutable credit sources chokes off incipient short-term changes in real interest rates. Monetary deviations are consequently pushed into nominal adjustments of prices and exchange rates.

However, this approach to exchange rate determination stops short of being wholly analogous to other monetary models of assets pricing—for example, the assets approaches to bond price determination of James Tobin or Karl Brunner. In particular, in these other models all transactors generally hold some or all of the assets under consideration, so that bond prices are determined by a process of portfolio balancing among assets substitutable in both supply and demand. In the assets approach to exchange rate determination, on the other hand, economic agents are implicitly viewed as holding only *one* asset (one money), in that the ultimate demand for a particular currency stock implicitly arises only from *domestic* sources. Monetary services can be provided only by the domestic currency, so that, though one optimizes over the set of currencies in obtaining the cheapest source of credit, the transactor always converts the proceeds of his acquisitions into domestic currency. In effect, the elasticity of substitution in demand among the various monies is, in the received monetary approach to exchange rate determination, assumed to equal zero. Any one agent's "portfolio" of highly liquid assets therefore consists of only one currency. Consequently, all other things being equal, incipient changes in the domestically determined supply of money inevitably generate exchange rate movements. Clearly, however, multinational trade and investment firms, as well as banks and foreign exchange market speculators, maintain money holdings denominated in several currencies. In so far as their particular institutional framework and the ability of the various assets to provide similar monetary services allow, these transactors optimize through substitutions among their money balances as expectations concerning the value of the currency portfolio change. Recent literature has developed the concept of currency substitution in the demand for money. Concentrating on potential differential returns to the various monies and exogenously stipulating various degrees of substitution, Lance Girton and Don Roper[5] show how currency substitution can moderate exchange rate movements. Marc Miles[6] has attempted empirically to identify parametric indicators of the degree of currency substitution in money demand.[7] Emphasizing the theoretical development of demand-side substitutions, however, these authors abstract from substitution in supply, so that a comprehensive currency portfolio approach to exchange rate determination remains to be enunciated. Moreover, a theory of the degree of currency substitution itself has not been fully developed.*

To assess better the questions of exchange rate stability and the independence of monetary policy under flexible exchange rates, the initial purpose of this study is to extend the assets or monetary approach to a balance of payments-exchange rates model into a more general (portfolio adjustment) model of exchange rate determination. This is done by taking explicit account of substitution among currencies in *both* the demand for and supply of money. To this end, first the money demand function is generalized to include foreign monies. A theory of the degree of currency substitution is obtained at the same time. Then, the portfolio approach to exchange rate determination—an assets model that includes currency substitution in demand—is developed. The study concludes with a discussion of the implications of the general model for the efficacy of international monetary policy divergence.

Summarizing, the application of this monetary synthesis to the question of policy independence strongly implies the meaninglessness of monetary autonomy under flexible exchange rates. Optimizing demanders of monetary services react in a manner that reinforces stable and harmonious policies but magnifies the undesirable effects of unstable and digressive policies.

CURRENCY SUBSTITUTION AND THE DEMAND FOR MONETARY SERVICES

Generalizing Money Demand

Casual observation suggests that a large proportion of exchange market transactions are conducted by banks and corporations that regularly deal in foreign exchange and hold balances of several currencies simultaneously. Foreign currencies perform monetary services for these transactors as they conduct their daily business of buying and selling goods and assets on an international scale. These transactors are the first to feel any wealth effects due to the change in

---

*Associated with the literature on currency substitutability are issues addressed by F. A. Hayek and Gordon Tullock on competition between monies.[8]

exchange rates, and consequently are continually optimizing at the margin in the foreign exchange market to the extent that institutional constraints allow.

Thus, for an open economy, a general money demand specification must take into account transactors who utilize several currencies in order to fulfill desired monetary services. Such a money demand function can be simply stated as follows:

$$M^d/p = \Phi \cdot f(y, i, u) \tag{1}$$

where M^d = quantity of *domestic* money (currency) demanded
  p = the domestic price level
  Φ = proportion of monetary services provided by domestic money $(0 < \Phi < 1)$
  y = permanent real income
  i = opportunity cost of holding money, and
  u = stochastic disturbance (log normally distributed)

In this function, the total demand for real monetary services, given by $f(\cdot)$, depends on a traditional set of determinants—permanent real income and the opportunity cost of holding money. This total demand is adjusted by Φ to yield the demand for domestic money.

In this function, residents' (domestic transactors') demand for money can be partly satisfied by foreign currency holdings ($1 - \Phi$ gives the proportion of monetary services provided by foreign money). Residents' allocations of their money holdings between foreign and domestic currencies will depend on the degree of substitutability between monies. In the extreme case of perfect substitutability, transactors would be indifferent between domestic and foreign currencies. Excess demand for domestic money would tend to be satisfied simply by increased private holdings of foreign money, with no change in the exchange rate.* This is the counterpart to the fixed exchange rate case in which currency substitution is perfect on the supply side. Alternately, the assumption of zero substitution among monies, implied in nearly all existing models of exchange rate determination, requires that exchange rates fully reflect all relative changes in excess money supply. Of importance from this brief discussion, then, is that the existence of a set of transactors able to substitute among currencies, even imperfectly, directly affects how exchange rates will adjust following events that change relative excess demands for money. Thus, the currency substitution question has important implications for the independence of monetary policy under flexible exchange rates.

---

*This assumes appropriate foreign monetary expansion. Otherwise, relative holdings remain the same; the attempt to increase holdings simply raises interest rates everywhere.

Currency Substitution: The Fundamental Scope

What, then, are the determinants of the substitution among currencies in the demand for money—that is, of the proportionality factor, Φ, in equation (1), which reflects the shares of foreign and domestic currencies held in real money balances? Basically, currencies are substitutes in demand to the extent that they provide similar monetary services to *any* transactor. Alternatively, the extent to which the monetary services rendered to the representative individual by any set of currencies differ is reflected in the degree to which the two assets are not perfect substitutes in demand. Thus, the fundamental scope for currency substitution is determined in a macroeconomic sense by the integration of world goods and capital markets. The state of global market integration in turn affects the allocation of the currency portfolio through both transactions and speculative reasons for demanding money.

Currencies are ultimately imperfect substitutes because domestic trade is denominated in domestic currency. Thus, for a large part of their usual transactions for goods and services, individuals acquiring foreign currencies must first go through the exchange markets to obtain the required domestic currency. However, increased integration of world markets for goods and services—making foreign goods and services more readily accessible (more effectively substitutable) to domestic residents—would tend to provide a wider role for foreign currencies in satisfying transactions demands for money. Indeed, the transactions demand for various forms of money for use in international trade is substantial. Transactors trading internationally have the opportunity to choose from a broad variety of substitutable goods and services denominated in a variety of currencies. Optimizing over changing costs of money balances, they substitute among currencies in their transactions demand portfolios as they reallocate demands for *goods* among substitute sources. Moreover, international corporations, incurring large flows of receipts and expenditures in several currencies, have wide latitude in deciding whether to convert to domestic currency or to hold foreign currencies for possible future international transactions.

Currency substitution in "speculative" money demand is determined by world capital market integration. In this context, utility-maximizing individuals—especially through nonbank intermediaries—can distribute their financial wealth among all available currencies and currency denominations of bonds, instead of just between domestic money and domestic currency-denominated bonds as in the traditional closed economy case. The high degree of world capital market integration and the ease of acquiring foreign deposits and foreign currency-denominated bonds suggest that "speculative" money demand portfolios are well diversified among the various currencies.

Generalizing, then, it is the integration of world markets for goods and financial assets that allows different currencies to perform similar monetary services and thus provides the institutional framework within which currency substitution is possible. Formulating this concept more rigorously, the elasticity of currency substitution is given by

$$\sigma = g(I) \tag{2}$$

where σ = elasticity of currency substitution in real money demand
      I = the intensity of integration of global goods and capital markets, arising from that institutional structure, and $d\sigma/dI > 0$

that is, an increase in world market integration increases currency substitutability.*

To simplify the analysis, we take the intensity of world market integration as constant for the relevant period of analysis. However, market integration can change as a result of secular forces and official policies. The primary institutional factors determining the level of I for any time period are the set of tariffs, quotas, and other barriers to trade of goods; the set of controls on international movements of capital, transportation, and other transactions costs; and the availability of information concerning external sources of and markets for goods, services, and financial assets. The first two sets of factors are officially determined, while the latter two change secularly over time. Symbolically,

$$I = h(T, C; \theta, \phi) \tag{3}$$

where T = barriers to trade
      C = capital controls
      θ = transportation and transactions costs, and
      ϕ = information availability;
and where $\partial I/\partial T < 0$
            $\partial I/\partial C < 0$
            $\partial I/\partial\theta < 0$, and
            $\partial I/\partial\phi > 0$

Increases in official barriers to trade or restrictions on capital movements decrease global market integration, while decreases in transportation costs or increases in information availability enhance it.

As the world market becomes more integrated, different currencies become more acceptable as payment for goods or assets, since any currency more readily provides monetary services to the transactor. Thus, increased world economic integration reduces the ultimate institutional rigidity making for nonsubstituta-

---

*Miles estimated the elasticity of currency substitution in money demand between U S and Canadian dollars showing it to be significantly greater than unity.[9]

bility—the acceptability on the part of sellers of goods and assets of only the domestic currency in their marketing operations.

According to the theory outlined in this section, then, those factors that tend to enhance market integration also expand the fundamental scope for currency substitution by improving the extent to which different currencies can provide similar monetary services. In the context of well-integrated world markets, currency substitution is therefore an increasingly important issue in international finance theory and policy. Empirical indications of substantial integration of world markets for goods, services, and financial assets—as reflected in the existence of a sizeable Eurocurrency market heavily involved in financing international flows of goods and services, and in the rapid growth of world trade, which now accounts for some 25 percent of world output—constitute a strong a priori case for taking account of currency substitution in exchange rate models and domestic monetary policy formulation.

Portfolio Substitution

Optimization over incipient changes in the relative cost of credit stimulates substitution in credit demand among the various currencies. Traditionally, these acquired balances were seen as always being fully converted back into domestic currency, in effect assuming that domestic money alone could supply monetary services to the transactor. The previous section shows that, in fact, monetary services are provided to individuals by several currencies in an integrated world economy. Consequently, transactors have reason to accept and hold both domestic and foreign monies in optimizing their money holdings, while continuing to substitute among these portfolio assets in order to minimize the overall opportunity cost of holding money balances. On this basis, optimizing shifts in demands for currency stocks tend to eliminate deviations in relative excess supplies of these monies. These adjustments tend to obviate changes in both interest rate differentials and exchange rates.

However, the transactor is now faced with a new optimization problem arising from the fact that currency substitution, though significant, is not perfect. That is, given the opportunity cost structure of holding the set of currencies, he must be alert to possible changes in the relative real values of the currencies he holds.* These potential changes arise from the possibility of differential rates of growth in the prices of goods and assets that the various currencies will purchase. To the extent that currencies are to any degree unique in their control over goods, with respect to their country of origin, the problem

---

*Throughout the discussion we abstract from the money-bond portfolio decision. Attention is concentrated on substitution among currencies aimed at maintaining the overall real value of the *money* portfolio.

of adjusting balances of a currency expected to depreciate in real value arises.*
This institutional characteristic or residual imperfection in the world economy,
caused by the absence of perfect integration, represents the fundamental nonsubstitutability among currencies.

Under floating rates, capital gains and losses to holding currency stocks, if
anything, tend to occur *ahead* of actual changes in differential inflation, because
possible future changes in the relative purchasing power of currencies over goods
or financial assets tend to be quickly reflected in current exchange rates.[10]

Given the structure of relative opportunity costs of holding money and the
basic scope for currency substitution, changes in the real value of currency
portfolio holdings are most immediately brought about by exchange rate
changes. Thus, possible exchange rate changes are of continuing concern to
holders of currency portfolios as they attempt to maintain the overall real value
of their money balances. It therefore seems clear that given the basic institutional factors determining the intensity of world market integration that allows
substitution, the actual share of foreign currency in residents' real money balances will also depend on exchange rate expectations. Furthermore, an increase
in uncertainty associated with the set of exchange rate expectations, all other
things being equal, will encourage a portfolio shift away from domestic currency—
now a relatively more risky asset in the currency portfolio—by risk-averse
transactors.†

Formally, the share of foreign currencies in the total real money holdings
of residents for any given set of relative credit conditions depends upon exchange
rate expectations and the confidence with which these expectations are held,
conditional upon the institutional structure determining currency substitutability.

$$\Phi = j(E^0, V \mid I) \qquad\qquad (4)$$

---

*Thus, for example, incipiently higher inflation rates in New York do not provoke
the running down of Second Reserve District notes in individuals' domestic currency portfolios, since Second District notes control Third, . . . District goods. It is the fact that
Second District notes control other district goods—currency substitutability is perfect—
which guarantees that speculative arbitrage will lead to similar inflation rates in both districts.

†The presentation we are using illustrates the implications of portfolio substitution in
a model in which the covariances of returns on all other assets are held constant. Thus, we
can represent the portfolio optimization decision by looking at the behavior of the exchange
value of only one currency vis-a-vis an unspecified foreign currency. As the uncertainty
(taken as originating only from domestic sources) associated with the set of home currency-
foreign currency exchange rates rises, the fundamental scope for currency substitution
encourages a marginal shift into the foreign currency, whose exchange value, though simultaneously becoming more uncertain with respect to the *domestic* currency, is unchanged in
its perceived variability with respect to all other currencies. Thus, the total variance of the
portfolio is reduced by moving out of the home currency, even as (given the basic scope for
substitution) money demand services are maintained.

where E^O = the expected exchange rate, in units of domestic currency per unit of foreign currency, relative to the current spot rate

V = the uncertainty associated with exchange rate expectations

and where $\partial\Phi/\partial E^O < 0$

$\partial\Phi/\partial V < 0$

Expectations of exchange rate appreciation unambiguously tend to increase domestic money holdings. The effects of increased uncertainty on the share of domestic money in the currency portfolio result in a shift away from the risky asset. That is, if the exchange risk of holding the domestic money increases, then, all other things being equal, the marginal transactor alters the composition of his currency portfolio in favor of the less risky asset, toward foreign money.*

Following the rational expectations approach, market participants are assumed to use information efficiently, including information about the underlying economic structure.[11] Given foreign inflation, exchange rate expectations would therefore be based first on expectations concerning future domestic and foreign inflation rates,[12] which depend primarily on their perceptions about relative monetary policies and real growth prospects.[13] For simplicity, taking permanent real income growth as the more stable component, these expectations generally result from changes in transactors' perceptions of current and future domestic monetary policies, given foreign monetary policy. Thus,

$$E^O = m(M^O | M^O_W, I) \tag{5}$$

where M^O = expected domestic monetary expansion, and

M^O_W = expected foreign monetary expansion (considered given), and
where $\partial E^O/\partial M^O > 0$

That is, given a state of world market integration that fundamentally allows currency substitution, expectations of "loose" domestic monetary policies relative to given foreign monetary policies provoke expectations of exchange rate depreciation.

In turn, the uncertainty associated with exchange rate expectations will depend on the perceived variability of domestic and foreign policies:

---

*We can cite as an example the recent (1976) Mexican experience. Prices in the tourist industry (an internationally traded and highly substitutable service) in Mexico have traditionally been denominated in both dollars and pesos, with a certain level of dollars to pesos held individually in the industry. The uncertainty surrounding the peso and its possible further depreciation changed this ratio dramatically as people moved toward dollar-denominated transactions much more heavily. Similarly, in border towns where most retail goods are, in effect, internationally traded, prices became widely quoted in dollars during the period of uncertainty following the initial de facto devaluation.

$$V = V[\text{Var}\ (M^O)|M^O_W, I] \tag{6}$$

where Var (M^O) = the variance associated with expectations about domestic
monetary policy
and where $\partial V/\partial$ Var $(M^O) > 0$

Increased variance raises the level of exchange uncertainty associated with portfolio holdings of domestic currency.

Substituting the specifications for exchange rate expectations, (5), and the associated uncertainty, (6), into the determination of the share of foreign currency holdings in residents' money balances, (4), yields

$$\Phi = k[M^O, \text{Var}\ (M^O)|M^O_W, I] \tag{7}$$

where $\partial\Phi/\partial M^O < 0$
$\partial\Phi/\partial$ Var $(M^O) < 0$

All other things being equal, an expected increase in the domestic money supply increases the portfolio share of real foreign money balances, to the extent that the domestic currency is expected to depreciate relative to foreign currencies. With respect to the variance of expectations, increased uncertainty concerning the real value of domestic money leads to a portfolio shift away from that asset. Increased domestic monetary policy variability requires a more careful monitoring of exchange rates, raising the relative cost of holding the domestic currency and reducing its usefulness for international transactions.

A GENERALIZED MODEL OF
EXCHANGE RATE DETERMINATION

The exchange rate model presented here is based on the demand and supply of money, monetary equilibrium, and assumptions concerning the integration of word markets for goods and assets. Thus, the model is a descendant of the monetary models of Harry G. Johnson, Robert A. Mundell, Arthur Laffer, Jacob Frenkel, Rudiger Dornbusch, and others.[14]

The money demand function, is given a specific form,

$$M^d/p = \Phi\ y^a e^{\gamma i} e^u \tag{7a}$$

The demand for domestic real money balances depends on the traditional determinants—permanent real income and the opportunity cost of holding money—and a factor of proportionality representing the shares of real monetary services provided by domestic and foreign monies. Converting this equation to growth terms yields,

$$g(M^d) - g(p) = g(\Phi) + ag(y) + \gamma d(i) + u, \tag{8}$$

where a = the real income elasticity of the demand for real money balances $(a > 0)$,

and where $g = (dx/dt)/x$ for all x (that is, the notation $g(x)$ represents the percentage change form of the relevant variable),

γ = the (semi-log) interest parameter of the demand for real money balance $(\gamma < 0)$.

The supply of money is determined by the monetary authorities and is expressed here in growth terms:

$$g(M^s) = g(M). \tag{9}$$

Monetary equilibrium is maintained such that

$$g(M^d) = g(M^s). \tag{10}$$

As the earlier discussion of currency substitution outlines, the analysis is based on the assumption of well-integrated and efficient world goods, services, and assets markets. The tendencies linking domestic and foreign price levels and interest rates are reflected in the equilibrium conditions of purchasing power parity and interest rate parity:

$$g(p) = g(p_w) + g(E), \text{ and} \tag{11}$$

$$i = i_w + g(E^o). \tag{12}$$

where the subscript w indicates a world market variable, and

E = the exchange rate expressed in units of domestic currency per unit of the foreign currency, and

E^o = exchange rate expectations.

Solving this five-equation system—that is, equations (8) – (12)—yields:

$$g(E) = -g(p_w) - ag(y) - \gamma d(i_w) - g(\Phi) - \gamma dg(E^o) + g(M) + u. \tag{13}$$

In this formulation, all other things being equal, factors increasing net money demand tend to cause exchange rate appreciation, while factors causing expansion in domestic money cause exchange rate depreciation. The inclusion of the share variable, Φ, follows from the demand for money specification. Thus, portfolio shifts in the currency compositions of transactors' money balances influence the exchange rate in a direct manner.*

To complete the model, the equation specifying the form of exchange rate expectations, (5), and the determinants of the domestic and foreign currency shares in real money balances, (7), are expressed here in growth terms and then substituted into equation (13). Thus, from equation (5),

$$dg[E^o|M^o_w,I] = mdg(M^o) \tag{14}$$

where $m = \partial E^o / \partial M^o > 0$.

From equation (7),

$$g(\Phi|I) = k_1 g(M^o) + k_2 g[Var(M^o)] \tag{15}$$

where $\Phi = k(M^o, Var(M^o), | M^o_w, I)$

showing how monetary policies affect the composition of the currency portfolio. Substituting these equations in (13) yields the final reduced-form equation,

$$g[E|g(M^o_w),I] = -g(p_w) - ag(y) - \gamma d(i_w) - k_1 g(M^o) - \gamma mdg(M^o)$$
$$-k_2[Var(M^o)] + g(M) + u \tag{16}$$

where $k_1, \gamma m, k_2 < 0$.

This expression is a generalized version of the monetary approach to exchange rate determination. As in the latter, a decrease in world prices, an increase in world interest rates, or a decrease in domestic real permanent income leads to exchange rate depreciation as the demand for domestic money rises, all other things being equal. Moreover, as in the received literature, actual or expected relatively expansive domestic monetary policy tends to depreciate the exchange rate, all other things being equal. In addition, however, equation (16) captures the effects of currency substitution in the demand for money. The coefficients on anticipated domestic monetary policy show clearly that transactors' capacity to change the composition of currency portfolios between domestic and foreign

---

*Put another way, the inclusion of a share variable more fully specifies the exchange rate equation. For example, an excess demand for money may be partially met through portfolio shifts; the effect of an excess demand (of domestic currency) need not be fully reflected in an exchange rate change. On the other hand, an outside shock affecting Φ would imply an exchange rate change, all other things being equal.

monies aggravates depreciation pressures (or the converse), pushing exchange rates beyond what would be implied by the model in the absence of currency substitution in money demand.* Furthermore, an increase in the variability of domestic monetary policy tends to depreciate the exchange rate, as transactors, able to substitute among currencies according to the given state of world market integration, shift their portfolio holdings toward less risky foreign monies.

Finally, equation (16) should be discussed in light of the recent literature dealing with the efficacy of monetary policy.[15] Recent studies show how monetary authorities can avoid the nominal implications of their policies only by conducting "innovative"–variable or uncertain–monetary policies. Real effects are possible only to the extent that nominal variables–wages, prices, interest rates, and, in this case, the exchange rate–do not quickly offset the change in the nominal money stock. When variability and uncertainty surround the course of monetary policy, transactors are hindered in their attempts to anticipate nominal money changes, resulting in such lags in the adjustment of the dependent nominal variables and, consequently, temporary real effects.

In the context of a currency portfolio approach to exchange rate determination, the increase in monetary variability makes the formation of exchange rate expectations more difficult, so that these expectations adjust to any fundamental policy shift more slowly than they otherwise would. In equation (16), then, increased variability serves to mask true changes in policy temporarily, and changes in expectations on monetary growth $[g(M^O)]$ will lag actual monetary changes. Monetary authorities can therefore elect to suffer the initial exchange rate depreciation associated with increasing the variability of their policies in order to gain some flexibility for achieving short-run real effects in policy deviations. The situation, then, is analogous to the conditions discussed in recent closed-economy literature: the nominal implications of monetary divergence in an open economy can be escaped only insofar as the policy is innovative–but this capacity for innovation is "bought" with an initial depreciation of the exchange rate.

THE INDEPENDENCE OF MONETARY POLICY
AND THE CURRENCY PORTFOLIO APPROACH

This analysis is conditional upon the state of world market integration. On one hand, the integration of international markets constrains the independence of monetary policies by dissolving distinctions among the world's monies. Thus,

---

*That is, the coefficients associated with expected domestic monetary growth (γm and k_1) are absolutely larger than for the case of no currency substitution. Further, it is shown that a move toward greater than expected money creation, $dg(M^O)$, aggravates the problem. Empirical tests of this hypothesis would presumably be based on sets of time series data, segregated in some manner according to the state of world economic integration.

for example, an expansionary monetary policy in any individual country simply expands the *world* money supply and has no country-specific effects. This has been the message of the received currency substitution literature.

On the other hand, if the possibility of monetary autonomy exists at all, it is due to the residual absence of integration of the world economy. But the above analysis shows that the capacity for altering the composition of portfolios of money holdings tends to frustrate even this potential. That is, the *apparent* scope for independent monetary policy—suggested by the extent to which control over substitutable goods and assets remains currency-specific—is eroded by the optimizing reactions of economic agents substituting among currencies in money demand. Indeed, consistent with recent literature on monetary policy in a closed economy, the monetary authorities can postpone the inevitable offsetting exchange rate effects of their policies only by making the policies variable and uncertain.

But currency portfolio substitution thus has further clear implications for monetary autonomy under flexible exchange rates. Since transactors can substitute from one currency to another, they are quick to reallocate their portfolios in response to any exchange rate changes that can be anticipated. Exchange markets can therefore be expected to reflect immediately the potential inflationary implications of divergent monetary policies, once perceived by holders of currency portfolios. These implications are thereby rapidly communicated to the public through the prominence of exchange rate changes, thus frustrating any real effects of the "independent" policy. Exchange rate stability among countries following predictably harmonious monetary policies naturally tends to be maintained by profit-maximizing commercial and professional speculators. On the other hand, the actions of these same transactors, who are able to adjust quickly the shares of foreign and domestic currencies in their portfolios, increase the exchange rate instability of currencies of countries following inharmonious monetary policies: countries following "independent" policies quickly reap the consequences of their actions in the exchange markets. Under a fixed exchange rate system, countries can maintain inconsistent monetary policies for however long they are willing to bear the implied reserves flow problems or are able to have these policies financed by international transfers of funds. Since the central bank carries the burden of adjustment under fixed exchange rates, the consequences of divergent policies can be hidden or ignored, at least temporarily. In a flexible exchange rate system, with private transactors bearing the burden of adjustment, the market acts swiftly, reflecting inharmonious policies in highly visible exchange rate changes. It is, perhaps, a sterner taskmaster than the self-imposed discipline of Bretton Woods.

The general model of exchange rate determination presented in this study, concentrating on currency portfolio adjustments in the face of changing conditions of costs of and returns to holding various currencies, shows that private optimization in an increasingly integrated world economy severely compromises the ability of flexible exchange rates to provide countries with a scope for conducting meaningfully autonomous monetary policies. The implications of the model are consistent with increasing evidence that the attempts undertaken since 1973 to use flexible rates as a shield for attempting independent monetary policies have been; in any real sense, largely futile.

NOTES

1. Rudiger Dornbusch, "Expectations and Exchange Rate Dynamics," *Journal of Political Economy* 74, 6 (December 1976): 1161-76.

2. J. Frenkel, "A Monetary Approach to the Exchange Rate," *Scandinavian Journal of Economics* (May 1976):200-61.

3. See, for example, Harry G. Johnson, "The Monetary Approach to the Balance of Payments," in *Further Essays in Monetary Economics* (Cambridge: Harvard University Press, 1973), pp. 229-49; Harry G. Johnson, "The Monetary Approach to the Balance of Payments Theory: A Diagramatic Analysis," *The Manchester School* 43 (1975):220-74; Arthur Laffer, "The Anti-Traditional General Equilibrium Theory of the Rate Growth and the Balance of Payments under Fixed Exchange Rates," manuscript, University of Chicago (1968); J. Richard Zecher, "Monetary Equilibrium and International Reserve Flows in Australia," *Journal of Finance* 29, 4 (December 1974):1322-30; John R. Rutledge, "Balance of Payments and Money Demand," manuscript, 1975; and Alexander K. Swoboda, "Monetary Approaches to the Balance of Payments Theory," in *Recent Issues in International Monetary Economics*, ed. E. Claassen and P. Salin (New York: North Holland, 1976), pp. 3-24.

4. Frenkel, op. cit.

5. Lance Girton and Don Roper, "Theory and Implications of Currency Substitution," *International Finance Discussion Papers*, Federal Reserve Board, No. 86, 1976.

6. Marc Miles, "Currency Substitution, Flexible Exchange Rates and Monetary Independence," *American Economics Review* 68 (June 1978).

7. For other literature that utilizes this concept of substitutability, see R. Boyer (this book, Chapter 13); Arthur Laffer, "Optimal Exchange Rates," paper presented at The American Economic Association Meeting, Atlantic City, September 1976; Guillermo Calvo and Alfredo Rodriguez, "A Model of Exchange Rate Determination Under Currency Substitution and Rational Expectations," *Journal of Political Economy* 85 (May–June 1977): 617-25; and W. Michael Cox, "The Impact of Substitute Currencies on International Monetary and Exchange Market Equilibrium," manuscript, Virginia Polytechnic Institute, 1976.

8. See Gordon Tullock, "Competing Monies," *Journal of Money, Credit, and Banking* (November 1975):491-97; and F. A. Hayek, *Denationalization of Money* (Hobart Special Papers, 1976).

9. Miles, op. cit.

10. See Dornbusch, op. cit.; and David T. King, "Monetary Autonomy and Flexible Exchange Rates," mimeographed, January 1977.

11. See, for example, John Rutledge, *A Monetarist Model of Inflationary Expectations* (Toronto: Lexington Books, 1974).

12. See David T. King, "The Performance of Exchange Rates in the Recent Period of Floating: Exchange Rates and Relative Rates of Inflation," *Southern Economic Journal* 43, no. 4 (April 1977):1582-87.

13. See Cox, op. cit.; Frenkel, op. cit.; Lance Girton and Don Roper, "A Monetary Model of Exchange Market Pressure Applied to the Post-War Canadian Experience," *American Economic Review* 67 (September 1977):537-48; Bluford H. Putnam and John Wood-

bury, "Exchange Rate Stability and Monetary Policy: A Case Study," Federal Reserve Bank of New York Research Paper No. 7718 (1976); and Nicholas Sargen, "Exchange Rate Stability and Demand for Money," paper presented at the meeting of The American Finance Association, Atlantic City, N.J., September 1976.

14. Johnson, "The Monetary Approach to the Balance of Payments," op. cit., and "The Monetary Approach to the Balance of Payments Theory: A Diagramatic Analysis," op. cit.; R. A. Mundell, *International Economics* (New York: Macmillan, 1968); Laffer, "Anti-Traditional General Equilibrium Theory," op. cit.; Frenkel, op. cit.; Dornbusch, op. cit.; Girton and Roper, op. cit.; Sargen, op. cit.; *Studies in the Monetary Approach to the Balance of Payments*, ed. J. Frenkel and Harry G. Johnson (London: Unwin, 1976); Donald S. Kemp, "A Monetary View of the Balance of Payments," *Federal Reserve Bank of St. Louis Review* 57, no. 4 (April 1975):14–20; Harold Fry, "A Monetary Approach to Afghanistan's Flexible Exchange Rate," *Journal of Money, Credit and Banking* 8 (May 1976): 219–25; Bluford H. Putnam and John J. Van Belle, "A Monetary Approach to Afghanistan's Flexible Exchange Rate: A Comment," *Journal of Money, Credit and Banking* 10, no. 1 (February 1978): 117–18; Rutledge, op. cit.; D. Sykes Wilford and Walton T. Wilford, "Monetary Approach to the Balance of Payments: On World Prices and the Reserve Flow Equation," *Weltwirtschaftliches Archiv* vol. 113, no. 1: 31–39; "A Note on the Monetary Approach to the Balance of Payments: The Small, Open Economy," *Journal of Finance* vol. 33, no. 1 (March, 1978):319–22; and Zecher, op.cit.

15. See R. J. Barro, "Rational Expectations and the Role of Monetary Policy," *Journal of Monetary Economics* 2 (1976):1–32; R. J. Barro and Stanley Fischer, "Recent Developments in Monetary Theory," *Journal of Monetary Economics* 2, no. 2 (April 1976): 133–68; E. S. Phelps and J. B. Taylor, "Stabilizing Powers of Monetary Policy under Rational Expectations," *Journal of Political Economy* 85, no. 1 (January 1977):163–90; and T. J. Sargent and Neil Wallace, "'Rational' Expectations, the Optimal Monetary Investment, and the Optimal Money Supply Rule," *Journal of Political Economy* 83, no. 2 (April 1975): 241–54.

Lance Girton
Don Roper

15

THE EVOLUTION OF
EXCHANGE RATE POLICY

The history of money has been characterized by an evolutionary process in which fiduciary monies have gradually replaced commodity monies. This study, on some of the forces in this evolutionary process, develops a hypothesis concerning a fundamental drive behind the policy of fixed exchange rates. The hypothesis is used to reinterpret several features of the experience with fixed exchange rates under the gold-exchange standard and the Bretton Woods system.

March 1973 is the date most frequently cited for the final collapse of the Bretton Woods system. Since then many countries have been experimenting with managed floats. In an effort to distinguish the temporary disturbances that they want to offset with intervention from secular trends that reflect differential inflation rates, authorities must turn to the implications of purchasing power parity. But previous statements of this doctrine do not yield unambiguous theoretical guidelines for intervention policy. Consequently, an alternative statement of purchasing power parity is presented here.

Present-day exchange market intervention, like the previous policy of fixed exchange rates, treats the exchange rate or the exchange rate path as a target variable rather than an an instrument of policy. We argue that a significant change in policy will occur as monetary authorities begin to reconsider exchange market intervention within the broader context of domestic stabilization policy.

The authors would like to thank Dayle Nattress, Lori Schuetz, and Ralph Smith for helpful comments.

A FUNDAMENTAL DRIVE
BEHIND FIXED EXCHANGE RATES

At the outset a sharp distinction must be drawn between arguments over whether exchange rates should be fixed and arguments about why exchange rates have, in fact, been fixed. The debate over fixed-versus-floating rates has been concerned with the former problem. These authors are unaware of any work that deals explicitly with the latter problem, although insights concerning this question can be gleaned from the voluminous historical literature on monetary questions. This section offers a tentative hypothesis concerning a force that the present authors consider important in the formulation of exchange rate policy over time. In the next section this hypothesis is used to offer a new interpretation of several features of the policy of fixed exchange rates.

This hypothesis can be related to the intellectual foundation of the doctrine of metallism. Cast in modern terms, metallism questions the concept of the demand for fiduciary money.* Why, metallism asks, would anyone accept paper money or deposit money unless such money is convertible into a commodity of intrinsic worth? The argument that person A accepts paper money in the belief that he can pass the paper on to person B is circular. Is B supposed to be willing to accept the paper money because he thinks it can be passed on to C, and from C to D and so on? This would lead back to A's being willing to accept intrinsically worthless paper money because A is willing to give intrinsically worthless paper money.

The present authors think metallists were correct to assert that the public would not, at least initially, voluntarily hold intrinsically worthless paper or deposit money.[2] Once the public became familiar with the convertibility fiduciary elements in their monetary system, however, they could be (and have, in fact, been) weaned from commodity money and from convertibility into a commodity.† The public could be induced to use the past as a guide to the future—to believe that paper money could be passed on to other persons in the future because they had previous successful experiences using the paper money—if the withdrawal of convertibility were sufficiently gradual.‡

---

*"Fiduciary" means that the face value is greater than the value of the money as a commodity. Paper and deposit monies are completely fiduciary whereas token and debased coins are partly fiduciary. Dictionaries emphasize the role of trust in defining "fiduciary." Here it is argued that the person who voluntarily accepts fiduciary money must believe or "trust" that the money can be passed on to other members of the community. An excellent discussion of "fiduciary" is found in Arthur Nussbaum.[1]

†Tullock has expressed a similar argument in his analysis of the development of paper money in China between 1000 and 1500: "After the people and government had become accustomed to the use of paper money ... it was possible to establish inconvertible currencies...."[3]

‡An example of the way convertibility can be withdrawn gradually or, at least, in stages is provided by the experience of the United States. Starting in March 1933 U.S. citizens were prohibited from converting U.S. currency into gold. In March 1968 the United States refused to convert foreign private holdings of U.S. currency into gold. And, after August 1971, foreign official institutions could no longer sell their U.S. dollars to U.S. monetary authorities for gold.[4]

It is argued here that the evolution of exchange rate policy has been strongly influenced by the need to create and maintain a demand for fiduciary money. A demand for fiduciary money could be generated by making the money unambiguously convertible when initially issued; then, if convertibility were withdrawn slowly and without notice, the demand could be maintained.

The incentive for profits or seigniorage induced banks of issue to lower their commodity reserves relative to their fiduciary liablilities. But the reduction of commodity backing undermined their ability to maintain convertibility. To maintain confidence in their fiduciary liabilities, money issuers have imitated characteristics of the gold standard to keep up appearances of convertibility. It was uncertain when convertibility into gold, or the appearance of convertibility, could be dropped without undermining confidence in fiduciary money. The natural response to this uncertainty was to err on the conservative side—to imitate characteristics of the gold standard until events forced the abandonment of such appearances.

The preceding argument is tantamount to asserting that policymakers have had the explicit, well thought out objective of setting up pretences of being on the gold standard. It is not the purpose here, however, to try to question what has been on the minds of monetary authorities during the twentieth century. A postivistic statement of the hypothesis of this study is that exchange rate policies have been designed as if policymakers have been trying to wean the public away from gold backing (to increase profits) by maintaining the appearances of the gold standard (to maintain confidence) and that this weaning process has been gradual (in response to uncertainty) in order to avoid confidence problems.

REINTERPRETING SOME FEATURES OF THE FIXED RATE POLICY

Before using this study's hypothesis to interpret certain features of the policy of fixed exchange rates, it is necessary to review briefly how the procedure for fixing exchange rates has changed over time. Under the gold standard, currency rates were fixed by private traders responding to market incentives. The banks of issue maintained a fixed parity, a buying and selling price for their currency into a commodity like silver or gold. If two money issuers maintained convertibility of their liabilities into the same commodity, then private traders in currency markets would choose between two routes for exchanging one currency for another. They would make a direct change in the currency market or,

---

States refused to convert foreign private holdings of U.S. currency into gold. And, after August 1971, foreign official institutions could no longer sell their U.S. dollars to U.S. monetary authorities for gold.[4]

if the market clearing rate differed from the ratio of the parities by more than the cost of shipping the commodity from one money issuer to the other, they would sell the cheap currency to its issuer for specie and ship the specie to the other issue to obtain the dear currency. It was the convertibility of the monies into a common commodity plus arbitrage that kept the narrow band around the rate of exchange in the currency markets.

The modern approach to fixing exchange rates has evolved along with the gold-exchange standard. The gold-exchange standard was instituted in some countries just prior to the turn of the century, and it received its greatest impetus after World War I, in response to the shortage of gold at pre-war parities and post-war price levels. Re-establishing the gold-exchange standard after World War II, monetary authorities placed ceilings and floors around the official exchange rate by standing ready, not to buy or sell gold, but to buy or sell a "reserve" currency, that is, by intervening directly in currency markets. These ceilings and floors were selected and enforced at the discretion of monetary authorities, not by private traders responding to arbitrage incentives.

One of the curiosities associated with the policy of pegging exchange rates by direct intervention in currency markets has been the historical determination of the size of bands placed around exchange rates. Since the band widths were chosen at the discretion of policymakers, the question of the optimal size of the band was faced at one time or another for each currency. One might have thought that band widths would have been determined according to a tradeoff between, say, the objective of facilitating international commerce (a narrow band) and the objective of maintaining flexibility for domestic monetary policy (a wide band). But policymakers treated the problem as presolved—with little or no discussion they selected band widths that resembled the gold standard.[5] According to this study's hypothesis, this choice of band width was part of the weaning process. By selecting modern band widths on the basis of the cost of gold arbitrage that prevailed before World War I, the allowable fluctuations in the exchange rate were of the same magnitude as the fluctuations that were possible under the gold standard. The absence of more discussion of this question supports the hypothesis that the desire to make the twentieth century fixed exchange rate system resemble the gold standard was an important objective. If this were the only objective in the minds of policymakers when selecting band widths, then they in fact optimized and there was no need for a discussion of tradeoffs.

One of the ways in which the appearance of a continued link with the gold standard has been maintained is through the retention of nineteenth century language. The language that was appropriate for the gold standard has been used in financial circles even through the international monetary crises of the 1970s. It is well known that the gold-exchange standard has been asymmetric with respect to exchange rate control. Except for the fact that most countries felt obligated to engage in some consultation with the International Money Fund they, rather than the United States, controlled dollar-exchange rates by direct intervention in currency markets. After August 1971 the official U. S. dollar price of gold, on record at the IMF, ceased to be of any importance, since official U. S. gold sales halted. Yet the language used gave the apperance that, through control over its official par value, the United States could affect the exchange rate in exactly the same manner that it could alter the exchange rate under the gold standard.

To illustrate the point, consider a press report of the 10 percent revaluation of the German mark against the dollar in February 1973. After the closing of exchange markets and emergency weekend meetings between German Finance Minister Schmidt and American authorities, the *Washington Post,* on February 14, reported the outcome in the following terms:

> Despite almost universal expectations that . . . [the weekend agreement] would have had to include some upward revaluation of the mark, the West German currency was left at its current fixed rate . . . The big mark question was whether Schmidt could resist upgrading the mark in the face of the massive $6 billion inflow of money that hit West Germany last week. . . .In a press conference today, the obviously triumphant finance minister contended that he had never considered revaluation. . . .

By concentrating on the official DM price of gold, the news obscured the fact that the exchange rate was, in fact, changed by Germany. By focusing on the legal gold parities rather than on the exchange rate, other news reports also referred to the United States as having "capitulated" by devaluing the dollar while the German monetary authorities "sat tight."* But the attention to the gold parities was misplaced because there were no official purchases or sales of gold at the old or the new parity either before or after the crisis. Moreover, the change in this legal price was not accomplished until later in 1973 when the U. S. Congress acted on the appropriate legislation.

The only economic significance of the U. S. parity change was to redirect political embarrassment from Bonn to Washington; and, of course, this is what Germany had negotiated for—a public announcement that shifted attention from the fact that Germany, not the United States, altered the all-important DM/dollar rate. Despite the convenience of the nineteenth century language for reallocating political adjustment burden from a non-center country to the

---

*Since so many currencies were revalued against the dollar in this period, it is useful to say that the dollar was devalued but misleading to say that the dollar was devalued by the United States.

The use of nineteenth century gold-standard language became less prevalent as the Bretton Woods system collapsed. The example given in the text is particularly interesting because it reflects the use of the language as late as 1973. It is easier to find examples in the 1960s than in the 1970s.

center country, there is no reason to think that it was designed for this purpose. According to the hypothesis of this study, the reason for the retention of nineteenth century language that focuses on official gold prices has been the need to retain as many trappings of the gold standard as possible to achieve a slow-but-sure weaning process.

The present hypothesis can also be used to resolve what might be called the "paradox of controls." This phrase is used to refer to the fact that controls on international transactions have been repeatedly introduced to improve countries' balance of payments positions. The introduction of these controls is paradoxical because they run counter to the alleged purpose of fixed exchange rates. From those persons responsible for monetary policy, the most pervasive argument for fixed exchange rates has concerned importance of stabilizing exchange rates to facilitate international commerce. Yet, when countries have had difficulties maintaining fixed exchange rates, they have invariably introduced a variety of controls, taxes, tariffs, and other impediments to international commerce. Many observers have noted that policymakers seem to have confused means with ends—that international transactions have been suppressed or distorted to achieve the end of fixed exchange rates. The authors take this paradox as more than a curiosity useful for tweaking friends in policy circles. It can be interpreted as a manifestation of the fundamental drive that, it is maintained here, underlies the policy of fixed exchange rates. A revaluation or devaluation is like the breaking of a promise—the promise of convertibility at the original price at which fiduciary liabilities were issued. Persons steeped in the tradition of banking, with knowledge of the crises associated with illiquid and inconvertible positions, have strong feelings about what the abandonment of convertibility or the appearance of convertibility means concerning the soundness of one's bank.

Finally, the hypothesis can be used to explain a striking irony in the fixed-versus-floating rate debate. As is well known, the commitment to fixed exchange rate constrains monetary policy. Equally well known is the fact that monetary authorities have refused to run monetary policy by a rule (for example, Friedman's x-percent rule). Therefore, it is ironic that those in charge of monetary policy have for so many years demanded that currency market intervention be subjected to the rule of fixed rates. Why, one must ask, have they been so determined to constrain themselves? According to the hypothesis, the monetary authorities have been willing to face this constraint to avoid the possible loss of public confidence that might occur if they gave up the image of the gold standard provided by fixed exchange rates.

One can make even more sense out of the paradox of controls and the irony of central bankers advocating fixed rates by imagining a simple world in which banks had only recently induced the public to hold their liabilities as currency. Consider a hypothetical world to illustrate the argument: Suppose there are two communities, each using gold as its medium of exchange, and, in response to the unexploited seigniorage opportunities, a bank of issue arisies in each community. To induce the public to accept their fiduciary liabilities, they initially maintain convertibility of their liabilities into gold and, as a consequence, the rate at which their liabilities are exchanged is fixed at the ratio of their gold parities. In order to increase their profits, the banks reduce their gold reserve ratios. This makes it difficult to maintain convertibility. But the banks are aware that the likelihood of a panic increases if convertibility is questionable. By cooperating to keep the exchange rate fixed, the banks can give the appearance of true gold-standard, convertibility no matter how low their gold reserve ratios. Given that the banks profits are much more dependent on the maintenance of confidence in their liabilities than on the volume of inter-community commerce to facilitate their ability to maintain a fixed exchange rate. Although this example is obviously too narrow and crude to be realistic depiction of the many currents underlying the behavior of our modern central banks, it explains, suprisingly well, two features of the traditional policy of fixed rates; the paradox of controls and the fact that monetary authorities have clung to fixed rates.

MANAGED FLOATING USING PURCHASING POWER PARITY

In the currency crises of the late 1960s and early 1970s, policymakers learned that the policy of fixed exchange rates was nearly impossible if each country was determined to pursue substantially different monetary policies, with their consequent differential inflation rates. The idea developed that, at least over the long run, exchange rate policy must be modified to allow for flexibility. The idea that exchange rates should be allowed to move with the differential inflation rate (since they could not be stopped from doing so) is influential in present-day intervention policy. Intervention in currency markets today is used to offset temporary and unnecessary exchange rate movements more often than it is to maintain a fixed exchange rate. The policy of fixed exchange rates has been, in part, replaced with a policy of smoothing the secular path of exchange rates.

To implement the new policy, monetary authorities must identify the short-term aberrations in exchange rate movements. Since the long-term movements are usually linked to the differential inflation rate, an important criterion for determining when to intervene is some version of purchasing-power parity.[6] This leads to an analysis of exactly what this doctrine has to offer for exchange rate policy.

To facilitate the discussion of Purchasing Power Parity (PPP) the following notation will be introduced:

P_i = money price of a basket of goods in country i
E = exchange rate

O = price of currency 2 in terms of currency 1
$X = P_1/EP_2$ = deflated or real exchange rate
$p_i = \ln P_i$ $\qquad$ $e = \ln E$ $\qquad$ $x = \ln X$

The usual statement of PPP, namely, that foreign and domestic prices tend to equality, rests on arbitrage in commodity markets. But even if the same goods sold for the same prices in a world without transport costs and tariffs, one would not expect the absolute PPP equation, $P_1 = EP_2$ or $X = 1$, to hold unless the price indices were constructed with identical weights. Also, the broader the measures of prices (for example, the more prices of nontraded goods that are included) the more difficult the equation is to justify. The usual theoretical justification for PPP with broad price indices is an argument that the relationship between the prices of traded and nontraded goods should be the same in the two countries. This further argument also rests on assumptions about the efficiency of private markets.

Since most price data are in the form of indices that compare current prices to a base year, the relative rather than the absolute version of PPP is usually employed and tested. The usual mathematical statement of the relative version is that, over some time period, X is constant or ΔX is zero. A constant real exchange rate, however, implies nothing about market efficiency. If, to take a far-fetched example to make the point, domestic prices were a hundred times greater than foreign prices (that is, $X = 100$), then the fact that X remained constant would indicate the continued failure of the market to equalize prices. To use the finding of a constant X to say something about commodity arbitrage requires additional information about the value of the real exchange rate. But this is the information necessary to test absolute PPP.

PPP, as it has been traditionally stated on the basis of commodity market arbitrage, is subject to a fundamental problem. The arbitrage theory of PPP has not yielded a testable economic hypothesis. It ranges from a tautology to an imprecise statement about price levels tending toward equality. To any evidence purporting to show that, after transport costs and tariffs are taken into consideration, the same good sells for different prices in different countries, the arbitrage theory of PPP can be defended with the argument that all market impediments must not have been taken into account or that the goods must not be identical after all. At this level, PPP is a tautology.[7] When PPP is interpreted as a statement about the relation between prices of a basket of goods for which it is impossible to take into account tariffs and transport costs, then it is an imprecise statement about prices tending to equality. Although no one expects the equation $X = 1$ to hold perfectly, it is unknown how near to unity arbitrage is supposed to make the value of X before one accepts or rejects PPP.[8]

To overcome this problem, an alternative theory of PPP based on classical monetary theory, or, more particularly, on the classical neutrality proposition, is proposed here.[9] Neutrality is a statement that real variables are invariant to monetary phenomena. Since both the level of the real exchange rate and changes in the real exchange rate are real variables, the neutrality theory of PPP, like the arbitrage theory of PPP, produces both an absolute and a relative version.

It is useful to develop the implications of neutrality by considering the following equation:

$$\Delta x = \Delta p_1 - \Delta e - \Delta p_2 = f(\text{real variables})$$

Since lower-case letters represent logarithms, their first differences represent percent changes in the variables. This equation represents the relative version of PPP based on neutrality since it specifies Δx as a function of real variables.* According to this equation, the percent change in E should *not* equal the differential inflation rate unless Δx were forced to zero by underlying real economic conditions.

The neutrality proposition applied to the real exchange rate is a stronger concept than is needed to capture the spirit of the PPP doctrine. A statement of PPP for which complete neutrality is a sufficient but not a necessary condition is that the real exchange rate between two regions is independent of whether the two regions have separate currencies or a common currency.[10] This means that the real exchange rate and movements in the real rate are independent of monetary shocks associated with the presence of multiple currencies.† Although this study has excluded consideration of any other monetary shocks, the theory of PPP will nevertheless be referred to here as a neutrality theory. Stated most succinctly, the neutrality theory of PPP states that the number of currencies does not matter for the behavior of the real exchange rate.

To illustrate the neutrality theory of PPP, consider the kind of situation to which PPP was applied following World War I. For a European country that suffered twice the inflation as the United States, for instance, PPP was used to argue that the European currency in question should be set at half its pre-war dollar value. But when policymakers were searching for new equilibrium exchange rates, it was argued (for example, by Keynes in 1923) that (the arbitrage

---

*More precisely, there are two conditions for neutrality, one concerning homogeneity and the other concerning the number of exogenous nominal variables. Homogeneity means that levels of nominal variables must enter real functions in ratio form, and that nominal rates (that is, rates of change or anticipations of rates of change of nominal variables) must enter real functions in difference form. The exogeneity condition is that the number of exogenous nominal variables cannot exceed one, and that the number of nominal rates cannot exceed one.

†Monetary shocks do not include shifts in the demand for money. Monetary shocks associated with the presence of multiple currencies would include, for instance, changes in nominal wages in one currency but not another currency, an official change in an exchange rate, and changes in the outstanding liabilities of a central bank.

version of) relative PPP was not an infallible guide, since real conditions had changed over the course of the war. Unlike the arbitrage theory of PPP, the neutrality theory of PPP allows for movements in real variables. Also, in contrast with the arbitrage version of PPP, the neutrality version can be postulated for any price indices. In other words, the basket of goods used to measure the purchasing power of one currency does not have to be identical with the basket used to measure the purchasing power of the other currency.

The neutrality theory of PPP can be recognized in more familiar terms as a natural rate hypothesis. It is the assertion that there exists a natural real exchange rate.

A distinction must be drawn between the existence of a natural real exchange rate and whether, assuming it exists, the natural real rate prevails at any point in time. This distinction can be developed by writing a PPP adjustment mechanism as a stochastic difference equation.* In a simple autoregressive process of the first order, for instance, x_t can be regarded as adjusting towards its natural rate, x_n, according to

$$\Delta x_t = -\lambda (x_{t-1} - x_n) + u_t$$

where u_t is white noise with a mean of zero. This is a stable process if λ lies between zero and two. This model is consistent with the existence of a natural real rate, x_n, which might never be realized, due to random shocks. But even if x_t were never equal to x_n, it might be possible to estimate the natural rate.

It has not been argued that PPP holds or that a natural real exchange rate exists. Only the implications of the classical neutrality proposition have been investigated here to obtain an alternative statement of PPP. This statement of PPP provides a theoretical solution to the question of the "natural" exchange rate referred to by Paula Tosini in her study of intervention guidelines.[11]

FUTURE EXCHANGE RATE POLICY

Robert Triffin has argued that during the long discussions over international monetary reform, there was "unanimous" agreement among officials that fixed exchange rates and a fixed price of gold would be "the pillars of any future system" and that changes in these pillars would "be beyond the pale of consideration."[12] Yet, the official abandonment of fixed rates and fixed gold

———————————

*In a dissertation at the University of Utah, Dayle Nattress has studied PPP adjustment equations in both continuous and discrete time models.

prices has been, according to Triffin, the most fundamental change that has occurred with the breakdown of the Bretton Woods system.

According to the hypothesis of this study, these pillars served the purpose of making the gold-exchange standard and the Bretton Woods system appear to provide the convertibility associated with the gold standard. Now that all pretenses have been dropped and the demand for fiduciary monies has not collapsed, there is no reason, according to the hypothesis, for monetary authorities to return to fixed parities. Given that the maintenance of gold-standard appearances no longer constrains exchange rate policy, it is useful to attempt some observations about the future course of intervention policy and the attitudes associated with such policies.

As the future unfolds one can expect to see a realignment of the former sides of the fixed-floating rate debate. Central bankers, rather than advocating exchange rate policies that constrain monetary policy, should become advocates of discretion; and economists who ordinarily argue for rules over authority should be expected to criticize the discretionary intervention made possible by the abandonment of fixed rates. The present authors regard Robert Mundell, in his advocacy of fixed rates, as more in the tradition of rules-over-authority than Milton Friedman, in his advocacy of floating exchange rates. Friedman played, perhaps, an unintended role in hastening the time at which monetary authorities abandoned the rule of fixed rates and found themselves with a new form of discretionary power.

This new-found flexibility in the conduct of monetary policy means that the potential use of monetary policy for stabilization policy is enhanced. Whatever the ultimate objectives of monetary policy, the potential for achieving these objectives is greater with the removal of the fixed exchange rate rule for intervening in the exchange market. The question of whether fixed or floating exchange rates are potentially superior for domestic stabilization is a nonissue. There may, of course, be particular instances in which the optimal monetary policy for achieving domestic objectives might involve stabilizing the exchange rate. But that must be sharply distinguished from the solution to the problem of optimal monetary policy under the constraint of exchange rate stabilization. This added flexibility in the use of monetary policy opens up an area of research concerning optimal intervention policy.[13] A PPP criterion might provide the optimal intervention rule for exchange rate smoothing. But when exchange market intervention is seen as another tool for achieving the whole constellation of monetary policy objectives, optimal intervention will generally violate any PPP guideline.

Over half a century ago, Irving Fisher (1911) and J. Maynard Keynes (1923) recommended deliberate alterations in the gold parity for domestic stabilization purposes. A proposal based on Fisher's plan almost became U.S. law in the early 1920s and, in the 1930s, the British Macmillan Committee made recommendations similar to Keynes' plan. These recommendations were rejected by the banking community because they would have required a complete reversal in thinking—they relegated exchange rates from the status of target to that of tool.[14] At the time that Fisher and Keynes were writing, the banking community was much more sensitive to confidence problems associated with changes in the gold parity. But it is likely that we will begin to see many more proposals for exchange rate manipulation, and monetary authorities are no longer prevented from giving serious consideration to such recommendations.

There is, however, one situation in which central banks might want to reinstitute fixed exchange rates to obtain more rather than less discretion. If the monopoly over note issue in each country were abolished and if currencies were sufficiently substitutable in the portfolios of ultimate wealth holders, then central banks would be forced to compete away their seigniorage to maintain the demand for their liabilities.[15] The abolition of their government-protected monopoly positions and the presence of currency substitution would either eliminate discretionary monetary policy or make that discretion not worth having.* In an effort to resecure their abilities to pursue (jointly, at least) discretionary monetary policy, central banks could fix exchange rates to keep the public from substituting into the currency with the lowest rate of depreciation.[16]

NOTES

1. Discussions of metallism can be found in Arthur Nussbaum, *Money in the Law; National and International* (Brooklyn: The Foundation Press, 1950), and in Ludwig von Mises, *The Theory of Money and Credit* (New Haven: Yale University Press, 1954).

2. This argument is also found in F. A. Hayek, *Denationalization of Money* (London: Institute of Economic Affairs, 1976), pp. 24-25.

3. An example of the way convertibility can be withdrawn gradually or, at least, in stages is provided by the experience of the United States. Starting in March, 1933 U.S. citizens were prohibited from converting U.S. currency into gold. In March, 1968, the United States refused to convert foreign private holdings of U.S. currency into gold. And, after August, 1971, foreign official institutions could no longer sell their U.S. dollars to U.S. monetary authorities for gold.

4. A detailed analysis of official gold policies is found in *Gold, Money and the Law*, ed. Henry G. Manne and Roger LeRoy Miller (Chicago: Aldine Publishing Co., 1975).

---

*Vera Smith has cited numerous examples showing that the monopolies enjoyed by central banks originated, in part, from the need by governments to obtain loans. In other words, there were many reciprocal arrangements under which the government would protect a bank from competition in the issuance of notes in return for a large government loan. Today this reciprocity is reflected by the fact that most central bank portfolios are dominated by government securities and that governments can place pressure on central banks to support the government bond markets. If this need of the government is sufficiently great, then there is little reason to suspect that government could be easily induced to remove the central banks' monopolies over the issuance of notes.[17]

5. To our knowledge, there has been only one published piece of research in which the question of the optimal band width has been systematically explored: see Robert Mundell, "The Exchange Rate Margins and Economic Policy," in *Money in the International Order*, ed. Carter Murphy (Dallas: Southern Methodist University Press, 1964).

6. The use of PPP as an intervention guideline has been discussed by First National City Bank in "Purchasing Power: A Polestar for Drifting Exchange Rates," *Monthly Newsletter* (November 1973).

7. In Lawerence H. Officer, "The Purchasing Power Parity Theory of Exchange Rates: A Review Article," *IMF Staff Papers* 23 (March 1976):8; and J. Maynard Keynes, *Tract on Monetary Reform* (London: Macmillan, 1923), p. 75, the respective authors noted that PPP can be reduced to a statement devoid of "operational content" and that PPP can be interpreted as a "truism."

8. The question of how far apart domestic and foreign prices (converted into domestic currency equivalents using the exchange rate) must be in order to reject the doctrine is the question that Balassa asked when examining Yeager's study; see Leland Yeager, "A Rehabilitation of Purchasing-Power Parity," *Journal of Political Economy* 66 (December 1958):516–30; and Bela Belassa, "The Purchasing-Power Parity Doctrine: A Reappraisal," *Journal of Political Economy* 72 (December 1964):584–96.

9. In a recent study of PPP, Moon Lee makes numerous references to the affinity between PPP and classical neutrality, but he never identifies the relation; see Moon Lee, *Purchasing Power Parity* (New York: Marcel Dekker, 1976). The neutrality proposition is distinct from the better-known neutrality-of-money theorem. This distinction is developed in Lance Girton and Don Roper, "The Theory and Implication of Currency Substitution," *International Financial Discussion Papers* (May 1976).

10. Hans A. Genberg, in "Aspects of the Monetary Approach to Balance-of-Payments Theory: An Empirical Study of Sweden," in *The Monetary Approach to the Balance of Payments*, ed. Jacob Frenkel and Harry G. Johnson (Toronto: University of Toronto Press, 1976), pp. 198–226, has compared the relation of prices between cities with different currencies. Although a precise test of the neutrality theory of PPP may be very difficult to construct, Genberg's study contains the only test that we can interpret as directed towards the neutrality-based PPP.

11. Paula Tosini, "Leaning Against the Wind: A Standard for Managed Floating," *Essays in International Finance* (Princeton: Princeton University).

12. Robert Triffin, "Jamaica: 'Major Revisions' of Fiasco?" in Edward Bernstein, *Essays in International Finance* (Princeton, N.J.: Princeton University), pp. 48–49.

13. An interesting example of how optimal intervention policy might be derived in a stochastic framework using a domestic stabilization objective is found in a recent paper by Russ Boyer, "Optimal Foreign Exchange Market Intervention," manuscript, 1976.

14. Although Fisher wanted to use the gold parity as a tool, he nevertheless proposed a strict rule that would not have allowed any discretion in monetary policy. His rule was that the U.S. parity (official dollar price of gold) be changed by the same percent and in the opposite direction as any change in the domestic price level. Keynes, op. cit., on the other hand, advocated that the English authorities reset the gold parity every week on the basis of their appraisal of changes in all conditions in the domestic economy. The reaction of the banking community to Fisher's plan is documented in Lance Girton and Don Roper, "J. Laurence Laughlin and the Quantity Theory of Money," *Journal of Political Economy* 86 (August 1978).

15. The argument that currency substitution would induce banks to compete away their profits by lowering their inflation rates (or by paying interest on their liabilities) is developed in L. Girton and D. Roper, "Theory and Implications of Currency Substitution," op. cit.

16. F. A. Hayek, op. cit., p. 82, has also recognized that, if central banks' monopolies over note issue were abandoned, floating rates might be necessary for retaining discipline over money issuers.

17. See Vera C. Smith, *Rationale of Central Banking* (London: P.S. King, 1936).

Charles D. Cathcart

16

A MONETARY APPROACH
TO THE EXCHANGE RATE
IN THE SHORT RUN

INTRODUCTION

The monetary approach posits that market-induced changes in the balance of payments and exchange rate are essentially monetary phenomena. In the standard analysis this is a long-run proposition that follows from two theories: the monetary theory of the price level and the purchasing-power-parity theory of the exchange rate. Most monetary approach studies are limited to the long run because purchasing-power parity is not ordinarily expected to hold in the short run. The question remains, however: if purchasing power parity does not hold, what does the monetary approach have to say about exchange rate determination in the short run? More specifically, can short-run changes in the exchange rate be ascribed directly to monetary disturbances in a money-demand, money-supply framework?

This study addresses these questions by showing, first, that if purchasing-power parity does not hold, the demand for nominal balances in an open economy may be specified as depending on the exchange rate and the expected rate of change in the exchange rate, independently of other variables. These dependencies, which are not existent in the long run, form the basis of a monetary analysis of exchange rate determination in the short run, exchange rate stability, and the adjustment of the exchange rate over time to a higher growth rate of the money stock. It is argued that monetary expansion affects the exchange rate in the direction implied by purchasing power parity but in advance of increases in the prices of domestic goods. Inflation in the prices of domestic goods later reduces pressure on the exchange rate, giving the impression of overshooting.

THE DEMAND FOR MONEY IN AN OPEN ECONOMY

The model begins with a fairly standard demand-for-money function incorporating the expected rate of inflation as the opportunity cost variable,

$$\text{Log} \frac{M^D}{PQ} = -a\pi^0 ; a > 0 \tag{1}$$

where M^D is the demand for nominal balances, P is the price level for final sales, Q is real final sales, and π^0 is the expected rate of inflation.

Households and firms hold cash balances for transactions in domestically produced goods, Q^H, and imported goods, Q^E. Domestic goods are priced directly in terms of the domestic medium of exchange and unit of account. Imported goods are originally priced in foreign exchange and, neglecting transportation costs, carry prices in domestic money equal to their foreign prices times the exchange rate. The price-level variable, therefore, may be segmented into the following components,

$$P = H(1 - \rho) + XE(\rho) \tag{2}$$

where H is the price level of final sales of domestically produced goods, ρ is the proportion of final sales accounted for by imports, X is the price of foreign exchange, and E is the foreign price level of imported goods.

For the short run ρ is assumed constant, reflecting rigidities in production and consumption. (Goods markets may not be in equilibrium in the short run.) During a period that we will identify as the inter run, ρ may change in response to market forces such as price differentials. In the long run, however, it is assumed that steady state relationships hold such that ρ is again constant. Therefore, except for the inter run, the time derivative of the logarithm of (2) may be expressed as follows:

$$\pi = \delta(1 - \phi) + \gamma\phi + \eta\phi \tag{3}$$

where π is the general rate of inflation, δ is the rate of inflation in domestically produced goods, ϕ is the proportion of the market value of final sales accounted for by imports $[\phi = \rho(XE/P)]$, γ is the rate of change in the exchange rate, and η is the rate of change in the foreign prices of imports.

In the long run, goods market arbitrage establishes purchasing-power parity such that $\gamma = \delta - \eta$. Therefore, in this case expression (3) collapses to

$$\pi = \delta \tag{4}$$

In other words, in the long run the exchange rate and foreign inflation have no independent, direct impact on the domestic inflation rate. Market participants forming expectations on π for this time frame, therefore, are able to ignore considerations related to the exchange rate and foreign inflation.

In the short run, however, various factors may operate on δ, γ, and η such that wide divergences from purchasing-power parity occur. The rate of change in the exchange rate, in particular, is subject to episodes of large swings. Such behavior has been interpreted by R. Dornbusch as an overreaction of the exchange rate to a change in the rate of monetary expansion—the overshooting hypothesis; a variation on Dornbusch's interpretation will be developed in a later section.[1]

Since inflation can be materially affected by the foreign sector in the short run, market participants forming expectations on the inflation rate for this period might prudently form expectations separately on η and δ .(One can note here that the impact on the domestic inflation rate of extreme exchange-rate changes, especially in small open economies, is a familiar concern to both policymakers and market participants.)

Our expected inflation term in (1), therefore, may be specified for the short run as

$$\pi^0 = \delta^0(1 - \phi) + \gamma^0\phi + \eta^0\phi \tag{5}$$

In this manner, the demand for money in an open economy may be said to depend in part on the expected rate of change in the exchange rate. And because the price level term in equation (1) is described by equation (2), the demand for nominal balances also depends on the level of the exchange rate.

THE EXCHANGE RATE, MONEY, INFLATION AND STABILITY

The next step is to solve for a rate-of-change relationship between the exchange rate and other relevant variables in a money-demand, money-supply model. Money demand is assumed to equal money supply. Substitution of (5) and (2) into (1) and the time differential of the logarithm of the result yields

$$\gamma = -\eta + a\gamma^0 + a\eta^0 + 1/\phi \left[\Theta - \lambda - (1 - \phi)\delta + a(1 - \phi)\delta^0\right] \tag{6}$$

where Θ is the rate of growth in the money supply, and λ is the rate of growth of real final sales.

Several important results are immediately apparent from (6). First, a higher rate of growth of the domestic money stock tends to cause appreciation in the price of foreign exchange. This is the usual conclusion except that it holds with other things constant including the rate of inflation of domestically produced goods. In fact, an increase in the inflation rate of domestically produced goods, δ, operates in a direction opposite to the one implied by the purchasing-power parity theorem. By tending to increase the demand for nominal balances, this increase exerts a downward influence on the price of foreign exchange. Thus the second result posits an inverse relationship between the rate of inflation for domestic goods, and the rate of change in the exchange rate in the short run.

Third, a one-time increase in the expected rate of change in the exchange rate will be associated with a temporarily higher rate of appreciation of foreign exchange, other things the same. This effect is important, of course, because it raises the possibility of an unstable interaction between exchange rate change and the demand for money—precisely the same type of interaction, in fact, that has been studied extensively for the general inflation rate and the demand for money.

Most studies of the stability of inflation rate and the monetary system have concluded that, except perhaps in some rare cases, stability exists. According to Cagan, Stein, and others, it exists because of frictions: lags in the adjustment of real cash balances or of expectations to actual rate changes.[2] A question arises, therefore: are these frictions as great with respect to real balances and the exchange rate as they are with respect to real balances and the prices of goods in their countries of origin?

Although much remains to be understood about expectational and adjustment lags, there are reasons to believe that these frictions are indeed smaller for interactions of the exchange rate and real balances. One of the reasons inflation expectations lag the actual rate of inflation would seem to be the lag in government statistics. In advance of government statistics there is a high cost of information regarding the actual rate of inflation. Moreover, after the release of government data, there is uncertainty regarding their meaning for prices of specific baskets of goods.

These factors would seem to be less important for the exchange rate. A major exchange rate change for most currencies is known to important market participants with virtually no delay or cost. The implication of an exchange rate change for the prices of specific goods is subject to some uncertainty since foreign exporters may absorb some of the change by taking smaller or larger profits, but this uncertainty would not be important for large changes.

Another difference may involve the lag in the adjustment of real cash balances to expected rate changes.* This lag may exist for inflation in goods prices because of incremental costs associated with the size or rapidity with which transactions in goods are effected. In other words, a decision to hold significantly more goods and less cash may be more costly to carry out all at once. Such an increase in cost might not be as much a factor, however, for a cash

---

*This model excludes this lag in equation (6); an allowance for it in (6) would not affect the earlier conclusions.

balance adjustment to an anticipated increase in the exchange rate, since this adjustment could be handled, of course, by the current sale of a large amount of domestic cash for foreign cash at little or no incremental cost; the cash could be spent on foreign goods over time.

For these various reasons, the interaction between real balances and the rate of change in the exchange rate may carry more potential for instability than does the interaction between real balances and inflation in the prices of domestic goods. It would seem, however, that actual cases of such instability still would be rare, requiring exceptional accelerations in the rate of expansion in the money supply.*

A PROCESS OF ADJUSTMENT TO HIGHER MONEY GROWTH

Equation (6) provides not only some interesting results for short-run, all-other-things-equal interdependencies, but a framework for a monetary explanation of the overshooting phenomenon. For money market equilibrium, a higher rate of growth of the money supply must create a compensating adjustment in one or more of the other variables affecting the demand for nominal balances. The equation itself provides no information about the variables that adjust at different points of time. However, based on notions of the relative flexibility of different variables and adjustment speeds in different markets, a reasonable pattern of adjustment may be suggested.

It is generally accepted that financial markets adjust to changes more rapidly than do goods markets. In fact, in the absence of intervention, financial asset prices (or yields) are sufficiently flexible to clear large financial markets almost instantaneously. This certainly applies as much to the foreign exchange market at it does to other financial markets. Consequently, if monetary changes do have a direct impact on the foreign exchange market, they will cause quick adjustments in the exchange rate.

As emphasized by M. Friedman and in conformity with portfolio theory, an increase in the rate of monetary expansion creates, in *direct* response, higher demands for a broad range of assets, real as well as financial.[4] Also, and especially important for these purposes, the range naturally extends to foreign assets. What are the immediate effects? Domestic interest rates may decline; and,

---

*The German hyperinflation experience following World War I might provide one such case. In the popular press the mark exchange rate was accorded a great deal of responsibility for inflation at the time.

Jacob A Frenkel has estimated a money-demand friction for the German episode using the forward exchange rate discount as an independent variable; however, Frenkel's approach was different from the one here in that he used the forward discount as a proxy for the overall expected rate of inflation.[3]

starting from a steady state, involuntary inventory decumulation and a rise in unfilled orders occurs in response to the increase in demand for domestic real assets.* At the same time, in response to the increase in demand for foreign real and financial assets the price of foreign exchange will rise, without any necessary prior rise in domestic prices or prior decline in interest rates.† A rise in real final sales and a rise in the price of foreign exchange raise the demand for money and establish equilibrium between money demand and money supply.

Over time the prices of domestic goods tend to rise in response to the rise in demand and higher output rates. As domestic goods' prices rise the demand for money rises; this in turn exerts downward pressure on the price of foreign exchange. The time pattern of the exchange rate, therefore, includes a change in direction. It is reasonable that the path of adjustment exhibit initially a substantial, sharp rise in the price of foreign exchange, considerably out of line with purchasing-power parity; this is then followed by a more gradual decline in the exchange rate, eventually to a level consistent with purchasing-power parity.

This path describes an overshooting by the exchange rate of a new purchasing-power parity relationship. Overshooting, however, might convey the wrong impression of the process that underlies the path, for it suggests that purchasing-power parity forces motivate exchange rate changes throughout. The whole process in fact is similar to the one that underlies the change in the direction of change in interest rates that can occur following an increase in the rate of monetary expansion.[5] The initial impact occurs because of different degrees of flexibility in the variables that are affected by the money supply and that tend to increase money demand. Eventually adjustments are determined by equilibrium goods market relationships.

NOTES

1. Rudiger Dornbusch, "Expectations and Exchange Rate Dynamics," *Journal of Political Economy*, 84 (December 1976): 1161–76.

2. Phillip Cagan, "The Monetary Dynamics of Hyperinflation," in *Studies in the Quantity Theory of Money*, ed. Milton Friedman (Chicago: University of Chicago Press,

---

*The reason for saying that interest rates *may* decline is that it is not clear that monetary expansion will always reduce interest rates. If markets are keying on monetary expansion as a guide to future inflation, the demand for financial assets may fall and the increase in the demand for domestic real assets and foreign real and financial assets may be even stronger.

†In Dornbusch's analysis, monetary expansion affects the exchange rate through a decline in the domestic interest rate. A lower interest rate is responsible for capital outflow. Although the interest rate does not enter into this study's demand-for-money function—it was omitted in order to focus directly on expected inflation—in this approach, a fall in the domestic rate of interest due to the liquidity effect would have a *dampening* effect on the appreciation of foreign currencies by raising the demand for domestic money.

1956); and J. L. Stein, "Monetary Growth Theory in Perspective," *American Economic Review* 60: 85-106.

3. Jacob A. Frenkel, "The Forward Exchange Rate, Expectations and the Demand for Money: The German Hyperinflation," *American Economic Review* 67: 653-70.

4. M. Friedman, *A Theoretical Framework for Monetary Analysis*, Occasional Paper 112 (New York: National Bureau of Economic Research, 1971).

5. See Phillip Cagan and Arthur Gandolfi, "The Lag in Monetary Policy as Implied by the Time Pattern of Monetary Effects on Interest Rates," *American Economic Review, Papers and Proceedings* 59 (May 1969):277-84; and W. E. Gibson, "Interest Rates and Monetary Policy," *Journal of Political Economy* 78 (May/June 1970):431-55.

David T. King

17

EXPECTATIONS AND
EXCHANGE RATE DYNAMICS

It is a well-established empirical proposition that, over the long run and independent of the exchange rate regime, exchange rates and international inflation rates offset each other. This tendency is not only natural but desirable, since otherwise, the relative price signals on which international trade is based would change because of nominal factors rather than trends in real comparative advantage. The long-run correlation between rates of price inflation in a given country and rates of monetary growth in excess of its real growth potential has also been frequently demonstrated. Together, these observations form the basis for the empirical validation of the monetary approach to exchange rate determination.[1] With money exogenously determinable and prices endogenous, exchange rates adjust to offset international differences in monetary accommodation. Put another way, exchange rates act, with domestic inflation, to maintain money neutrality in an international context, keeping real money (currency) supplies consistent with real productive potential, and thereby hold countries' demand for goods and services equivalent to supply over the long run. Exchange rates, like prices, are edogenous variables in the monetary approach. Thus, the proponents of target-based international stabilization policies, who argue for publicized commitments across countries to steadily declining medium- to long-run monetary aggregates growth, see exchange rate as neutral, responding passively to whatever inflation differentials are implied.*

The record of exchange rate fluctuation since the institution of generalized floating in 1973 has in fact demonstrated the quick response of exchange rates

---

*See for example recent contributions by members of the Shadow European Economic Policy Committee, coordinated by Karl Brunner and Alan Meltzer.

to changing inflation prospects. It has also, however, raised suspicion that exchange rates have often overadjusted to inflation differentials. Exchange rate change over this period has rarely been a smooth, continuous, unidirectional process, and wide swings have occurred in rates. When such adjustment is moderate and short-lived, it is potentially damaging only to the extent that rate volatility contributes to uncertainty and thereby represses investment and real growth. When it is extreme and presistent, however—resulting in lasting unwarranted changes in *real* exchange rates—it becomes truly "exogenous," and the equivalence of inflation and exchange rate change can end up maintained via feedbacks on domestic prices. One way or another, that is, exchange rates and differential inflation will offset each other; real exchange rate changes will not persist. Adjustment can be well-behaved, from money to prices and exchange rates, or prices can adjust through accommodating monetary policy to exogenous exchange rate change not justified by inflation developments. Alternatively, a country may refuse to accommodate the exogenous shock on prices in the latter case and adjust through a decline in real economic activity and an eventual recovery of the exchange rate.

The point is that exogenous exchange rate change is either inflationary or costly in terms of real growth. It thus presents a policy problem to all concerned with international markets and economic stabilization. Authorities have chosen to abandon, at least temporarily, monetary growth targets in the apparent belief that exchange rate appreciation was overdone—that is, so far beyond the country's relative inflation advantage as to compromise significantly its real growth prospects. Firms trading in international markets have gone so far as to move plant location to the country of market, apparently because exchange rate appreciation in excess of domestic cost advantage had so persistently left them unable to sell internationally at a reasonable profit. Countries facing exchange rates that were depreciating in excess of underlying inflation have been faced with the difficult choice of accepting higher rates of inflation or retarding real growth.

This study looks at the question of exchange rate overshooting—its causes, its costs, and how it can be minimized.

WHY EXCHANGE RATES OVERSHOOT

Some authors have analyzed exchange rate overshooting. Rudiger Dornbusch[2] shows how, given an unanticipated monetary disturbance, lagged price adjustment in goods markets leads spot exchange rates to move beyond the longer-term rate expectations reflected in the forward rate. In a similarly "mechanistic" approach, Jürg Neihans[3] theoretically demonstrates, in effect, the resistance of short-term exchange rate change to systematic analysis—adjustment to the new equilibrium can involve overshooting, undershooting, both, or neither. While these studies may help account for exchange rate fluctuation in periods of relative calm, other authors have concentrated more explicitly on the process of expectations adjustment. Most market observers would agree that the adjustment of expectations dominates exchange rate determination in the short to medium term. Stephen Kohlhagen[4] empirically incorporates an expectations specification that helps explain periods of instability in Canadian dollar rates. Ronald I. McKinnon[5] most directly introduces the present study, by emphasizing the importance of uncertainty in accounting for spot rate volatility through its effect on the international substitutability of financial assets—that is, on the sufficiency of stabilizing speculation.

Assume a small domestic economy with two assets—goods and money—and a flexible exchange rate. Suppose a foreign economy (comprising the rest of the world) is pursuing a steady zero-inflation rate monetary policy. Now suppose the domestic economy, starting from a similar point, initiates a permanently more expansive monetary policy.

The exchange rate consequences are straightforward. As domestic residents attempt to spend rising nominal incomes, domestic prices rise (since domestic output is already at potential). In addition, domestic residents bid for foreign exchange with which to purchase foreign goods. Foreigners faced with offers of the domestic currency, however, are unwilling to hold increased quantities of it at current exchange rates, since they foresee a capital loss equivalent to the rationally predictable rise in domestic inflation and the associated depreciation of the country's currency that will ultimately be induced by international arbitrage. That is, the domestic currency's real value, measured in terms of either domestic or foreign goods, is expected to decline. Foreigners refuse to sell foreign currency until its price falls to offset the expected inflation. This adjustment, along with the rise in domestic inflation, maintains the real value of the currency stock and keeps the economy's demand at a sustainable level.

If these adjustments are less than perfect, the policy will allow the country some temporary real income gain in the transitional period between the shift in policy and the ultimate adjustment of all transactors' inflation perceptions. Lagged expectations adjustment among domestic agents, especially in the labor market, stimulates "overemployment," and lagged adjustment of foreign investors expectations allows the country to run a current account deficit. Indeed, it may finally be the change in the current account balance that prompts the adjustment of inflation anticipations. Monetary developments are difficult to assess, even when policy targets are in effect. The current account can provide information about the state of excess demand in the economy. In this respect, the signals to which international transactors are attentive are broader-based than those available to domestic agents, and it therefore appears natural that labor-market participants, for example, would look to exchange rate behavior as an input in wage negotiations.

The same profit-loss assessment helps explain the problem of overshooting, which is best illustrated by considering a cyclical problem. Start again with similar, zero-inflation monetary policies on long-run output trends in the domestic and foreign economies. Now suppose the domestic economy suffers an exogenous supply shock that results in a decline in real output below potential. Monetary policy is unchanged, however; income is supported at a full employment sustainable level. The country can satisfy its demand during the cyclical downturn only by importing from abroad, that is, by running a current account deficit. Whether or not the country is able to sustain its long-run real income depends on whether foreign investors are willing to hold financial assets of the deficit country at unchanged exchange rates. In the pure monetary model, that depends on their perceptions of relative monetary policies. If they understand that money is in excess supply only in relation to temporarily depressed money demand, and not in relation to sustainable output, they will not anticipate price effects and will be willing to hold increased quantities of the currency. Indeed, to the extent that bidding for foreign currencies by domestic residents tends to lower the domestic currency's rate, real capital gains opportunities appear for investors foreseeing the ultimate output recovery and the reversal of incipient depreciation pressures.

The uncertainties ignored in this scenario are the basis for the overshooting of exchange rates. This can be appreciated by first recalling that for all allocations that require any waiting before collection of return, the economically relevant signals are *certainty equivalent* returns, and not just expected returns in a mean sense. In other words, action is determined by the state of the probability distribution of yield as a whole, encompassing of course its expectation, but also its variance (a reflection of uncertainty) and perhaps its skewness as well (reflecting probability bias). The resulting certainty equivalent is the return that, if offered today, would make the transactor just willing to call off the bet. For this study's purposes, if transactors are risk-averse, the existence of uncertainty about the actual state of monetary policy (inflation pressure) is enough to move exchange rates away from appropriate values even if monetary policy is actually stable in a long-run sense. Even if the *expectation* of the typical transactor is that monetary policy is non-inflationary, non-zero variance in the probability distribution of monetary trends—perhaps the result of past variability—is enough to move rates when investors rationally base their exchange rate expectations on a monetary approach. It may be expected, rightly, that the current account deficit associated with the cyclical downturn is "sustainable"—that is, reversible. But uncertainty about this outcome reduces the certainty equivalent return to absorbing currency balances as their cost starts to fall, meaning that the deficit will be less than financed, and that exchange rates will oscillate with current account balances.

In practice, over the floating period monetary trends have often been difficult to discern. The use of publicized policy targeting has become widespread only over the past three years, and even now the credibility attached to these pronouncements varies with exchange market participants' perceptions about the political will and power of the central bank or administration in question. The state of the current account balance has therefore remained an important signal of excess demand and, consequently, exchange rate prospects. But this indicator is flawed, as suggested above. The increase in the current account deficit associated with a purely *cyclical* excess demand problem warrants no exchange rate adjustment; only that associated with inflationary demand stimulus does. Several factors have led, unfortunately, to an over-concentration on this uncertain indicator in assessing the exchange rate outlook: unwillingness of central banks to commit themselves, in public concert with each other, to long-run monetary aggregate growth stabilization policies; instabilities over the short to medium run in the relationship between money and income; and misperceptions of the nature of appropriate exchange rate adjustment. The first two factors explain the uncertainty of expectations about monetary policy and the shifting of attention to the current account balance as an inflation indicator, while the last point reflects the widely held notion that exchange rates are supposed to adjust to eliminate current account imbalances—which, as has been shown here, is quite incorrect in the case of cyclical imbalances.*

The uncertainty about monetary policy, the use of the current account balance as an indicator of excess demand pressure, and misperception about the adjustment role of exchange rates have made the international investment required to keep exchange rate adjustment appropriate a highly risky area. In consequence, certainty equivalent returns of taking such foreign exchange positions tend to deteriorate with current account deficit size, and exchange rates have moved with those balances. The public sector counterpart to this behavior has been a tendency toward reserve accumulation or decumulation according to the behavior of the current account, as central banks absorbed risk that the market was unwilling to take on, lengthening currency positions to moderate (profitably) unwarranted movement.

IS OVERSHOOTING SERIOUS?

Since the future is never certain, individuals willing to tie their incomes to it deserve to be rewarded—that is, risk is inescapable, and certainty can be bought only at a price that satisfies the ultimate open-position-taker.† Thus, it

---

*Cyclical imbalances can include deficits associated with very long-run development of output or progress in reducing excess demand. Thus developing countries' current account deficits in themselves do not explain such countries' depreciations, and, on a radically different note, the immense structural problems of adjustment to the oil price rise suggest strongly that the U.S. oil deficit, though persistent, is not irreversible, and need not in itself call for any exchange rate adjustment.

†This "price" is the difference between the yield expected with uncertainty if the position is left open (the risk taken) and the yield implied in the speculator's current (certain) price offer for the asset in question.

is normal that exchange rates fluctuate to some extent with current account balances. Cyclical "misfortune" cannot be entirely escaped.

It does not necessarily follow from this that all exchange rate fluctuation is normal and efficient in the sense that it is at a welfare minimum. As shown in the previous section, inordinate uncertainty can be expected to lead to exchange rate changes that may depart significantly from appropriate values. The costs of such departures are potentially severe:

1. Excessive exchange rate volatility reduces certainty equivalent returns to international trade, frustrating investment, trade growth, and welfare.

2. Movement of exchange rates beyond appropriate levels for significant periods of time begins to shift demand and supply flows away from the fundamentally efficient pattern.

3. Associated with such lasting real exchange rate changes are direct additions to inflation through imports and excess demand in deficit countries, and price deflation and declines in demand in surplus countries. These exogenous factors disturb domestic economic stabilization and present policy dilemmas for domestic monetary authorities. Since policymakers are, defensibly, hardly ever willing to allow price shocks to be absorbed completely in a decline in real income, persistent unwarranted exchange rate movements can be expected on a net global basis to add to inflation and probably to decrease employment somewhat.*

Have departures from appropriate exchange rates been significant enough over the floating period to create such problems? This question is difficult to address empirically given the relative brevity of the period in question and the various forces at work during it. On the other hand, a few obvious empirical facts are quite relevant.

1. In terms of pure magnitude, exchange rate swings have been big. An extreme example is the 15 percent depreciation of the Canadian dollar against the U.S. dollar over 1977. Against the same currency, the Japanese yen appreciated over 30 percent during the same period. These two countries have important trading relationships. In other cases, such as the mark and sterling, large rate changes have been wholly reversed only to swing back again.

2. Major companies have shifted production facilities to market countries—with obvious direct home-country employment effects—to escape exchange rate appreciation that kept rates of sale price increase on international markets below domestic cost increase.

3. Monetary authorities have been forced to depart—typically with great reluctance—from monetary policies when exchange rate change became intoler-

---

*If prices are less fluid downward than upward, temporary employment benefits in inflating countries will be more than offset by temporary employment losses in deflating surplus countries.

able. Important examples are Canada, Germany, and Switzerland in 1977–78. These policy moves would clearly not have been undertaken had exchange rates simply been offsetting underlying relative cost developments. They were adopted because rates went so far beyond underlying inflation differentials that authorities concluded that the output or inflation risk inherent in exchange rate protection had become smaller than the risks associated with further exchange rate movement.

It is very important to emphasize that these shortcomings are not the result of markets that are irrational or inefficient, but can be blamed on the extreme uncertainty that has been associated with national inflation prospects, or, put another way, with the sustainability of the pattern of current account balances. Two examples illustrate the difficulties of making such assessments. Until late in 1976, market participants lacked a credible basis for forming expectations about U.K. monetary policy. Conditioned by past events, their probability distributions of the U.K. monetary stance were probably biased toward expansionism, especially given the information gap between the Bank of England and the market. Thus, even though the United Kingdom in fact began to voice monetary moderation during the summer, the lack of clarity of this commitment led most market participants to continue to key on current account prospects as the best available indicator of U.K. policy. As the authorities began to institute moderation more actively, this indicator became an incorrect signal of inflation prospects; the current account deficit was in fact becoming "reversible." The credibility gap concealed this truth and led to a continued and rapid marking-down of sterling that, now truly "adding to" U.K. inflation, began to feed into domestic wage settlements directly. The seriously destabilized macroeconomic situation ultimately forced the United Kingdom into a clear monetary commitment, under the "enforcement" of the International Money Fund. This information proved dramatically efficient in restoring sterling rates and wage inflation levels more appropriate to the actual monetary stance of the Bank of England.

Although it has proven very difficult to substantiate empirically, exchange market participants became officially convinced by mid-1977 that U.S. exporters were in a disadvantageous competitive situation vis-a-vis their principal trading partners. In other words, although on apparent relative monetary grounds U.S. inflation was only mildly above that of Germany and Japan, market participants were encouraged to conclude, in effect, that these trends understated the true advantage of the latter countries. Thus, the U.S. current account deficit, which had previously been regarded as primarily cyclical in nature, came to be looked on as significantly resulting from relative cost divergence; it was therefore considered unsustainable. Though oil is a monopolistically supplied good largely untraded among industrialized countries, and whose price is, moreover, dollar-denominated, the energy-related deficit also began to be viewed with alarm as reflecting an excessive U.S. dependence on foreign goods, despite the fact that the rise in oil imports was clearly related in part to the short- to medium-term cyclical surge in U.S. growth and in part to the longer-term structural nature of adjustment of the U.S. economy to the higher relative price of oil. Market participants were invited by many commentators to view this problem as requiring the short-run expedient of exchange rate depreciation. The United States would have to pay for its oil through an overadjustment of its competitive position vis-a-vis the industrialized countries with which it competes in many exports. These attitudes severely destabilized the process of expectations formation in the exchange markets and generated a progressive and fundamentally unwarranted depreciation of the dollar. The process was aggravated by mounting uncertainties about the course of monetary policy itself. In the first place, the merging dollar-depreciation-based inflation shock on an economy that was in any case expanding well on its own created monetary growth pressures that compromised the achievement of targets. Additonally, the prospects for inflation were thrown into some uncertainty by the change in chairmanship of the Federal Reserve Board. Indeed, it was not until the spring of 1978, coincident with firm anti-inflationary and conservative monetary statements by the new chairman, that the dollar finally stabilized. But in its wake lay a significantly higher U.S. inflation rate, significantly lower-than-expected growth in Germany and Japan, and a significant increase in world liquidity, associated with fruitless central bank attempts to preserve more appropriate rate levels.

AVERTING OVERSHOOTING

As just suggested, central banks' attempts to stabilize exchange rates are often unsuccessful. However, the public transactor, as a market participant different primarily in his degree of risk-aversion, at times can play an important and welfare-enhancing role in helping to maintain exchange market efficiency. Perhaps the more important question is not *whether* the central bank should exercise its responsibilities as "risktaker of last resort," but how it should finance the associated positions. If they are financed by the net creation of new central assets that are transferred to the private sector, the inflationary results of the associated expansion of liquidity may offset the benefits of exchange rate stabilization, and will certainly erode them. If, on the other hand, public transactors take positions by simply shifting the currency denomination of their own existing liabilities—an attractive prospect for a country whose currency is depreciating inappropriately, since foreign interest rates are artificially low and dollar countervalues of borrowing artificially high—private capital inflows are directly stimulated and liquidity creation is no more than it would have been in normal circumstances. Since countries experiencing cyclical current account deficits are normally also experiencing cyclical budget deficits, the liabilities in question are already there.

More fundamentally, however, the stabilization of expectations adjustment tends to obviate the need for public position-taking. As the above discussion has suggested, the instability of the expectations adjustment process is dependent largely on the state of uncertainty surrounding underlying inflation trends. Logic and experience indicate that this situation is best improved via the publicized commitment to monetary aggregate goals. The credibility of these goals and their contribution to exchange market orderliness would be enhanced if they were regularly presented in consistent and concerted fashion. It is reasonable to expect more movement in this direction. Certainly such movement must accompany any attempt to target exchange rate change tolerence ranges or to widen relationships of the "snake" type. Most central banks now announce their aggregates intentions, and recent experience has heightened concern about the potential costs of exogenous exchange rate shocks.

Finally, market participants and analysts in both the public and private sectors must understand the concept of appropriate exchange rate adjustment and the difference between cyclical and excessive current account deficits and surpluses.

NOTES

1. See Jacob A. Frenkel, "A Monetary Approach to the Exchange Rate: Doctrinal Aspects and Empirical Evidence," *Scandinavian Journal of Economics* 78, 2 (1976):200–24.

2. Rudiger Dornbusch, "Expectations and Exchange Rate Dynamics," *Journal of Political Economy* 84 (December 1976):1161–76.

3. Jürg Niehans, "Exchange Rate Dynamics with Stock/Flow Interaction," *Journal of Political Economy* 85 (December 1977):1245–58.

4. Stephen W. Kohlhagen, "The Stability of Exchange Rate Expectations and Canadian Capital Flows," *Journal of Finance* 32 (December 1977):1657–70.

5. Ronald I. McKinnon, "Instability in Floating Exchange Rates: A Qualified Monetary Interpretation," mimeographed, as summarized in Susan Schadler, "Sources of Exchange Rate Variability: Theory and Empirical Evidence," IMF *Staff Papers* 24 (July 1977): 253–96.

John J. Van Belle

18

MONEY ILLUSION AND
ITS INFLUENCE ON
INTERNATIONAL ADJUSTMENT

The monetary approach to international adjustment follows directly from the consistent application of domestic monetarist analysis to the international sphere. The integration of money and value theory through Patinkin's real balance effect not only represents an important element in domestic monetary theory but also provides a key to understanding the monetary approach to balance of payments theory. Individuals in an economy who view their real cash balances as excessive will increase their expenditures as they adjust toward their desired level of real balances. Conversely, individuals with inadequate real cash balances will reduce their expenditures to build their cash balances up to the desired level. In addition to providing a direct link between the expansion of the domestic money supply and a real stimulus to the domestic economy, the adjustment of real cash balances is—according to the monetary approach—the crucial element fueling the balance of payments adjustment mechanism. In fact, Harry G. Johnson objected to the absorption approach to the balance of payments and viewed it as "a halfway house to the correct analysis because of its myopic focus on expenditure flows, which obscured the recognition that a continuing balance of payments deficit will eventually correct itself without devaluation by reducing the economy's real balances, unless, of course, real balances are continually renewed by domestic credit expansion.[1]

Under a regime of fixed exchange rates, the real balances of a country whose international payments are in deficit are directly reduced by the outflow of funds to finance the deficit, but with flexible exchange rates, the deficit country's real balances are reduced indirectly through the depreciation of its currency (as well as through faster domestic inflation).* The impact on the surplus country's real balances is symmetrical. Real balances in a surplus country are directly raised by an inflow of international reserve under fixed exchange rates, but rise indirectly through the appreciation of its currency (and slower inflation) when exchange rates are flexible. The essence of the balance of payments adjustment mechanism is that, all other things being equal, the payments imbalance leads to opposite changes in real cash balances in the surplus and deficit countries.† The adjustments of individuals to their desired level of real cash balances lead in turn to an acceleration of spending (raising imports of goods, services, and assets) in the surplus country, and a reduction of spending (lowering imports of goods, services, and assets in the deficit country. The altered expenditure patterns tend to correct the international payments imbalance. The individual transactors in the economy base their cash balance adjustments (and thus their expenditure patterns) on their *perceived* levels of existing and desired real cash balances. Since money illusion drives a wedge between the actual and perceived levels of real balances, its existence distorts the balance of payments adjustment mechanism. Previous studies of the relationship between money illusion and balance of payments adjustments have reached the conclusions that money illusion facilitates the adjustment mechanism,[2] and that money illusion impedes the adjustment mechanism.[3] The purpose of this brief study is to clarify the apparent inconsistency of previous discussions and to produce a coherent framework for understanding the impact of money illusion on the adjustment mechanism.

The confusion concerning the relationship between money illusion and the balance of payments adjustments stems primarily from two factors. First, money illusion is a loosely used generic term; it encompasses divergent phenomena that are often uncritically lumped together. Second, the various forms of money illusion can affect either the payments or the receipts side of an individual's balance sheet. This second factor is important because money illusion has opposite effects depending upon which side of the balance sheet it affects. The classical form of money illusion was based on ignorance, specifically the inability to recognize that there was a difference between nominal and real values. An example of this form of illusion was "documented" by Mark Twain. Workers in Bagdegamus thought they were better off than the workers in Camelot because they had higher nominal wages. However, prices were so much higher in Bagde-

---

*An international payments deficit refers to an outflow of central bank international reserves or, correspondingly, a net deficit on nonofficial current and capital transactions in the balance of payments. However, the analysis of this study concerning payments adjustment can also be applied to the current account alone.

†It should be obvious that domestic monetary growth will also have a significant impact on real balances, and that the monetary policies of the countries involved may also either impede or facilitate the balance of payments adjustment mechanism.

gamus that they actually had lower real wages. Camelot's workers were able to avoid money illusion because they listened to the Connecticut Yankee, who observed that "a man who hasn't had much experience and doesn't think is apt to measure a nation's prosperity or lack of prosperity by the mere size of the prevailing wages; if the wages be high the nation is prosperous; if low, it isn't. Which is an error. It isn't what sum you get, it's how much you can buy with it that's the important thing and it's that that tells whether your wages are high in fact or only in name."[4] A more sophisticated version of this form of money illusion attributes the misperception (or merely lagged perception) of the real value of cash balances to the high cost of obtaining information about price changes rather than to ignorance. A modern variation of money illusion, which may be dubbed "revealed illusion," is derived from an examination of individuals' behavior patterns (demand curves). In his pathbreaking work on the real balance effect, Don Patinkin stressed this method of delineating money illusion. He viewed illusion as existing whenever excess demand functions did not depend solely on relative prices and real wealth inclusive of initial real balances.[5] If the demand curves contain distortions similar to those produced by the classical "ignorance" illusion, then money illusion is deemed to exist even if there is actually neither misunderstanding of the distinction between nominal and real balances nor any misperception of prices. The most common strain of this "revealed illusion" is the denomination of labor contracts in terms of domestic money, which causes a lagged adjustment of wages to changes in the price level.[6] Even when labor contracts contain explicit cost-of-living escalator clauses (implying that the distinction between nominal and real wages is understood), they are still classified as a form of money illusion because the wage adjustments are made only periodically, normally annually, and thus remain lagged. This "revealed illusion" is in reality an institutional rigidity, stemming from the complexity and cost of paying salaries in real terms. To be accurate, payment of wages in real rather than nominal terms would require a price index reflecting the consumption pattern of each worker, and the index would have to be continually updated as prices and consumption patterns changed. It should be recognized that money illusion in the form of labor contracts denominated in domestic money terms hits the receipts side of the individual's balance sheet, while the more traditional form of illusion has an impact on the expenditure side.

Having delineated two divergent forms of money illusion, one can now turn toward an examination of their impact on the balance of payments adjustment mechanism. The classical form of illusion is considered first. In an era of rising prices, this illusion generally involves either a lagged (diminished) perception of the effect of price increases on real incomes and real cash balances, or a total disregard of these price effects. This would represent an underestimation of the decline in real incomes and real cash balances due to inflation and would thus overstate the actual level of real balances, slowing down the reduction in spending needed to build actual real balances up to their desired level. Since prices will generally be rising faster in the deficit country than in the surplus country, this distortion will be more significant for the deficit country and will therefore, all other things being equal, inhibit the balance of payments adjustment mechanism.* A variation of this classical form of illusion, mentioned in the literature, is the failure to recognize fully the effects of exchange rate changes on real income. This illusion underestimates a decline in real incomes and real cash balances in the deficit (depreciating currency) country while underestimating an increase in the real incomes and real cash balances in the surplus (appreciating currency) country. This tends to restrain the rise in spending in the surplus country as well as the decline in expenditures in the deficit country, both of which adjustments are needed to correct the payments imbalances. In line with this discussion, analysts who have focused on the classical form of illusion have concluded that money illusion obstructs the adjustment process. It must be recognized however, that this study is limited to the common case where prices are rising and the illusion understates the price change. For the analysis to be complete, situations with declining prices and money illusion where the misperception of price (exchange rate) changes involves an overestimation rather than an underestimation must also be considered. With falling prices, illusion underestimating the price changes underestimates the rise in real incomes and cash balances implied by the lower prices, slowing the rise in expenditures needed to reduce real cash balances to the desired level. Since prices would generally be falling faster in the surplus country than in the deficit country, this distortion would be more significant for the surplus country and would therefore impede the balance of payment adjustments. So whether rising prices or falling prices are involved, classical illusion tends to obstruct the balance of payments adjustment mechanism.

If classical money illusion results from the failure to recognize the distinction between nominal and real values, then it can only underestimate the extent of price changes. However, if the illusion is generated by high costs associated with obtaining accurate price information, then the individual's price misperceptions could be either underestimates or overestimates. In the infrequent cases where price changes were overestimated, the change in real incomes and real cash balances would be overestimated and the results of the above analyses for both price increases and price decreases would be reversed. Thus, this rare form of classical illusion would facilitate the balance of payments adjustment mechanism.

---

*Again, the balance of payments adjustment under fixed exchange rates is the flow of international reserves, and, in the flexible rate case, an exchange rate change instead of a reserve flow. In terms of the standard monetary approach models such as those described by Michael Connolly, "The Monetary Approach to an Open Economy" (this book, Chapter 1), money illusion would be incorporated in the model by relaxing the restriction that the elasticity of actual price changes with respect to money demand is unitary. When this restriction is relaxed, the elasticity may be less than unity.

An examination of the specie "revealed illusion" indicates that its most prevalent form—the lagged adjustment of wages to changes in the price level—also facilitates the balance of payments adjustments. Assuming that this form of money illusion is the only type of illusion in the economy, the price and exchange rate changes would have their full effect on real incomes and real cash balances, and the balance of payments adjustment mechanism could function without obstruction. To understand how "revealed illusion" aids the adjustment process, one of the ceteris paribus assumptions must first be relaxed. So far, it has been indicated that depleted real cash balances were replenished by reducing expenditures. Another method of achieving this end would be to secure higher levels of nominal income. By delaying or closing off this source of increased real balances, "revealed illusion" forces expenditure adjustments to bear more of the burden for shifting real cash balances to their desired levels. If instead the reduced real balances were instantaneously replenished through higher nominal incomes, then, all other things being equal, the initial expenditure levels would be maintained and the payments imbalance would persist until the aggregate level of real incomes and real cash balances in the deficit country was reduced by unemployment. The decline in aggregate real cash balances of the deficit country is a necessary part of the balance of payments adjustment mechanism. In the literature, references to facilitation by money illusion (that is, "revealed illusion") of the adjustment mechanism referred to the fact that, by allowing individuals' real incomes and real cash balances to decline, the illusion precluded the need for unemployment in achieving the necessary aggregate decline. The fact that "revealed illusion" also accelerated the speed of the process was for some observers a secondary consideration.*

Money illusion's impact on the balance of payments adjustment mechanism will depend on whether the illusion is "classical" or "revealed," or, put differently, on whether the illusion strikes the expenditure or the receipt side of an individual's balance sheet; in cases of classical illusion, whether it underestimates or overestimates the price and exchange rate changes; and, in cases of revealed illusion, whether the changes in nominal income lag or lead the price changes. Since more than one form of illusion can exist at the same time, no definitive statement can be made concerning money illusion's actual net effect.

---

*For completeness, it should be noted that if—recognizing the distinction between nominal and real values—labor unions, or workers in general, include an overestimate of future price increases in their wage demands that are validated, then the institutional structure of periodic nominal wage increases would not involve a lagged or reduced adjustment to price increases, but rather a leading or augmented adjustment to higher prices. In such situations, the conclusions of the above analysis would be reversed, and "revealed illusion" would obstruct rather than aid the adjustment process. In the present institutional setting, it may be as difficult to decide whether wage adjustments lead or lag price adjustments as it is to decide whether the chicken or the egg came first.

However, the general relationship between the various money illusions and the balance of payments adjustments can be succinctly stated. Money illusion that underestimates (or delays) changes in real income and real cash balances facilitates the balance of payments adjustments, while illusion that overestimates (or accelerates) changes in real income and real cash balances impedes these adjustments.

NOTES

1. H. G. Johnson, "Money, Balance-of-Payments Theory, And the International Monetary Problem," *Essays In International Finance*, Publication no. 124 (November 1977):10.

2. Support for this view can be found in R. A. Mundell, "A Theory of Optimum Currency Areas," *American Economic Review* 51 (November 1961):509–17; and W. M. Corden, "The Adjustment Problem," in *European Monetary Unification and Its Meaning For the United States*, ed. L. B. Kraus and W. S. Salant (Washington, D.C.: 1973).

3. Support for this view can be found in J. C. Murphy and S. K. Das, "Money Illusion and Balance-of-Payments Adjustment," *Journal of Political Economy* 84, no. 1 (February 1976):73–82.

4. Mark Twain, *A Connecticut Yankee In King Arthur's Court* (New York: Harper and Brothers, 1889), p. 279.

5. See Don Patinkin, *Money Interest and Prices*, 2d ed. (New York: Harper and Row, 1965), p. 22.

6. See Murphy and Das, op. cit., for the explicit classification of this phenomenon as money illusion.

BIBLIOGRAPHY

This bibliography has been constructed especially for the researcher interested in the monetary approach to international adjustment. Complete citations of all studies referenced by the essays in this volume, plus numerous other studies dealing with the monetary approach, have been organized into categories with identifications of whether the study contains empirical work or not.

The bibliography is divided into two primary parts: monetary approach studies and background references. Within the monetary approach part, there are three categories: fixed exchange rates, flexible exchange rates, and portfolio substitution. Furthermore, studies containing empirical work are marked to indicate which empirical investigations are related to industrial (I) or developing (D) economies. In dividing the bibliography into sections some arbitrary decisions were made. For example, an article by Lance Girton and Don Roper encompassing both fixed and flexible exchange rate regimes fit into more than one section. This example was listed in the fixed exchange rate section. Also, as with any attempt such as this, there are errors and omissions, and the editors apologize for these mistakes.

The second part of the bibliography lists background studies that the contributors to this volume found particularly useful. These listings are divided into three categories: historical, purchasing power parity, and general studies. These sections are not comprehensive in any sense.

A summary of the contents of the bibliography follows:

MONETARY APPROACH STUDIES

Fixed Exchange Rates

Aghevli, B. "Money, Prices and the Balance of Payments: Indonesia 1968-73." *Journal of Development Studies* 13 (January 1977): 37-57. (D)

Aghevli, B., and M. Kahn. "The Monetary Approach to Balance of Payments Determination: An Empirical Test." In *The Monetary Approach to the Balance of Payments*, 275–90. Washington, D.C.: International Monetary Fund, 1977. (D)

Akhtar, M. A. "Some Common Misconceptions about the Monetary Approach to International Adjustment." In *The Monetary Approach to International Adjustment*, edited by Bluford H. Putnam and D. Sykes Wilford. New York: Praeger Publishers, 1978. (I)

Akhtar, M. A., B. H. Putnam, and D. S. Wilford. "Fiscal Constraints, Domestic Credit, and International Reserve Flows." *Journal of Money, Credit, and Banking* 11 (May 1979). (I)

Beals, R., and A. Collery. "A Monetary Approach to the Balance of Payments of a Small Country: The Case of Jamaica." 1971. Mimeographed. (D)

Blejer, M. I. "The Short-Run Dynamics of Prices and the Balance of Payments." *American Economic Review* 67 (June 1977): 419–28. (D)

Borts, G., and J. A. Hanson. "The Monetary Approach to the Balance of Payments." In *Short Run Macroeconomic Policy in Latin America*, edited by Jere Behrman. National Bureau for Economic Research, forthcoming. (D)

—— "The Monetary Approach to the Balance of Payments." Unpublished working paper, Brown University, 1975.

Boyer, Russell S. "Commodity Markets and Bond Markets in a Small, Fixed-Exchange-Rate Economy." *Canadian Journal of Economics* 8 (February 1975): 1–23.

Collery, Arnold. "International Adjustment, Open Economies, and the Quantity Theory of Money." *Princeton Studies in International Finance* no. 28 (June 1971).

Connolly, Michael. "The Monetary Approach to an Open Economy: The Fundamental Theory." In *The Monetary Approach to International Adjustment*, edited by Bluford H. Putnam and D. Sykes Wilford. New York: Praeger Publishers, 1978.

Connolly, Michael, and D. Taylor. "Testing the Monetary Approach to Devaluation in Developing Countries." *Journal of Political Economy* (August 1976): 849–59. (D)

——. "Adjustment to Devaluation with Money and Non-Traded Goods." *Journal of International Economics* (August 1976): 289–99. (D)

———. "Exchange Rate Changes and Neutralization: A Test of the Monetary Approach Applied to Developed and Developing Countries." Manuscript, 1978. (D)

Courchene, Thomas. "The Price-Specie Flow Mechanism and the Gold Exchange Standard: Some Exploratory Empiricism Relating to the Endogeneity of Country Money Balances." In *The Economics of Common Currencies*, edited by H. G. Johnson and A. K. Swoboda. London: Allen and Unwin, 1973. (I)

Cox, W. Michael. "An Incomplete Information Model of the Monetary Approach to the Balance of Payments." Mimeographed, University of Western Ontario, 1978.

———. "Rational Expectations and the Monetary Approach to the Balance of Payments: The Canadian Experience." In *The Monetary Approach to International Adjustment*, edited by Bluford H. Putnam and D. Sykes Wilford. New York: Praeger Publishers, 1978. (I).

Cox, W. Michael, and Halbert White. "Unanticipated Money, Output, and Prices in the Small Economy." Mimeographed, University of Rochester, 1978.

Cox, W. Michael, and D. Sykes Wilford. "The Monetary Approach to the Balance of Payments and World Monetary Equilibrium." Mimeographed, 1977. (I & D)

Currie, D. A. "Some Criticisms of the Monetary Analysis of Balance of Payments Correction." *Economic Journal* 86 (September 1976): 508-22.

Frenkel, J. "Adjustment Mechanisms and the Monetary Approach to the Balance of Payments: A Doctrinal Perspective." In *Recent Issues in International Monetary Economics*, edited by E. M. Claassen and P. Salin. Amsterdam: North-Holland, 1976.

Frenkel, J., and Harry G. Johnson, eds. *The Monetary Approach to the Balance of Payments*. London: Allen and Unwin, 1976. (D & I)

———. "The Monetary Approach to the Balance of Payments: Essential Concepts and Historical Origins." In *The Monetary Approach to the Balance of Payments*, edited by Jacob Frenkel and Harry G. Johnson, 21-45. Toronto, Canada: University of Toronto Press, 1976.

Frenkel, J., and C. A. Rodriguez. "Portfolio Equilibrium and the Balance of Payments: A Monetary Approach." *American Economic Review* 65 (September 1975): 674-88.

Genberg, H. "Aspects of the Monetary Approach to Balance of Payments Theory: An Empirical Study of Sweden." In *The Monetary Approach to the*

Balance of Payments, edited by Jacob Frenkel and Harry G. Johnson, 298–325. Toronto, Canada: University of Toronto Press, 1976. (I)

Girton, Lance, and Don Roper. "A Monetary Model of Fixed and Flexible Exchange Rates Applied to the Post-War Canadian Experience." *American Economic Review* 67 (September 1977): 537–48. (I)

Girton, Lance, and Dayle Nattress. "The Monetary Approach to the Balance of Payments, Stocks and Flows, and Walras' Law." *Intermountain Economic Review* 8 (Fall 1977).

Guitian, Manuel. "Credit Versus Money as an Instrument of Control." In *The Monetary Approach to the Balance of Payments*, 227–4 2 Washington, D.C.: International Monetary Fund, 1977. (D)

Haberler, G. "The Monetary Approach to the Balance of Payments Theory: By Frenkel and Johnson," review, *Journal of Economic Literature* 14 (December 1976): 1324–28.

Hahn, F. H. "The Monetary Approach to the Balance of Payments." *Journal of International Economics* 7 (August 1977): 231–41.

Johnson, Harry G. "The Monetary Approach to the Balance of Payments." In *Further Essays in Monetary Economics*, 224–41. Cambridge: Harvard University Press, 1973.

———. "The Monetary Approach to Balance of Payments Theory." In *International Trade and Money*, edited by M. Connolly and A. Swoboda, 206–24. London: Allen and Unwin, 1973.

———. "Money and the Balance of Payments." *Banca Nazionale del Lavoro-Quarterly Review* no. 116 (March 1976): 3–18.

———. "Elasticity, Absorption, Keynesian Multiplier, Keynesian Policy, and Monetary Approaches to Devaluation Theory: A Simple Geometric Exposition." *American Economic Review* 66 (June 1976): 448–52.

———. "The Monetary Approach to the Balance of Payments: A Nontechnical Guide." *Journal of International Economics* (August 1977): 289–98.

———. "The Monetary Approach to Balance of Payments Theory and Policy: Explanation and Policy Implications." *Economica* 44 (August 1977): 217–29.

———. "Money, Balance-of-Payments Theory, and the International Monetary Problem." *Essays in International Finance* no. 124 (November 1977).

———. "The Monetary Approach to the Balance of Payments Theory: A Diagrammatic Analysis." *The Manchester School* (1975): 220–74.

Jonson, P. D. "Money and Economic Activity in the Open Economy: The United Kingdom, 1880–1970." *Journal of Political Economy* 84 (October 1976): 979–1012. (I)

Kahn, Mohsin S. "The Determination of the Balance of Payments and Income in Developing Countries." In *The Monetary Approach to the Balance of Payments*, 243–74. Washington, D.C.: International Monetary Fund, 1977.

———. "A Monetary Model of Balance of Payments: The Case of Venezuela." *Journal of Monetary Economics* 2 (July 1976): 311–32. (D)

Keleher, Robert. "Of Money and Prices: Some Historical Perspectives." In *The Monetary Approach to International Adjustment*, edited by Bluford H. Putnam and D. Sykes Wilford. New York: Praeger Publishers, 1978.

Kemp, Donald S. "A Monetary View of Balance of Payments." *Federal Reserve Bank of St. Louis Review* 57, no. 4 (April 1975): 14–22. Reprinted in *The Monetary Approach to International Adjustment*, edited by Bluford H. Putnam and D. Sykes Wilford. New York: Praeger Publishers, 1978.

Komiya, R. "Economic Growth and the Balance of Payments." *Journal of Political Economy* 77 (January-February 1969): 35–48.

Kouri, Pentti J. K. "The Exchange Rate and the Balance of Payments in the Short Run and in the Long Run: A Monetary Approach." In *Flexible Exchange Rates and Stabilization Policy*, edited by Jan Herin, Assar Lindbeck, and Johan Myhrman, 148–72. Boulder, Colorado: Westview Press, 1977.

Kouri, Pentti J. K., and M. G. Porter. "International Capital Flows and Portfolio Equilibrium." *Journal of Political Economy* 82 (August 1974): 443–67. (I)

Kreinen, M., and L. Officer. "Survey of Empirical Evidence on Monetary Approach to Open Economies." In *Essays in International Finance*. Princeton, N.J.: Princeton University, forthcoming.

Lachman, D. A. "A Monetary Approach to the South African Balance of Payments." *South African Journal of Economics* 43 (September 1975): 271–83. (D)

Laffer, Arthur. "The Anti-Traditional General Equilibrium Theory of the Rate Growth and the Balance of Payments under Fixed Exchange Rates." Mimeographed, University of Chicago, 1968. (I)

————. "Monetary Policy and the Balance of Payments." *Journal of Money, Credit, and Banking* 4 (February 1972): 13–22.

Magee, S. "Empirical Evidence on the Monetary Approach to the Balance of Payments and Exchange Rates." *American Economic Review* 66 (May 1976): 163–70.

McClosky, Don, and J. Richard Zecher. "How the Gold Standard Worked, 1880–1913." In *The Monetary Approach to the Balance of Payments*, edited by Jacob Frenkel and Harry G. Johnson, 357–85. Toronto, Canada: University of Toronto Press, 1976.

Miller, N. C., and S. S. Askin. "Monetary Policy and the Balance of Payments in Brazil and Chile." *Journal of Money, Credit, and Banking* 8 (May 1976): 227–38. (D)

Mundell, Robert A. *International Economics.*London: Macmillan, 1968.

Mussa, Michael. "A Monetary Approach to Balance-of-Payments Analysis." *Journal of Money, Credit, and Banking* 6 (August 1974): 331–51.

————. "The Exchange Rate, the Balance of Payments and Monetary and Fiscal Policy Under a Regime of Controlled Floating." In *Flexible Exchange Rates and Stabilization Policy*, edited by Jan Herin, Assar Lindbeck, and Johan Myhrman, 97–116. Boulder, Colorado: Westview Press, 1977.

————. "Tariffs and the Balance of Payments: A Monetary Approach." In *The Monetary Approach to the Balance of Payments*, edited by Jacob Frenkel and Harry G. Johnson, 187–221. Toronto, Canada: University of Toronto Press, 1976.

Myhrman, Johan. "Balance of Payments Adjustment and Portfolio Theory: A Survey." In *Recent Issues in International Monetary Economics*, edited by E. Claassen and P. Salin. Amsterdam: North-Holland, 1976.

Nobay, A. R., and Harry G. Johnson. "Monetarism: A Historic-Theoretic Perspective." *Journal of Economic Literature* 15 (June 1977): 470–85.

Otani, I., and Y. C. Park. "A Monetary Model of the Korean Economy." *International Monetary Fund Staff Paper* 23 (March 1976): 164–99.

Porter, M. G. "The Interdependence of Monetary Policy and Capital Flows in Australia." *Economic Record* 24 (August 1974): 120–50. (I)

Prais, S. J. "Some Mathematical Notes of the Quantity Theory of Money in an Open Economy." In *The Monetary Approach to the Balance of Payments*, 147–62. Washington, D.C.: International Monetary Fund, 1977.

Putnam, Bluford H. "Non-traded Goods and the Monetary Approach to the Balance of Payments." Federal Reserve Bank of New York Research Paper #7714, 1976. (I)

Putnam, Bluford H., and D. Sykes Wilford. "Money, Income and Causality in the U.S. and the U.K.: A Theoretical Explanation of Different Findings." *American Economic Review* 68 (June 1978): 423-27. Reprinted in *The Monetary Approach to International Adjustment*, edited by Bluford H. Putnam and D. Sykes Wilford. New York: Praeger Publishers, 1978.

———. "Monetary Equilibrium and International Reserve Flows: An Empirical Treatment of the Money Supply Identity Issue." Mimeographed, 1975. (I)

———. "International Reserve Flows: Seemingly Unrelated Regressions." *Weltwirtschaftliches Archiv* 114 (June 1978): 211-26. Reprinted in *The Monetary Approach to International Adjustment*, edited by Bluford H. Putnam and D. Sykes Wilford. New York: Praeger Publishers, 1978. (I).

Ramanathan, R. "Monetary Expansion, Balance of Trade and Economic Growth." *Economic Record* 51 (March 1975): 31-39. (D)

Rhomberg, Rudolf R. "Money, Income, and the Foreign Balance." In *The Monetary Approach to the Balance of Payments*, 163-84. Washington, D.C.: International Monetary Fund, 1977.

Rhomberg, Rudolf R., and H. Robert Heller. "Introductory Survey." In *The Monetary Approach to the Balance of Payments*, 1-114. Washington, D.C.: International Monetary Fund, 1977.

Rodriguez, Carlos A. "Money and Wealth in an Open Economy Income-Expenditure Model." In *The Monetary Approach to the Balance of Payments*, edited by Jacob Frenkel and Harry G. Johnson, 222-36. Toronto, Canada: University of Toronto Press, 1976.

Rutledge, John. "Balance of Payments and Money Demand." Mimeographed, Clairmont College, 1975. (I)

Swoboda, Alexander K. "Equilibrium, Quasi-Equilibrium, and Macroeconomic Policy Under Fixed Exchange Rates." *Quarterly Journal of Economics* 86 (February 1972): 162-71.

———. "Monetary Policy Under Fixed Exchange Rates: Effectiveness, the Speed of Adjustment and Proper Use." *Economica* 40 (May 1973): 136-54.

———. "Monetary Approaches to Balance-of-Payments Theory." In *Recent Issues in Monetary Economics*, edited by E. Claassen and P. Salin. Amsterdam: North-Holland, 1976.

——. "Gold Dollars, Euro-Dollars and the World Money Stock." *American Economic Review* 68 (September 1978).

Tsiang, S. C. "The Monetary Theoretic Foundation of the Modern Monetary Approach to the Balance of Payments." *Oxford Economic Papers* 29 (November 1977): 319–38.

Van Belle, John J. "Money Illusion and its Influence on International Adjustment." In *The Monetary Approach to International Adjustment*, edited by Bluford H. Putnam and D. Sykes Wilford. New York: Praeger Publishers, 1978.

Whitman, Marina v. N. "Global Monetarism and the Monetary Approach to the Balance of Payments." *Brookings Papers on Economic Activity* no. 3 (1975): 491–536.

Wilford, D. Sykes. *Monetary Policy and the Open Economy: Mexico's Experience.* New York: Praeger Publishers, 1977. (D)

Wilford, D. Sykes, and Walton T. Wilford. "Monetary Approach to the Balance of Payments: On World Prices and the Reserve Flow Equation." *Weltwirtschaftliches Archiv* 113, no. 1 (1977): 31–39. (D)

——. "On the Monetary Approach to the Balance of Payments: The Small, Open Economy." *The Journal of Finance* 33 (March 1978): 319–23. (D)

——. "Efectos de la Creacíon de Crédito Sobre la Balanza de Pagos en El Salvador." *Caribbean Studies*, forthcoming.

Wilford, D. Sykes, and J. Richard Zecher. "Monetary Policy and the Balance of Payments in Mexico 1955–75." *Journal of Money, Credit, and Banking* 11 (1979), forthcoming. (D)

Wilford, Walton T. "Some Observations on the Monetary Approach to Balance of Payments and the Third World." In *The Monetary Approach to International Adjustment*, edited by Bluford H. Putnam and D. Sykes Wilford. New York: Praeger Publishers, 1978.

Witte, James G., and Barbara Henneberry. "A Monetary-Real Approach to Balance of Payments Theory: Old-New Synthesis for Old-New Problems." Mimeographed, Indiana University, April 1977.

Zecher, J. Richard. "Monetary Equilibrium and International Reserve Flows in Australia." *Journal of Finance* 29 (December 1974): 1523–30. (I)

Flexible Exchange Rates

Artus, Jacques R. "Exchange Rate Stability and Managed Floating: The Experience of the Federal Republic of Germany." *International Monetary Fund Staff Papers* 23 (July 1976): 312-33. (I)

Artus, Jacques R., and Andrew W. Crockett. "Floating Exchange Rates, Rate Management Policies, and the Need for Surveillance." In *Essays in International Finance*. Princeton, N.J.: Princeton University, Press, 1978.

Barro, R. "A Simple Flexible Exchange Rate Model with Uncertainty and Rational Expectations." Mimeographed, November 1975.

Basevi, Giorgio, and P. de Grauwe. "Vicious and Virtuous Circles: A Theoretical Analysis and a Policy Proposal for Managing Exchange Rates." *European Economic Review* 3 (1978).

Bilson, John F. O. "The Monetary Approach to the Exchange Rate: Some Empirical Evidence. *International Monetary Fund Staff Papers* (March 1978: 48-75. **(I)**

———. "Rational Expectations and the Exchange Rate." In *The Economics of Exchange Rate—Selected Studies*, edited by J. Frenkel and Harry G. Johnson. Reading, Mass.: Addison-Wesley, 1978. (I)

———. "A Simple Long Run Model of Exchange Rate Determination." Mimeographed, International Monetary Fund, April 1977.

———. "Recent Developments in Monetary Models of Exchange Rate Determination." Mimeographed, International Monetary Fund, 1978. (I)

Black, S. W. "International Money Market and Flexible Exchange Rates." *Princeton Studies in International Finance* no. 32. In *Essays in International Finance*. Princeton, N. J.: Princeton University Press, 1978.

———. *Floating Exchange Rates and National Economic Policy*. New Haven: Yale University Press, 1977.

Blejer, M. I. "The Monetary Approach to Devaluation: A Graphical Presentation." *Weltwirtschaftliches Archiv* 113 (1977): 348-52.

Boyer, Russell. "Optimal Foreign Exchange Market Intervention." Mimeographed, University of Western Ontario, January 1976.

——. "Revaluation and Portfolio Balance." *American Economic Review* 62, 2 (March 1977): 54–63.

Cathcart, Charles D. "Exchange Rate Stability from a Monetary Perspective." In *The Monetary Approach to International Adjustment*, edited by Bluford H. Putnam and D. Sykes Wilford. New York: Praeger Publishers, 1978.

Connolly, M., and J. da Silveira. "An Application of the Girton-Roper Monetary Model of Exchange Market Pressure to Postwar Brazil." Mimeographed, 1978. (D)

Cooper, Richard N. "Monetary Theory and Policy in the Open Economy." In *Flexible Exchange Rates and Stabilization Policy*, edited by Jan Herin, Assar Lindbeck, and Johan Myhrman, 14–31. Boulder, Colorado: Westview Press, 1977.

Dornbusch, R. "Real and Monetary Aspects of the Effects of Exchange Rate Changes." In *National Monetary Policies and the International Financial System*, edited by R. Z. Aliber. Chicago: University of Chicago Press, 1974.

——. "Devaluation, Money and Non-Traded Goods." *American Economic Review* 61 (December 1973): 871–80.

——. "The Theory of Flexible Exchange Rate Regimes and Macroeconomic Policy." In *Flexible Exchange Rates and Stabilization Policy*, edited by Jan Herin, Assar Lindbeck, and Johan Myhrman, 123–43. Boulder, Colorado: Westview Press, 1977.

——. "Capital Mobility, Flexible Exchange Rates and Macroeconomic Equilibrium." In *Recent Issues in International Monetary Economics*, edited by E. Claassen and P. Salin. Amsterdam: North-Holland, 1976.

——. "Expectations and Exchange Rate Dynamics." *Journal of Political Economy* 84, no. 6 (December 1976): 1161–76.

Dornbusch, R., and Paul Krugman. "Flexible Exchange Rates in the Short Run." *Brookings Papers on Economic Activity* 3 (1976): 537–75.

Frenkel, Jacob A. "Inflation and the Formation of Expectations." *Journal of Monetary Economics* 1 (October 1975): 403–21.

——. "A Monetary Approach to the Exchange Rate: Doctrinal Aspects and Empirical Evidence." In *Flexible Exchange Rates and Stabilization Policy*, edited by Jan Herin, Assar Lindbeck, and Johan Myhrman, 68–92. Boulder, Colorado: Westview Press, 1977.

Fry, Harold. "A Monetary Approach to Afghanistan's Flexible Exchange Rate." *Journal of Money, Credit, and Banking* 8 (May 1976): 219-25. (D)

Genberg, H., and H. Kierzkowski. "Short Run, Long Run and Dynamics of Adjustment Under Flexible Exchange Rates." Discussion paper, GIIS-Ford Foundation International Monetary Research Project. Geneva, June 1975.

Girton, Lance, and Don Roper. "The Evolution of Exchange Rate Policy." In *The Monetary Approach to International Adjustment*, edited by Bluford H. Putnam and D. Sykes Wilford. New York: Praeger Publishers, 1978.

Humphrey, Thomas, and Thomas Lawler. "Factors Determining Exchange Rates: A Simple Model and Empirical Tests." Federal Reserve Bank of Richmond *Economic Review* (May-June 1977): 10-15. Reprinted in *The Monetary Approach to International Adjustment*, edited by Bluford H. Putnam and D. Sykes Wilford. New York: Praeger Publishers, 1978. (I)

King, David. "Monetary Autonomy and Flexible Exchange Rates." Mimeographed, January 1977.

——. "Uncertainty, Flexible Exchange Rates and the Planning Horizon." In *The Monetary Approach to International Adjustment*, edited by Bluford H. Putnam and D. Sykes Wilford. New York: Praeger Publishers, 1978.

Mussa, Michael. "The Exchange Rate, the Balance of Payments, and Monetary and Fiscal Policy Under a Regime of Controlled Floating." *Scandinavian Journal of Economics* 78 (1976): 229-48.

Niehans, Jürg. "Exchange Rate Dynamics with Stock/Flow Interaction." *Journal of Political Economy* 85 (December 1977): 1245-58.

Putnam, Bluford H. "Interest Rates, the Money Supply, and Exchange Rates." In *The Monetary Approach to International Adjustment*, edited by Bluford H. Putnam and D. Sykes Wilford. New York: Praeger Publishers, 1978.

Putnam, Bluford H., and John J. Van Belle. "A Monetary Approach to Afghanistan's Flexible Exchange Rate: A Comment." *Journal of Money, Credit, and Banking* 10 (February 1978): 117-18. (D)

Putnam, Bluford H., and John Woodbury. "Exchange Rate Stability and Monetary Policy: A Case Study." Federal Reserve Bank of New York Research Paper #7718 (1976). (I)

Sargen, Nicholas. "Exchange Rate Stability and Demand for Money." Paper presented at the meeting of the American Finance Association, September 1976, Atlantic City, N.J. (I)

———. "An Empirical Analysis of a Monetary Model of Exchange Rate and Reserve Fluctuations." Mimeographed, November 1975. (I)

Portfolio Substitution

Boyer, R. "Nickels and Dimes." Federal Reserve Board of Governors. Mimeographed.

———. "Substitutability Between Currencies and Between Bonds: A Theoretical Analysis of Gresham's Law." Mimeographed, University of Western Ontario, 1973.

———. "Currency Mobility and Balance of Payments Adjustment." In *The Monetary Approach to International Adjustment*, edited by Bluford H. Putnam and D. Sykes Wilford. New York: Praeger Publishers, 1978.

Calvo, Guillermo, and Alfredo Rodriguez. "A Model of Exchange Rate Determination Under Currency Substitution and Rational Expectations." *Journal of Political Economy* 85 (May-June 1977): 617–25.

Cox, W. Michael. "The Impact of Substitute Currencies on International Monetary and Exchange Market Equilibrium." Mimeographed, Virginia Polytechnic Institute, 1976.

Evans, Paul, and Arthur Laffer. "Demand Substitutability Across Currencies." Mimeographed, University of Southern California, 1977.

Girton, Lance, and Don Roper. "Theory and Implications of Currency Substitution." *International Finance Discussion Papers* no. 86. Federal Reserve Board, 1976.

Hayek, F. A. *Denationalization of Money*. London: Institute of Economic Affairs, 1976.

King, David T., B. H. Putnam, and D. S. Wilford. "A Currency Portfolio Approach to Exchange Rate Determination: Exchange Rate Stability and Monetary Independence." In *The Monetary Approach to International Adjustment*, edited by Bluford H. Putnam and D. Sykes Wilford. New York: Praeger Publishers, 1978.

Klein, Benjamin. "Competing Monies: A Comment." *Journal of Money, Credit, and Banking* 8 (November 1976): 513–19.

Laffer, A. "Optimal Exchange Rates." Paper presented at the American Economic Association Meeting, September 1976, Atlantic City, N.J.

Miles, Marc A. "Currency Substitution—The Case of the United States." Mimeographed, Rutgers University, 1978.

———. "Currency Substitution, Flexible Exchange Rates, and Monetary Independence." *American Economic Review* 68 (June 1978): 428–36.

———. "Currency Substitution: Perspective, Implications, and Empirical Evidence." In *The Monetary Approach to International Adjustment*, edited by Bluford H. Putnam and D. Sykes Wilford. New York: Praeger Publishers, 1978.

Putnam, Bluford H., and D. Sykes Wilford. "How Diversification Makes the Dollar Weaker." *Euromoney* (October 1978): 201–04.

Tullock, Gordon. "Competing Monies." *Journal of Money, Credit, and Banking* 7 (November 1975): 491–97.

———. "Competing Monies: A Reply." *Journal of Money, Credit, and Banking* 8 (November 1976): 520–25.

BACKGROUND REFERENCES

Historical

Angell, James W. *The Theory of International Prices*. New York: Augustus M. Kelley, 1965.

Blaug, Mark. *Economic Theory in Retrospect*. Homewood, Ill.: R. D. Irwin, 1968.

Bloomfield, Arthur I. "Adam Smith and the Theory of International Trade." In *Essays on Adam Smith*, edited by Andrew Skinner and Thomas Wilson. Oxford: Clarendon Press, 1975.

Cannan, Edwin, ed. *The Paper Pound of 1797–1821: The Bullion Report*. New York: Augustus M. Kelley, 1969.

Cassel, Gustav. *The Theory of Social Economy*. New York: Augustus M. Kelley, 1967.

———. *Money and Foreign Exchange After 1914*. New York: Macmillan, 1922.

Daugherty, Marion R. "The Currency-Banking Controversy: Part I." *Southern Economic Journal* 9 (October 1942): 140–55.

———. "The Currency-Banking Controversy: Part II." *Southern Economic Journal* 9 (January 1943): 241–51.

DeJong, F. J. *Development of Monetary Theory in the Netherlands*. Rotterdam: Rotterdam University Press, 1973.

Eagly, Robert V. "Adam Smith and the Specie-Flow Doctrine." *Scottish Journal of Political Economy* 17 (February1970): 61–68.

——. "The Swedish and English Bullionist Controversies." In *Events, Ideology, and Economic Theory*, edited by Robert V. Eagly, 13–31. Detroit: Wayne State University Press, 1968.

——. *The Swedish Bullionist Controversy*. Philadelphia: American Philosophical Society, 1971.

Einzig, P. *The History of Foreign Exchange*. London: Macmillan, 1962.

Ellis, Howard S. *German Monetary Theory, 1905–1933*. Cambridge, Mass.: Harvard University Press, 1937.

Fetter, Frank W. *Development of British Monetary Orthodoxy 1797–1875*. Cambridge, Mass.: Harvard University Press, 1965.

Fetter, Frank W., and Derek Gregory. *Monetary and Financial Policy*. London: Irish University Press, 1973.

Fisher, Irving. *The Purchasing Power of Money*. New York: Macmillan, 1911.

Girton, Lance, and Don Roper. "J. Laurence Laughlin and the Quantity Theory of Money." *Journal of Political Economy* 86 (August 1978).

Gregory, T. E. "Introduction" in *A History of Prices* by Thomas Tooke, vol. 1. New York: Adelphi, 1928.

Haberler, Gottfried. *The Theory of International Trade*. London: Hodge, 1937.

——. *A Survey of International Trade Theory*, rev. ed. Special Papers on International Economics no. 1. International Finance Section, Princeton University, 1961.

Henneberry, Barbara, and James G. Witte. "Variable Gold Parities from a Classical Viewpoint: Hume Versus the Monetarists." Mimeographed, Indiana University, November 1974.

Hollander, Jacob. "The Development of the Theory of Money from Adam Smith to David Ricardo." *Quarterly Journal of Economics* 25 (May 1911): 429–70.

Hume, David. *Writings on Economics*. Edited with an introduction by Eugene Rotwein, 1955. Reprint. Freeport, N.Y.: Books for Libraries Press, 1972.

Jevons, W. Stanley. *The Theory of Political Economy*, 4th ed. London: Macmillan, 1924.

Laughlin, J. Laurence. *The Principles of Money*. New York: Charles Scribner's Sons, 1903.

Letiche, J. M. "Isaac Gervaise on the International Mechanism of Adjustment." *Journal of Political Economy* 60 (February 1952): 34–43.

Mill, John Stuart. *Principles of Political Economy*. London: Longmans, Green, 1926.

Myhrman, Johan. "Experiences of Flexible Exchange Rates in Earlier Periods: Theories, Evidence, and a New View." In *Flexible Exchange Rates and Stabilization Policy*, edited by Jan Herin, Assar Lindbeck, and Johan Myhrman, 37–64. Boulder, Colorado: Westview Press, 1977.

O'Brien, D. P. *The Classical Economists*. Oxford: Clarendon Press, 1975.

Ohlin, B. *Interregional and International Trade*, rev. ed., 1933. Cambridge, Mass.: Harvard University Press, 1967.

Petrella, Frank. "Adam Smith's Rejection of Hume's Price-Specie-Flow Mechanism: A Minor Mystery Resolved." *Southern Economic Journal* 34 (January 1968): 365–74.

Pigou, A. C. *Industrial Fluctuations*, 2nd ed. New York: Augustus M. Kelley, 1967.

———. "Some Problems of Foreign Exchanges." *Economic Journal* 30 (1920): 460–72.

Ricardo, David. *The Works and Correspondence*. Edited by Piero Sraffa. London: Cambridge University Press, 1951.

Robbins, Lionel. *Robert Torrens and the Evolution of Classical Economics*. London: Macmillan, 1958.

Robertson, Dennis H. *Money*. London: Cambridge University Press, 1922.

Rowe, J. W. F. "An Index of Industrial Production." *Economic Journal* 37 (June 1927): 173–87.

St. Clair, Oswald. *A Key to Ricardo*. New York: Kelley and Millman, 1957.

Sayers, R. S. "Ricardo's Views on Monetary Questions." *Quarterly Journal of Economics* 67 (February 1953): 30–49.

SeKine, Thomas T. "The Discovery of International Monetary Equilibrium by Vanderlint, Cantillon, Gervaise, and Hume." *Economica Internazionale* 26 (March 1973): 262–82.

Smith, Adam. *An Inquiry into the Nature and Causes of the Wealth of Nations.* Edited by Edwin Cannon. New York: Random House, 1937.

———. *Lectures on Justice, Police, Revenue and Arms.* New York: Kelley and Millman, 1956.

Staley, Charles E. "Hume and Viner on the International Adjustment Mechanism." *History of Political Economy* 8 (Summer 1976): 252-65.

Thornton, Henry. *An Enquiry into the Nature and Effects of the Paper Credit of Great Britain.* New York: Augustus M. Kelley, 1962.

Tooke, Thomas. *A History of Prices.* Vol. 4. New York: Adelphi, 1928.

Tullock, Gordon. "Paper Money—A Cycle in Cathay." *Economic History Review* 9 (June 1956): 393-407.

Twain, Mark. *A Connecticut Yankee in King Arthur's Court.* New York: Harper and Brothers, 1889.

Vickers, Douglas. "Adam Smith and the Status of Theory of Money." In *Essays on Adam Smith*, edited by Andrew Skinner and Thomas Wilson. Oxford: Clarendon Press, 1975.

Viner, Jacob. *Canada's Balance of International Indebtedness 1900-1913.* Cambridge, Mass.: Harvard University Press, 1924.

———. *Studies in the Theory of International Trade.* New York: Augustus M. Kelley, 1965.

Wicksell, Knut. *Interest and Prices.* New York: Augustus M. Kelley, 1965.

———. "International Freights and Prices." *Quarterly Journal of Economics* 32 (February 1918): 404-10.

———. *Lectures on Political Economy.* Vol. 2, *Money.* New York: Augustus M. Kelley, 1971.

Purchasing Power Parity

Balassa, Bela. "The Purchasing-Power Parity Doctrine: A Reappraisal." *Journal of Political Economy* 72 (December 1964): 584-96.

Bunting, F. H. "Purchasing Power Parity Theory Reexamined." *Southern Economic Journal* 5 (January 1939): 282-301.

Cassel, Gustav. "The Present Situation of the Foreign Exchanges." *Economic Journal* 26 (March 1916): 62-65.

——. "Comment." *Economic Journal* 30 (March 1920): 44–45.

——. *The World's Monetary Problems*. London: Constable and Co., 1921.

——. *Money and Foreign Exchange after 1919*. London: Macmillan, 1930.

Citibank. "Purchasing Power: A Polestar for Drifting Exchange Rates." *Monthly Letter* (November 1973).

Genberg, Hans. *World Inflation and the Small Open Economy*. Geneva: Graduate Institute for International Studies, 1975.

Haberler, G. *The Theory of International Trade*. London: Hodge, 1950.

Isard, Peter. "How Far Can We Push the 'Law of One Price'?" *American Economic Review* 67 (December 1977): 942–48.

Keynes, J. M. *A Tract on Monetary Reform*. London: Macmillan, 1923.

King, David T. "Purchasing Power Parity and Exchange Rate Flexibility: 1973–1975." *Southern Economic Journal* 43 (April 1977): 1582–87.

Lebon, Jules. "The Real and Nominal Effects of Devaluation: The Relative Price Effects on Exchange Rate Changes." Mimeographed, 1976.

Lee, Moon. *Purchasing Power Parity*. New York: Marcel Dekker, 1976.

Magee, Stephen P. "Contracting and Spurious Deviations from Purchasing Power Parity." In *The Economics of Exchange Rates—Selected Studies*, edited by J. Frenkel and H. G. Johnson. Reading, Mass.: Addison-Wesley, 1978.

Officer, Lawrence H. "The Purchasing Power Parity Theory of Exchange Rates: A Review Article." *International Monetary Fund Staff Papers* (March 1976): 1–60.

Richardson, J. D. "Some Empirical Evidence on Commodity Arbitrage and the Law of One Price." Mimeographed, 1977.

Thomas, L. B. "Behavior of Flexible Exchange Rates: Additional Tests from the Post-World War I Episode." *Southern Economic Journal* 15 (October 1973): 167–82.

Wilford, D. S. "Price Levels, Interest Rates, Open Economies and a Fixed Exchange Rate: The Mexican Case, 1954–74." *Review of Business and Economic Research* 12 (Spring 1977): 52–65.

Yeager, Leland. "A Rehabilitation of Purchasing-Power Parity." *Journal of Political Economy* 66 (December 1958): 516–30.

General Studies

Akhtar, M. A. "Demand Functions for High-Powered Money in the United States." Mimeographed, Federal Reserve Bank of New York, 1977.

Alexander, Sidney S. "Effects of a Devaluation on a Trade Balance." *International Monetary Fund Staff Papers* (April 1952): 263-78.

————. "Effects of a Devaluation: A Simplified Synthesis of Elasticities and Absorption Approaches." *American Economic Review* (March 1959): 22-42.

Aliber, R. "Speculation in the Foreign Exchanges: The European Experience, 1919-1926." *Yale Economic Essays*, 1952.

————. "The Firm Under Fixed and Flexible Exchange Rates." In *Flexible Exchange Rates and Stabilization Policy*, edited by Jan Herin, Assar Lindbeck, and Johan Myhrman, 177-90. Boulder, Colorado: Westview Press, 1977.

Anderson, L., and Jerry Jordan. "The Monetary Base—Explanation and Analytical Use." Federal Reserve Bank of St. Louis *Review* 50, 8 (August 1968): 7-11.

Artis, M. J., and M. K. Lewis. "The Demand for Money in the United Kingdom: 1963-1973." *The Manchester School* 44 (June 1976): 147-81.

Artus, Jacques. "The 1967 Devaluation of the Pound Sterling." *International Monetary Fund Staff Papers* 22 (November 1975): 595-640.

Barro, R. J. "Rational Expectations and the Role of Monetary Policy." *Journal of Monetary Economics* 2 (January 1976): 1-32.

Barro, R. J., and Stanley Fischer. "Recent Developments in Monetary Theory." *Journal of Monetary Economics* 2 (April 1976): 133-68.

Basevi, G. "A Model for the Analysis of Official Intervention in the Foreign Exchange Markets." In *International Trade and Money*, edited by A. Swoboda and M. Connolly, 107-26. London: Allen and Unwin, 1972.

Black, S. "International Money Markets and Flexible Exchange Rates." *Princeton Studies in International Finance* no. 32, 1973.

Boorman, John T. "The Evidence on the Demand for Money: Theoretical Formulations and Empirical Results." In *Current Issues in Monetary Theory and Policy*, edited by Thomas M. Havrilesky and John T. Boorman. Arlington Heights, Ill.: AHM Publishing, 1976.

Bordo, M., and E. Choudri. "The Behavior of the Prices of Traded and Non-Traded Goods: The Canadian Case 1962-74." Mimeographed, 1977.

Branson, W. "Stocks and Flows in International Monetary Analysis." *International Aspects of Stabilization Policies, Federal Reserve Bank of Boston*, Conference Series no. 12, 1974.

Brunner, Karl, and A. H. Meltzer. "Predicting Velocity: Implications for Theory and Policy." *Journal of Finance* 18 (May 1963): 319-54.

————. "Some Further Investigations of Demand and Supply Functions of Money." *Journal of Finance* 19 (May 1964): 240-83.

————. "Comment on the Long Run and Short Run Demand for Money." *Journal of Political Economy* 76 (November 1969): 1234-40.

————. "The 'Monetarist Revolution' in Monetary Theory." *Weltwirtschaftliches Archiv* 105 (1970): 1-30.

————. "A Fisherian Framework for the Analysis of International Monetary Problems." In *Inflation in the World Economy*, edited by Michael Parkin and George Zis. Toronto, Canada: University of Toronto Press, 1976.

————. "Money Supply in Process and Monetary Policy in an Open Economy." In *International Trade and Money*, edited by M. B. Connolly and A. K. Swoboda. London: Allen and Unwin, 1973.

Cagan, P. "The Monetary Dynamics of Hyperinflation." In *Studies in the Quantity Theory of Money*, edited by M. Friedman. Chicago: University of Chicago Press, 1956.

Cagan, Phillip, and Arthur Gandolphi. "The Lag in Monetary Policy as Implied by the Time Pattern of Monetary Effects on Interest Rates." *American Economic Review, Papers and Proceedings* 59 (May 1969): 277-84.

Campos, Roberto de Oliviera. "Economic Development and Inflation with Special Reference to Latin America." In *Development Plans and Programmes*, 129-37. Paris: Organization for Economic Cooperation and Development (OECD) Development Center, 1964.

Claassen, E., and P. Salin, eds. *Recent Issues in International Monetary Economics*, Vol. 2, *Studies in Monetary Economics*. New York: North-Holland, 1976.

Cleveland, Harold Van B., and Bruse W. H. Brittian. *The Great Inflation: A Monetarist View*. Washington, D.C.: National Planning Association, 1976.

Corden, W. M. "The Adjustment Problem." In *European Monetary Unification and Its Meaning for the United States*, edited by L. B. Krause and W. S. Salant. Washington, D.C.: Brookings Institution, 1974.

Cornell, B. "Spot Rates, Forward Rates and Exchange Market Efficiency." *Journal of Financial Economics* 5 (1977): 55–65.

Courchene, T. J. *Money, Inflation, and the Bank of Canada*. Montreal: C. D. Howe Research Institute, 1976.

Dornbusch, R., S. Fischer, and P. A. Samuelson. "Comparative Advantage, Trade, and Payments in a Ricardian Model with a Continuum of Goods." *American Economic Review* 67 (December 1977): 823–39.

Einzig, P. *The Theory of Forward Exchange*. London: Macmillan, 1937.

———. *A Dynamic Theory of Forward Exchange*. London: Macmillan, 1962.

———. *The History of Foreign Exchange*. London: Macmillan, 1962.

Eltis, W. A. "How Public Sector Growth Causes Balance-of-Payments Deficits." *International Currency Review* 7 (January-February 1975): 27–30.

Feige, Edgar L., and Douglas K. Pearce. "The Substitutability of Money and Near-Monies: A Survey of Time-Series Evidence." *Journal of Economic Literature* no. 2 (June 1977): 439–69.

Fisher, I. *The Theory of Interest*. New York: 1930.

Frenkel, Jacob A. "The Forward Exchange Rate, Expectations and the Demand for Money: The German Hyperinflation." *American Economic Review* 67 (September 1977): 653–69.

Frenkel, Jacob A., and Richard M. Levich. "Covered Interest Arbitrage: Unexploited Profits?" *Journal of Political Economy* 83 (April 1975): 325–38.

———. "Transactions Costs and Interest Arbitrage: Tranquil Versus Turbulent Periods." *Journal of Political Economy* 85 (December 1977): 1209–26.

Friedman, Milton. "The Case for Flexible Exchange Rates." In *Essays in Positive Economics*, edited by M. Friedman. Chicago: University of Chicago Press, 1953.

———. "The Demand for Money: Some Theoretical and Empirical Results." *Journal of Political Economy* 67 (August 1959): 327–51.

———. *A Program for Monetary Stability*. New York: Fordham University Press, 1960.

———. "Interest Rates and the Demand for Money." *Journal of Law and Economics* 9 (October 1966): 71–85.

———. "The Optimum Quantity of Money." In *The Optimum Quantity of Money and Other Essays*. Chicago: Aldine, 1969.

———. *A Theoretical Framework for Monetary Analysis*. Occasional Paper 112. New York: National Bureau of Economic Research, 1971.

Friedman, Milton, and Robert Roosa. *The Balance of Payments: Free Versus Fixed Exchange Rates*. Washington, D.C.: American Enterprise Institute, 1967.

Gervaise, Isaac. *The System or Theory of the Trade of the World*. Baltimore: Johns Hopkins University, 1954.

Gibson, W. E. "Interest Rates and Monetary Policy." *Journal of Political Economy* 78 (May-June 1970): 431–55.

Girton, Lance, and D. W. Henderson. "Financial Capital Movements and Central Bank Behavior in a Two Country, Short-Run Portfolio Balance Model." *Journal of Monetary Economics* 2 (January 1976): 33–61.

Goodhart, C. A. E. *Money, Information and Uncertainty*. London: Macmillan, 1975.

Grubel, H. G. "The Demand for International Reserves: A Critical Review of the Literature." *Journal of Economic Literature* 9 (December 1971): 1148–66.

Haberler, G. *The Theory of International Trade*. London: William Hodge, 1936.

———. "The Choice of Exchange Rates After the War." *American Economic Review* 35, no. 2 (1945): 308–18.

———. *A Survey of International Trade Theory*. Special Papers in International Economics 1 (July 1961). International Finance Section, Princeton University.

Halsen, J. A., and J. L. Waelbroeck. "The Less Developed Countries and the International Monetary Mechanism." *American Economic Review* 66 (May 1976): 171–76.

Hamburger, M. J. "The Demand for Money in an Open Economy: Germany and the United Kingdom." *Journal of Monetary Economics* 3 (January 1977): 25–40.

Johnson, Harry G. "Towards a General Theory of the Balance of Payments." In *Readings in International Economics*, edited by Richard E. Caves and Harry G. Johnson. Homewood, Ill.: Irwin, 1968.

———. "The Case for Flexible Exchange Rates, 1969." Federal Reserve Bank of St. Louis *Review* 51 (June 1969): 12–24.

———. *Essays in Monetary Economics*. Cambridge, Mass.: Harvard University Press, 1973.

Johnson, Harry G., and A. K. Swoboda, eds. *The Economics of Common Currencies*. London: Allen and Unwin, 1973.

Jonson, P. D., and H. Kierzkowski. "The Balance of Payments: Analytic Exercise." *The Manchester School* 43 (June 1975): 105–33.

Keynes, John Maynard. *Tract on Monetary Reform*. London: Macmillan, 1924.

Kohlhagen, Stephen W. "The Stability of Exchange Rate Expectations and Canadian Capital Flows." *Journal of Finance* 32 (December 1977): 1657–70.

Krueger, Anne O. "Balance-of-Payments Theory." *The Journal of Economic Literature* 17 (March 1969): 1–26.

Laidler, D., and J. M. Parkin. "The Demand for Money in the United Kingdom, 1955–67: Preliminary Estimates." In *Readings in British Monetary Economics*, edited by H. G. Johnson et al. London: Clarendon Press, 1972.

———. "Inflation: A Survey." *Economic Journal* 85 (December 1975): 741–809.

Lucas, Robert. "Some International Evidence on Output-Inflation Tradeoffs." *American Economic Review* 63 (June 1973): 326–34.

Machlup, F. "Relative Prices and Aggregate Spending in the Analysis of Devaluation." *American Economic Review* 45 (June 1955): 255–78.

Manne, Henry G., and Roger LeRoy Miller, eds. *Gold, Money and the Law*. Chicago: Aldine, 1975.

Mises, Ludwig von. *The Theory of Money and Credit*. New Haven: Yale University Press, 1954.

Modigliani, Franco, and R. Sutch. "Innovations in Interest Rate Policy." *American Economic Review* 56 (May 1966): 178–97.

Mundell, Robert A. "A Theory of Optimum Currency Areas." *American Economic Review* 51 (November 1961): 509–17.

———. "The Exchange Rate Margins and Economic Policy." In *Money in the International Order*, edited by Carter Murphy. Dallas: Southern Methodist University Press, 1964.

———. *Monetary Theory*. Pacific Palisades, California: Goodyear, 1971.

Murphy, J. C., and S. K. Das. "Money Illusion and Balance-of-Payments Adjustment." *Journal of Political Economy* 84, no. 1 (February 1976): 73–82.

Nurkse, Ragnar. *International Currency Experience*. Geneva: League of Nations, 1944.

Nussbaum, Arthur. *Money in the Law: National and International*. Brooklyn: The Foundation Press, 1950.

Patinkin, Don. *Money, Interest and Prices*, 2d ed. New York: Harper and Row, 1965.

Phelps, E. S., and J. B. Taylor. "Stabilizing Powers of Monetary Policy under Rational Expectations." *Journal of Political Economy* 85, no. 1 (January 1977): 163–90.

Pippenger, John. "Balance-of-Payments Deficits Measurement and Interpretation." Federal Reserve Bank of St. Louis *Review* 55 (November 1973): 6–14.

Polak, J. J. "Monetary Analysis of Income Formation and Payments Problems." In *The Monetary Approach to the Balance of Payments*. Washington, D.C.: International Monetary Fund, 1977.

Porter, M. "Capital Flows as an Offset to Monetary Policy: The German Experience." *International Monetary Fund Staff Papers* 19 (July 1972): 395–424.

Robinson, Joan. "The Foreign Exchanges." In *Readings in the Theory of International Trade*, Committee of the American Economic Association, 83–103. Philadelphia: Blakiston, 1949.

Samuelson, Paul. "An Exact Hume-Ricardo-Marshall Model of International Trade." *Journal of International Economics* (February 1971): 1–18.

Sargent, T. J., and Neil Wallace. "'Rational' Expectations, the Optimal Monetary Investment, and the Optimal Money Supply Rule." *Journal of Political Economy* 83, no. 2 (April 1975): 241–54.

Schadler, Susan. "Sources of Exchange Rate Variability: Theory and Empirical Evidence." *International Monetary Fund Staff Papers* 24 (July 1977): 253–96.

Smith, Vera C. *Rationale of Central Banking*. London: P. S. King, 1936.

Sohmen, E. *Flexible Exchange Rates.* Chicago: University of Chicago Press, 1969.

Spencer, Roger W. "Channels of Monetary Influence: A Survey." Federal Reserve Bank of St. Louis *Review* 56 (November 1974): 8–26.

Spraos, J. "The Theory of Forward Exchange and Recent Practice." *The Manchester School* 21 (May 1953): 87–117.

———. "Speculation, Arbitrage and Sterling." *Economic Journal* 69 (March 1959): 1–21.

Stein, J. L. "Monetary Growth Theory in Perspective." *American Economic Review* 60 (March 1970): 85–106.

Stockman, Alan C. "Risk, Information and Forward Exchange Rates." In *The Economics of Exchange Rates–Selected Studies*, edited by J. Frenkel and H. G. Johnson. Reading, Mass.: Addison-Wesley, 1978.

Tanner, J. E., and V. Bonomo. "Gold, Capital Flows, and Long Swings in American Business Activity." *Journal of Political Economy* 76 (January-February 1968): 44–52.

Thorn, Richard S., ed. *Monetary Theory and Policy*. New York: Random House, 1966.

Tosini, Paula. "Leaning Against the Wind: A Standard for Managed Floating." *Essays in International Finance* no. 126. Princeton, N.J.: Princeton University, December 1977.

Triffin, Robert. "National Central Banking and the International Economy." *Review of Economic Studies* 14 (February 1947): 53–75.

———. "Jamaica: Major Revision or Fiasco?" In "Reflections on Jamaica," *Essays in International Finance* no. 115. Princeton, N.J.: Princeton University, April 1976.

Van Belle, John J. "Money Illusion and Its Influence on International Adjustment." In *The Monetary Approach to International Adjustment*, edited by Bluford H. Putnam and D. Sykes Wilford. New York: Praeger Publishers, 1978.

Viner, Jacob. *Studies in the Theory of International Trade*. New York: Harper and Brothers, 1937.

Wilford, W. T., and R. Moncarz. *Essays in Latin American Economic Issues*. New Orleans: Division of Business and Economic Research, Louisiana State University, 1970.

Williamson, Jeffery G. *American Growth and the Balance of Payments 1820–1913.* Chapel Hill, N.C.: University of North Carolina Press, 1964.

Willms, Manfred. "Controlling Money in an Open Economy: The German Case." Federal Reserve Bank of St. Louis *Review* 53, 4 (April 1971): 10–27.

Yeager, Leland B. *International Monetary Relations:Theory, History, and Policy,* 2d ed. New York: Harper and Row, 1976.

Zecher, J. Richard, C. Burrows, and L. McGregory. "Determinants of the Australian Money Supply Since 1950." Paper presented at Congress of Australian and New Zealand Association for the Advancement of Science, August 1972.

INDEX

empirical studies, 14–16; fundamental propositions, 51–54; historical, 21–42; implications for
monetary policy, 53–54
monetary equilibrium equations,
135, 209
monetary expansion, 104, 233–34
monetary independence, 200
monetary model, small, open economy, 7
monetary policy, 211–13; future
course of, 225–26; independence
of, 202; for stabilization policy,
225
monetary services, demand for, 202
money, actual and desired, 50;
affecting prices, 139; causality of,
Sim's test, 65; definition of, 171;
fiduciary, 216–17; stock and
exchange rate, 119–20, 135, 147;
trading in, 184; transactions
demand for, 136, 203
money demand, 6–7, 139, 140;
as endogenous or exogenous, 123–
24; equations, 7, 57–59, 66, 73,
86, 99–100, 117–19, 135, 136,
138–39, 164, 180, 185, 190–91,
202, 208, 231; function, 122–23,
185, 201–02, 208–09, 231–32
money illusion, 246–50; classical,
246–47; revealed illusion, 247
money market equilibrium, 234
money stock, adjusts to quantity
demanded, 9; changes in, 8;
foreign reserves, 9
money supply, 50, 168; equation,
7–8, 57–58, 66–67, 68–69, 72–73,
86, 99, 117–19, 120–21, 138–39,
165, 167; and high-powered
money, 99; rate of growth, 231–
34; in relation to domestic liabilities, 165; in relation to prices,
19–20; relative, 140

natural rate hypothesis, 224
nominal interest rate, equations, 137;
relative, 140–41

OPEC, 63
opportunity cost, 196, 205;
inflation, 230

price expectations equations, 138
price-level variable, 230
prices, 61, 139; linear homogeneity in, 102, 109; relative, 53
(*see* money)
purchasing power parity, 8–9, 72,
148, 150–52, 154–55, 158, 180,
190, 209; arbitrage theory, 222;
equations, 8, 72–73, 87, 136,
138–39, 180, 209, 230; neutrality
theory of, 223–24, relative price,
53

quantity theory, 148, 149–52, 154–
55, 158, 180; of money, reverse
causation, 33–34 (*see also*
Laughlin, Mill, and Ricardo)

rational expectations, 85–97, 138
real bills doctrine, 154, 156
real cash balance, adjustment of,
245–50; decline in, 249; equations, 136
real interest rate parity, 137
reduced form models, 124
reserve currency country, 54-55, 60–
61, 66–67; closed economy, 67;
domestic credit, 75; nominal
money stock of, 66; prices, 69;
reserve flows, 67
reserve flows, equations, 9, 58–59,
60, 68–69, 74–75, 76, 87, 88,
101–02, 109, 118; foreign, 105;
neutralization of, 54; reduced form
equations, 9, 58–60, 68–69, 74-76,
87–88, 101–02, 109, 118
reserves, nondomestic influences on,
101
Ricardo, David, historical perspective, 27–30

seemingly unrelated regression, 72, 74–
75; integrated financial systems,

ABOUT THE EDITORS
AND CONTRIBUTORS

EDITORS

BLUFORD H. PUTNAM, economist in the International Economic Forecasting Division, Economics Group, Chase Manhattan Bank, has responsibilities concerning exchange rate forecasting and analysis of international economic issues. Previously, he worked in the International Research Department of the Federal Reserve Bank of New York. Putnam received his B.A. from Eckerd College and his Ph.D. from Tulane University. Research studies in the areas of fixed and flexible exchange rates have been published in the *American Economic Review*, the *Journal of Money, Credit, and Banking*, and *Weltwirtschaftliches Archiv*.

D. SYKES WILFORD holds a B.S. from the University of Tennessee, an M.A. from Vanderbilt University, and a Ph.D. from Tulane University. He has been a faculty member at the University of New Orleans, consultant to the Agency for International Development, international economist for the Federal Reserve Bank of New York, and is presently an economist with the Chase Manhattan Bank. Wilford has written numerous articles and one book in the area of the monetary approach to international adjustments. Articles appearing in *American Economic Review, Journal of Finance,* and *Weltwirtschaftliches Archiv* deal directly with this question.

CONTRIBUTORS

M. A. AKHTAR is an economist at the Federal Reserve Bank of New York. His previous experience includes teaching at the University of South Carolina, Guilford College, and Jacksonville State University. Akhtar has published in macromonetary economics, history of economic theory, and international economics in such journals as *History of Political Economy, Scottish Journal of Political Economy,* and *Indian Economic Journal.* He received his Ph.D. from the University of South Carolina.

RUSSELL S. BOYER received his Ph.D. in economics from the University of Chicago in 1971, writing his thesis in the area of growth and the balance of payments. He has been at the University of Western Ontario since that time, and is currently an associate professor in the Economics Department. During a leave of absence he spent a year as a Research Fellow with the International Monetary Research Programme at the London School of Economics. His research interests continue to be in international financial economics, with emphasis recently on stabilization policies in open economies. His articles have appeared in the *American Economic Review* and the *Canadian Journal of Economics.*

CHARLES D. CATHCART is presently an economist with the Chase Manhattan Bank N.A. His responsibilities include forecasting interest rates and other financial variables, tracking monetary policy, and participating in the formulation of forecasts for the overall economy. At Chase, he has also served in the International Forecasting Division of the Economics Group and was involved there with foreign exchange analysis. Cathcart taught at Pennsylvania State University before coming to Chase. He possesses a Ph.D. degree from the University of Virginia, an M.A. from the University of California, and a B.A. from the University of Denver. He is the author of publications on hyperinflation, international capital flows, and the demand for money. Articles relative to work in this volume have appeared in the *Journal of Money, Credit, and Banking* and *Weltwirtschaftliches Archiv.*

MICHAEL B. CONNOLLY is a professor of economics at the University of South Carolina. He has held previous teaching positions at the University of Florida from 1972 to 1978 and at Harvard from 1968 to 1972. His articles appeared in the *American Economic Review,* the *Journal of Political Economy,* the *Quarterly Journal of Economics,* and the *Journal of International Economics.* He holds a B.A. from the University of California at Berkeley, and an M.A. and a Ph.D. from the University of Chicago.

W. MICHAEL COX is currently a visiting assistant professor of economics at the University of Western Ontario, London, Ontario, on leave from Virginia Polytechnic Institute, Blacksburg, Virginia. During the academic year 1977–1978 he was a visiting assistant professor of economics at the University of Rochester, Rochester, New York. Cox earned a B.A. in economics from Hendrix College, Conway, Arkansas in 1972 and a Ph.D. in economics from Tulane University, New Orleans, Louisiana in 1976. His current research interests are international finance and domestic monetary and macroeconomic theory.

LANCE GIRTON, with a Ph.D. from the University of Chicago, has been employed as an economist in the International Finance Division of the Federal Reserve Board in Washington, D.C. since 1971. He has been an adjoint associate professor at George Washington University and a visiting professor at the University of Utah. His research specialty is in international monetary theory and finance, with publications in the *American Economic Review* and the *Journal of Monetary Economics*, among others.

THOMAS M. HUMPHREY is a research officer with the Federal Reserve Bank of Richmond, where he is responsible for general economic policy research. His interests are mainly in the areas of monetary policy, international economics, and history of thought. Humphrey holds a B.S. and an M.A. from the University of Tennessee and a Ph.D. from Tulane University. Besides publishing in the *Economic Review* of the Federal Reserve Bank of Richmond, he has published articles related to his contribution in this collection in the *Southern Economic Journal, History of Political Economy,* and *Banca Nazional de Lavaro Quarterly Review.* He has taught at several universities, including Tulane, Auburn, Virginia, and Virginia Commonwealth.

ROBERT E. KELEHER, a graduate of the University of Illinois, Northern Illinois University, and Indiana University, was an economist at First Tennessee National Corporation in Memphis, Tennessee from 1974 to 1976. Presently he is a financial economist at the Federal Reserve Bank of Atlanta, where he specializes in monetary and regional studies.

DONALD S. KEMP is currently international economist with Harris Trust and Savings Bank (Chicago). His main responsibilities include exchange rate and international money market forecasting. Previously Kemp was an economist with the Federal Reserve Bank of St. Louis and published several articles in their *Economic Review.* He received his Ph.D. from Tulane University.

DAVID T. KING is presently on leave from the Federal Reserve Bank of New York to the Organization for Economic Cooperation and Development (OECD). His main interests at the OECD, as the economist responsible for following fiscal and monetary policy of Canada and the United States, are in international monetary policy and exchange rate analysis. King holds a Ph.D. from Tulane University and a B.A. from Southern Methodist University. He is the author of a number of research papers dealing with international monetary policy. Work pertinent to this collection has appeared in the *Southern Economic Journal.*

THOMAS A. LAWLER is a research associate with the Federal Reserve Bank of Richmond. He holds a B.A. and is currently pursuing graduate studies at the University of Virginia. Lawler's research interests include both domestic and international monetary topics, and he has published several articles in the Federal Reserve Bank of Richmond's *Economic Review.*

MARC A. MILES is currently an assistant professor of economics at Rutgers College, Rutgers University. Miles holds a B.A., an M.A., and a Ph.D. from the University of Chicago, as well as an M.Sc. from the London School of Economics. Previously Miles was a research economist in the Balance of Payments Division of the Federal Reserve Bank of New York. In addition to a recently published article in the *American Economic Review*, Miles has completed one book, *Devaluation, the Trade Balance and the Balance of Payments,* and is currently putting the final touches on a second book, *International Economics in an Integrated World*, which he is co-authoring with Arthur B. Laffer.

DON ROPER received his Ph.D. from the University of Chicago. He served as an economist in the International Finance Division of the Federal Reserve Board of Washington, D.C. from 1969 until 1975. He has taught at the University of Stockholm, the University of Texas at Austin, the University of California at Berkeley, and the Australian National University, and is presently a professor at the University of Utah. His research specialty is international monetary theory, with articles appearing in such journals as the *American Economic Review* and *Economica Internazional.*

JOHN VAN BELLE received his Ph.D. from the University of Virginia in 1973, and since then has worked as an economist in the Balance of Payments Division at the Federal Reserve Bank of New York and as a senior market analyst in the Corporate Counselling Division at Citibank. He has published several articles on international developments in such journals as *Economic Inquiry, Journal of Money, Credit, and Banking,* the *Southern Economic Journal, Challenge,* and *Euromoney.*

WALTON T. WILFORD is a professor and Chairman of the Department of Economics and Finance at the University of New Orleans. Prior to his coming to UNO, Professor Wilford was a faculty member at the Universities of Georgia and Idaho, and was in Central and South America as an economist with the State Department. His main area of interest is in development economics. Publications pertinent to his work on developing economies have appeared in the *Journal of Finance, Economic Development and Cultural Change,* the *National Tax Journal,* and the *Western Economic Journal.* Professor Wilford's Ph.D. is from Southern Methodist University.

J. RICHARD ZECHER is a professor and Dean of the College of Business Administration at the University of Iowa. Before coming to Iowa, Zecher served as a faculty member at the University of Chicago, Monash University, and Tulane University; also, he has been senior staff economist at the Council of Economic Advisors, consultant to the securities industry and the U.S. Treasury, and Chief Economist and Director of Economic Policy Research at the Securities Exchange Commission. Zecher has published articles in numerous journals such as the *American Economic Review,* the *Journal of Money, Credit, and Banking,* and the *Journal of Finance.* He received his Ph.D. from Ohio State University.

332.45
MON

The Monetary
approach to
international
adjustment

DATE			
APR 7 '88			